TO LIVE FREELY IN THIS WORLD

To Live Freely in This World

Sex Worker Activism in Africa

Chi Adanna Mgbako

NEW YORK UNIVERSITY PRESS

New York and London

NEW YORK UNIVERSITY PRESS
New York and London
www.nyupress.org

References to Internet websites (URLs) were accurate at the time of writing. Neither the author nor New York University Press is responsible for URLs that may have expired or changed since the manuscript was prepared.

ISBN: 978-1-4798-1756-6 (hardback)
ISBN: 978-1-4798-4906-2 (paperback)

For Library of Congress Cataloging-in-Publication data, please contact the Library of Congress.

New York University Press books are printed on acid-free paper, and their binding materials are chosen for strength and durability. We strive to use environmentally responsible suppliers and materials to the greatest extent possible in publishing our books.

Manufactured in the United States of America

10 9 8 7 6 5 4 3 2 1

Also available as an ebook

For my beautiful parents, Iyom Enyikwoku Deborah Mgbako and Eze Iddi Dr. Ambrose Mgbako

CONTENTS

ACKNOWLEDGMENTS

Researching and writing this book was a powerful personal and professional experience, and many people graciously and enthusiastically helped me bring it to life.

My warmest thanks, and most profound debt, go first and foremost to the sex workers in Botswana, Kenya, Mauritius, Namibia, Nigeria, South Africa, and Uganda who created a space for me in their communities, believed in the importance of this project, and graced it with their participation. They have granted me the enormous privilege of documenting and illuminating their stories. They are the soul of this book, and I hope it will always stand as a testament to their inspiring activism.

This project would not have taken flight without the expert and dedicated assistance of those who helped facilitate my fieldwork. Tosh Legoreng in Botswana, John Mathenge and Phelister Abdalla in Kenya, Marlene Ladine in Mauritius, Felicita Hikuam in Namibia, Pat Abraham in Nigeria, Kholi Buthelezi in South Africa, and Daisy Nakato in Uganda were my entry points to a whole universe of wonderful activists and organizations. They have my profound respect and unfailing gratitude.

Elizabeth Gyori and Nimrah Najeeb provided consistently excellent research assistance and cheered me on throughout the entire writing and editing process. Katy Glenn Bass graciously provided meticulous feedback on draft chapters as I wrote them. I will forever be thankful for Elizabeth, Nimrah, and Katy's generous editorial and emotional support, which propelled me forward with confidence as I embarked on the sometimes daunting and always thrilling task of writing my first book.

I am extraordinarily grateful to the scholars and advocates—all of whom do urgent, purposeful, and inspiring work—who read and commented on the manuscript in whole or in part. Aziza Ahmed, who has generously supported this project from its early stages, gave the entire manuscript a thorough and wise reading. Lori Adorable provided wonderfully rich and incisive feedback on many chapters. Melinda Chateauvert, Clare Huntington, and Sienna Baskin offered probing and thoughtful insights, and Darby Hickey graciously reviewed several chapters.

Thanks are also due to David Henry Sterry, Hakima Abbas, Jennifer Gordon, and Matthew Greenall, who provided astute suggestions on the proposal; Gideon Engelbrecht for his beautiful digital artwork; and the global community of sex workers and allies on Twitter, who are an endless well of information, insight, and inspiration.

I am thrilled that this book found its home at NYU Press, and I thank my editor, Clara Platter, for enthusiastically embracing this project. I am also grateful to the anonymous reviewers for their invaluable and provocative insights that enriched the final manuscript.

For almost a decade, I have had the sheer good fortune of making the Leitner Center for International Law and Justice at Fordham Law School my professional home. It has been one of the great gifts of my life. My deepest thanks to Jim Leitner and Tracy Higgins for their friendship and support for the work of the Walter Leitner International Human Rights Clinic, which I have had the honor of directing since its founding and where the seeds of this book were first planted. Jim and Tracy's astonishing generosity has played a defining role in my professional growth and enduring happiness—I will never be able to thank them enough. Thanks to my cherished friends and colleagues, Jeanmarie Fenrich and Paolo Galizzi, for their unwavering personal and professional support. I am also grateful to Rita Astoor for the helpful research she always delivered with characteristic good cheer, and to Martin Flaherty and Liz Wickeri for their encouragement.

At Fordham Law School, I am enormously grateful to Sheila Foster, who granted me the sabbatical that allowed me the time, space, and freedom to write this book. Fordham also provided the research funding that made much of the fieldwork possible. I also thank my Fordham colleagues for their useful comments on the proposal at an early workshop for this project. Over the years, many Fordham students and alumni contributed to this book by conducting research, transcribing audio interviews, and assisting me in the field. I send my gratitude to all of them, with extra-special thanks to Beth Gavin, Nita Narayan, Rebecca Marlin, Scarlett Carmago, Grace Lee, Sungin Jung, Katie Waizer, Justin Brown, and Tessa Juste.

All my love and thanks to my wonderful family for their tender and steadfast encouragement. My beloved brothers, Drs. Obi, Chudi, and Fofie Mgbako, are my closest friends, and they have fiercely supported me in everything I have ever done. It is a supreme joy journeying through life hand-in-hand with them. Heartfelt thanks also to my sister-in-law, Maritza Mgbako, and my nephews, Kieren and Bryson Mgbako. Finally, and most important, I thank my utterly remarkable parents, Eze Iddi Dr. Ambrose Mgbako and Iyom Enyikwoku Deborah Mgbako. From the time I was young, my parents nurtured and supported my global adventures and Africanist leanings. They have been the shining, unwavering light throughout my life. With all that I am, and from the depths of my heart, I dedicate this book to them.

ACRONYMS AND ABBREVIATIONS

AMwA   Akina Mama wa Afrika

ARASA   AIDS and Rights Alliance of Southern Africa

ASWA   African Sex Workers Alliance

AWLI   African Women's Leadership Institute

BHESP   Bar Hostess Empowerment and Support Program (Kenya)

BONELA   Botswana Network on Ethics, Law and HIV/AIDS

CATW   Coalition Against Trafficking in Women

HIV/AIDS   Human Immunodeficiency Virus/Acquired Immune Deficiency Syndrome

HOYMAS   Healthy Options for Young Men on HIV, AIDS, and STIs (Kenya)

HRAPF   Human Rights Awareness and Promotion Forum (Uganda)

ILO   International Labour Organization

KASH   Keeping Alive Societies' Hope (Kenya)

KESWA   Kenya Sex Workers Alliance

LGBT   lesbian, gay, bisexual, and transgender

MSM   men who have sex with men

NGO   nongovernmental organization

NSWP   Global Network of Sex Work Projects

NZPRA   New Zealand Prostitution Reform Act

PILS   Prévention Information et Lutte contre le Sida (Mauritius)

RNRT   Rights Not Rescue Trust (Namibia)

STI   sexually transmitted infection

SWAA   Sex Worker Academy for Africa

SWEAT   Sex Workers Education and Advocacy Taskforce (South Africa)

UN   United Nations

UNAIDS   Joint United Nations Programme on HIV/AIDS

UNDP   United Nations Development Programme

UNFPA   United Nations Population Fund

UN WOMEN United Nations Entity for Gender Equality and the Empowerment of Women

WHO World Health Organization

WLC Women's Legal Centre (South Africa)

WONETHA Women's Organization Network for Human Rights Advocacy (Uganda)

WOPI Women of Power Initiative (Nigeria)

Introduction

"We Have Voices"

There's really no such thing as the "voiceless." There are only
the deliberately silenced, or the preferably unheard.
—Arundhati Roy

Peninah Nyambura's battered and lifeless body was discovered in the
twilight months of 2012 stuffed in a drainage ditch in Thika, a small
industrial town twenty-five miles outside of Nairobi, Kenya's capital.
Peninah was a Kenyan sex worker and the mother of a thirteen-year-old
daughter. She was only thirty years old. Hers was the fourth murder of
a sex worker in Thika in two years, but police turned a blind eye to the
killings haunting the community.

The day of Peninah's funeral, more than 300 Kenyan sex workers con-
verged on Thika to lead a peaceful protest and demand a police investigation into her murder. As they marched, Peninah's body lay in a hearse
that followed the mournful, defiant procession. When they reached the
police commissioner's gate, Peninah's daughter slowly, bravely moved to
the front of the crowd. The protesters grew silent so that her words, soft
yet firm, would linger: "The murderer killed the person who put food on
my table. He killed the only source of money for me to go to school. He
killed the only person who supported me. The only one who loved me."

Sex workers continued to protest that day, despite police officers'
brandishing their guns and threatening the protesters with tear gas, because Peninah was a human being; she was loved and needed, and her
life deserved recognition. "As we marched, we sang," says Phelister Abdalla, a Kenyan sex workers' rights activist, "so that people would know
we have voices."

Phelister and I are in Freedom Corner in Nairobi's Uhuru Park as
she recounts Peninah's story, flanked on all sides by healthy cypress and

Phelister Abdalla. Nairobi, Kenya. Photograph by author.

eucalyptus trees planted by the Kenyan environmental and women's rights crusader Wangari Maathai before her death. It's early morning, and the ground is still wet from last night's torrential rainfall; the sky is overcast, a muted silver. The city is slowly, grudgingly coming to life. Yesterday, there was a bombing in a Somali immigrant neighborhood, and the memory of violence still hovers in the air, which is eerily fitting because today is December 17, 2012, the International Day to End Violence against Sex Workers. In cities around the world, sex workers and their allies will cluster in intimate gatherings, light candles, and read aloud the names of sex workers who have been victims of violence. I've found my way through the winding streets of the city to Freedom Corner for a protest march organized by Kenyan sex workers' rights activists to mark the occasion.

I'm not sure what to expect. How will ordinary people in Nairobi react to the sight of sex workers, unmasked and unbowed, marching through the streets of this most cosmopolitan of African cities in the middle of the work day, demanding their rights? Will this inspiring sight cause them to raise their fists into the air in solidarity? Or will they hurl insults in Swahili—"*Malaya!*" [Prostitute!]—at the protesters?

At Freedom Corner, red umbrellas—the global symbol of the sex workers' rights movement, signifying the beauty and strength of vibrant inclusivity—are strewn all over the dew-laced grass. Signs that read "Only Rights Can Stop the Wrongs!" lie next to the umbrellas. Slowly, sex workers and their allies gather under Wangari's trees, quietly conversing, waiting to begin. They are wearing "Save us from Saviors" pins and t-shirts that read, "No to stigma and discrimination. Yes to life." They inflate condoms and attach them to their clothes. Bright red condom packets with "LOVE" in gold lettering stick out of their sun visors. I notice people carrying rainbow-striped flags, the international symbol of the LGBT rights movement, as an activist proudly tells me, "The sex worker movement and the queer movement basically coexist in Kenya." I'm comforted by the deep solidarity on display.

As we wait, as the sun begins to pierce the dull grayness, as sex workers and their allies continue to gather until we grow hundreds strong, people speak of why we march today. I hear the horrible stories of violence against Kenyan sex workers, starting with Peninah's story, which Phelister recounts to me in rapid-fire bursts, the directness of her gaze never leaving me. Sex workers in Thika had tenderly referred to Peninah as "Mama Ann" because of how much she looked out for them. She was known for the beautiful blue- and silver-checkered scarf she often wore elegantly draped over her shoulders. So when sex workers discovered a bruised corpse in a drainage ditch near the town's center with that same scarf shrouding its face, they immediately knew it was Mama Ann.

Phelister soon excuses herself to hurry off to attend to last-minute preparations for the march, and I meet Amani, a twenty-five-year-old male sex worker with short dreadlocks and a sweetly mischievous grin. He's using a folded red umbrella as a cane to help steady his walk as he limps over to me. I immediately notice the cast on his left ankle, the fresh purple and black bruises on the left side of his face and upper arms, his bloodshot eye. Several days ago, Amani was out strolling in the early evening when municipal officers, known as city council *askaris*, began to harass him and demand money. "When I refused their requests for bribes, the *askaris* beat me with the butt of a gun for thirty minutes in the middle of the street," Amani says.

* * *

Peninah's and Amani's stories are not outliers. Daily human rights abuses against Kenyan sex workers are replicated in other African countries and throughout the world. When Bongani refused to comply with a police officer's demand for sexual favors in exchange for avoiding arrest in South Africa, he dumped her miles outside of town in a remote and dangerous location in the middle of the night. Anna survived a sexual assault by a client in Namibia, and when she mustered the courage to report it to the police, they refused to file her complaint. "It's impossible for a prostitute to be raped," an officer told her. When Dembe tried to access testing for sexually transmitted infections at a government-run health clinic in Uganda, the nurses ridiculed her in front of other patients. She was so traumatized by the experience that she hasn't tried to go to a clinic in months.

Studies from throughout the continent echo these disturbing vignettes and document abuses against female and male sex workers, cisgender[1] and transgender, in the form of endemic police abuse; abuses by clients who take advantage of sex workers' lack of access to justice after violent victimization; lack of labor rights resulting in unsafe working conditions; and social stigma, leading to discrimination in health care services.[2] Why are these horrendous abuses so rampant?

Anti-prostitution scholars and activists have long argued that every exchange of sexual services for payment is an inherently violent and coercive act that degrades women. For many of these activists, the idea of a consenting adult sex worker is inconceivable.[3] They implicitly and explicitly argue that trafficking and sex work are one and the same, a dangerous conflation that has led to abuses of sex workers in the name of fighting trafficking.[4] Despite anti-prostitution activists' claims, when we actually listen to the multiplicity of sex worker voices and acknowledge that we can't universalize their experiences, we learn that violence is not inherent to prostitution.

In the economically unequal world of global capitalism, where the vast majority of workers have highly limited economic opportunities, some people do in fact make the rational decision to pursue sex work. The abuses they experience in that work don't occur because the selling of sexual services is necessarily degrading or dehumanizing. The source of the abuses lies elsewhere. It is, instead, structural: Laws and policies criminalizing sex work deeply marginalize sex workers, their clients, and the industry; push sex work underground and into the shadows; and ensure that sex workers have little power over their labor, therefore remaining vulnerable to abuse and discrimination. Throughout Africa and the rest of the world, where most governments criminalize sex work and most societies stigmatize sex workers, this continues to be the case.[5]

And yet in the midst of the chronic violence, grinding stigma, and unrelenting discrimination that accompany criminalization, something surprising and beautiful has emerged. African sex workers, refusing to swallow the bitterness of their suffering, have sparked a sex workers' rights movement that is spreading like a brushfire across the continent. Theirs is the latest manifestation of a global sex worker movement, birthed in Europe and the United States more than forty years ago, that has spread throughout the world.[6] It is also the continuation of a rich tradition of informal local sex worker activism. These vibrant, defiant voices should not be ignored, and yet too often they are indeed disregarded.

In the spring of 2005, when I was in my final semester as a graduate student at Harvard Law School, I took a seminar course on international women's rights. I especially loved the opportunity to hear directly from women's rights activists—the Ghanaian campaigner fighting against the harmful traditional practice of female genital cutting, the Nepalese lawyer advocating for women's increased political participation in her country, the U.S. human rights defender championing reproductive freedom. But our class on prostitution was different. Gone were the voices directly from affected communities that had so illuminated other parts of the course. Instead, we read a slew of articles by the *New York Times* columnist Nicholas Kristof on what struck me as his misguided efforts to liberate "sex slaves" from brothels in Southeast Asia by purchasing them.[7] We read nothing from sex workers themselves.

I was a young, budding human rights advocate, and I believed fiercely in the notion of individual and community agency. The silencing of these voices unsettled me. Were sex workers the world over incapable of speaking about the complexity of their own lives? That day in class I instinctively knew that these voices must exist, and I vowed to find them.

A decade later, as a human rights professor and advocate who works in solidarity with sex worker activists and has a special affinity for the

African sex work context in part because of my Nigerian heritage and professional Africanist leanings, I've experienced first-hand the vitality of the global sex workers' rights movement. Despite attempts by anti-prostitution activists to discredit the movement,[8] sex worker activism continues to spread in Asia and the Pacific, Europe, Latin America, North America, and the Caribbean. And now in Africa as well, red umbrellas are aflutter.

* * *

Back in Nairobi, we protest for Peninah and Amani and sex workers fighting for their rights in Africa and throughout the world. Suddenly we receive word that it's time for the march to begin. We all line up—sex workers and allies, men and women, cisgender and transgender, gay and straight—excitement pulsing through the crowd, red umbrellas opening en masse, the sunlight flowing through them, flecking the crimson with hints of gold. Blown-up condoms glow. A pulsing drumbeat fills the air. More than 500 of us begin to march, pumping red umbrellas, condoms, and rainbow flags into the sky. The rhythmic chants begin, loud and strong, like a booming heartbeat: "Sex workers' rights are human rights!" "Sex work is work!" "Stop killing us!"

Leaving Freedom Corner, we march down Koinange Street, Nairobi's informal red-light district. We arrive at the Supreme Court of Kenya, and as we cluster in front, the chants die down. We raise our red umbrellas high in silence, a poignant plea for justice. We march to the gates of City Hall, home of the *askaris*, the civil service officers who regularly abuse and harass Kenyan sex workers, and the chants begin anew. A group of *askaris* stands behind the steel gates staring at the protesters with dead eyes. Amani limps to the front until he's at the gate, face to face with the *askaris*, shouting, "I'm suing you for what you did to me!" He's pointing at them as he screams, as the chants behind him grow louder, more impassioned, accentuating his fearlessness. We march past the Parliament building, stopping traffic along the way as television crews and journalists appear. Scores of pedestrians stop and watch in silence with wide, curious eyes. Hours later, when we end the march back at Freedom Corner, we are exhausted and utterly exhilarated. The first December 17 protest march in Nairobi three years prior was an intentionally silent march, a message that Kenyan sex workers existed but had been robbed of their voices. Today they stomped through the streets of Nairobi, loud, fearless, and demanding what every human being deserves—freedom from violence.

* * *

Anti-prostitution activists may think that the sex workers who marched in Nairobi want nothing more than to be rescued from prostitution. But if asked, they will tell you that what they want is respect for their human rights. And it's not only in Kenya where African sex workers refuse to remain silent. A chorus of sex workers' voices is rising across the continent. South African sex workers are leading a sophisticated national legal reform campaign to decriminalize sex work. Ugandan sex worker activists have withstood fierce government crackdowns. In Namibia, the movement is forming strong alliances with LGBT activists. Brothel-based sex workers in Nigeria, taking to the streets of Lagos in the hundreds, have protested unfair working conditions. Sex worker activists throughout Africa are demanding the end of criminalization and the recognition and protection of their human rights to safe working conditions, health and justice services, and lives free from violence, discrimination, and stigma.

These efforts are bolstered by the fact that in the past few years, influential labor, global health, human rights, and women's rights organizations have embraced sex workers' rights. United Nations agencies have issued guiding principles and studies espousing the language and goals of the sex workers' rights movement. The World Health Organization (WHO) has encouraged organizations to "[s]upport community mobilization of sex workers to respond to violence and discrimination," and in 2012 and 2014, WHO released guidelines urging states to work toward the decriminalization of sex work.[9] In 2012, the United Nations Development Programme (UNDP) and the United Nations Population Fund (UNFPA) released an important survey regarding sex work and the law in almost fifty countries in Asia and the Pacific that called for the repeal of punitive laws related to the sex industry.[10] In 2013, the United Nations Entity for Gender Equality and the Empowerment of Women (UN Women) recognized "the right of all sex workers to choose their work."[11] In its *Guidance Note on HIV and Sex Work*, the Joint United Nations Programme on HIV/AIDS (UNAIDS) clearly argued that discrimination, stigmatization, and harassment from law enforcement increase sex workers' vulnerability to HIV/AIDS, and in a 2014 briefing note it asserted that "Criminalisation of sex workers or their clients negates the right to individual self-determination, autonomy and agency."[12] In 2014, the International Labour Organization (ILO) released a report stressing the importance of sex worker peer education programs.[13] United Nations Special Rapporteurs on extreme poverty, the right to health, and the right to be free from torture have all laid human rights violations against sex workers squarely at the door of criminalization, stigma, and discrimination.[14]

International independent experts in global health have also joined the influential voices supporting the goals of the sex workers' rights movement. *The Lancet*, one of the world's most respected general medical journals, has decried the marginalization of sex workers in global HIV efforts and in a July 2012 editorial further argued that the "conflation of sex work with human trafficking, and the disregard of sex work as work, has meant that sex workers' rights have not been properly recognised."[15] *The Lancet* also released a series of scientific reports in 2014 arguing that the decriminalization of sex work could significantly reduce HIV infections in female sex workers.[16] In a 2012 watershed report, leading health and human rights experts sitting on the Global Commission on HIV and the Law, including distinguished HIV/AIDS activist Stephen Lewis and U.S. Congresswoman Barbara Lee of California, powerfully argued, "Sex workers are not fully recognised as persons before the law and are rendered incapable of holding or exercising the range of human rights available to others."[17] They continued by noting, "Where sex workers organise, where the police don't harass them and they are free to avail themselves of quality HIV services, sex workers have lower rates of STIs [sexually transmitted infections], more economic power and a greater ability to get education for their children."[18] The Commission called for the full decriminalization of sex work.[19]

In 2013, Human Rights Watch, the world's leading international human rights organization, publicly affirmed that it had "concluded that ending the criminalization of sex work is critical to achieving public health and human rights goals," and in its 2014 World Report it reiterated its "push for decriminalizing voluntary sex work by adults."[20] The Open Society Foundations, one of the largest grant-making foundations in the world, has long supported grassroots sex workers' rights activism, including the campaign to decriminalize sex work in South Africa.[21]

The global membership of the Association for Women's Rights in Development (AWID), which every four years convenes one of the largest global gatherings of women's rights activists outside of the UN, for the first time ever in 2013 elected an out sex worker, Kthi Win, to its international board of directors.[22] This milestone followed Kthi's appearance at the 2012 AWID international forum in Istanbul, where before a hushed audience of more than 2,000 women's rights advocates from more than 140 countries, with quiet confidence Kthi bravely stated: "The key demand of the sex workers' movement . . . is simple. We demand that sex work [be] recognized as work. But we have one other key demand, specific to certain parts of the women's movement. We demand that we [not be] treated as victims."[23] The membership's election of Kthi to its board following this appearance was a ringing endorsement of the idea that sex workers' rights and feminism are not mutually exclusive. On June 2, 2014, in honor of the International Day for Sex Workers, the Global Coalition on Women and AIDS (GCWA), an international consortium of civil society groups focusing on women's rights, released a strong statement calling for "transformative laws which protect sex workers."[24]

The fact that the global health and human rights communities are increasingly reaching a consensus about the deep harms of sex work criminalization is significant—the more evidence and clear-sighted reasoning, and not emotion, inform the debate, the more lives will be saved. These positive developments are proof that sex worker activists in Africa and throughout the world are making important, persuasive assertions and garnering acknowledgment and support from influential players on the world stage.

To Live Freely in This World is the first book to fully document the history and continuing activism of the sex workers' rights movement in Africa, which is the newest and most vibrant manifestation of the global sex workers' rights struggle.[25] Based on participant observation and in-depth interviews with more than 200 sex workers, activists, and allies in seven African countries as diverse as Botswana, Kenya, Mauritius, Namibia, Nigeria, South Africa, and Uganda, the book explores how this young movement is blossoming, confronting challenges, and contributing an African perspective to feminist debates about sex work.[26]

Whereas anti-prostitution activists have long claimed that all sex workers are inherently violated people in need of rescue by virtuous saviors,
this book tells a different story. It serves as powerful proof that African sex worker activists are determining their social and political fate
through strategic, informed choices.

This book also seeks to help fill a large void in both sex work studies
and African feminist scholarship. The extensive body of literature per-
taining to sex workers' rights has heavily focused on the United States,
Europe, Asia, and Asia-Pacific and has lacked a comprehensive study
on sex work activism in Africa. African feminist scholars, with a few
notable exceptions, have largely remained silent on the issue of sex work.
Sylvia Tamale, a Ugandan legal scholar focusing on African sexualities,
has argued that the patriarchal state criminalizes sex work as a way of
controlling African women's sexual activity. She contends that criminalization has been a public health disaster that ignores African women's
economic realities, and she champions the need for a progressive African feminist agenda that embraces the decriminalization of sex work as
a response to the patriarchal state's injurious nature and indignities.[27]
Marlise Richter, a South African scholar focusing on sexual and reproductive health and rights, has argued for an Africanist sex-positive[28]
approach to sex work and bemoans the lack of African feminist engagement with the issue, especially in light of devastating rates of HIV/AIDS
in sex worker communities in sub-Saharan Africa, the continent most
heavily affected by the epidemic:

> It is curious that, while the prevalence of female sex workers and pro-
> portion of female sex workers to the general population are higher in
> sub-Saharan Africa than in any other region of the world, African femi-
> nisms have not grappled much with the issue of sex work. This is of par-
> ticular concern against the backdrop of the staggering prevalence of HIV
> amongst sex workers in Africa—sex workers generally have a 10–20 fold
> higher HIV prevalence than the general population—and the on-going
> human rights violations against sex workers. Sex work and sex workers'
> rights are conspicuously absent from most discussions on gender in Af-
> rica, and many feminist and gender practitioners avoid the issue like the
> plague—thus perpetuating the stigma and silence that surround the sex
> industry in Africa.[29]

Although leading African feminists such as Hope Chigudu and Solome Nakaweesi-Kimbugwe have stood in staunch solidarity with African sex workers and played significant roles in the early development of sex workers' rights movements in eastern Africa,[30] African feminists' general silence regarding sex work has been louder than these examples of solidarity. This study, which centralizes African sex workers' understanding of their work, feminist analysis, and fight for their rights, is not only an act of solidarity with them but seeks to address the gap in feminist knowledge regarding sex work in the African context.

Although this book focuses on the struggle for sex workers' rights in Africa, it is important to note that abuses against sex workers aren't confined to the Global South—they are equally prevalent in the Global North. In New York City, where I live, sex workers routinely experience abuse and lack access to justice when they are the victims of violence. In one study, 80 percent of street-based sex workers reported being the victims of violence and noted that police refused to take crimes committed against them seriously.[31] Sex workers have experienced police confiscation of their condoms from Washington, D.C., to Russia.[32] The International Day to End Violence against Sex Workers was inspired by the serial murders of sex workers in Seattle, Washington, that went unsolved for decades.[33] Studies have also documented entrenched violence and discrimination against sex workers in Britain, France, and other countries in the Global North.[34]

Elsewhere in the world, police abuse of sex workers is also ubiquitous: In a survey of 200 sex workers in eleven countries in eastern Europe and central Asia, 41.7 percent of respondents reported physical assault by law enforcement.[35] A survey of brothel-based and mobile Cambodian sex workers revealed that more than 57 percent reported being raped by police officers.[36] And in 2013, Human Rights Watch released a report that received global media attention for its documentation of widespread police torture, beatings, and arbitrary detention of sex workers in China.[37]

I chose to highlight the African context not because human rights abuses against African sex workers are unique—far from it—but because their response to this abuse is distinguished by an activism that is young and robust and therefore deeply compelling. In only the past several years, the African branch of the global sex workers' rights movement has exploded. Through the fresh stories of African sex worker activists, the book will highlight this unique moment. And by locating this counter-narrative in the Global South, it will challenge disempowering and one-dimensional depictions of "degraded Third World prostitutes" that are often the focus of anti-prostitution activists' savior impulses.[38]

The book tells the story of the African sex workers' rights movement by exploring the following themes: African sex worker advocates' perspectives on longstanding feminist debates regarding prostitution, including their insistence on the acceptance of sex work as labor and the recognition of their human agency even amidst limited economic opportunities (chapter 1); how social stigma and the criminalization of sex work result in human rights abuses against African sex workers, including police abuse, denial of access to justice, client abuse, lack of labor rights, and health care discrimination (chapter 2); and how whorephobia and sex work criminalization intersect with transphobia, homophobia, trafficking and sex work conflation, HIV stigma, and discriminatory laws to create multiple overlapping stigmas against African queer and trans sex workers, migrant sex workers, and HIV-positive sex workers (chapter 3).

The book then traces the history of African sex worker activism in various countries at different stages of organizing, highlighting informal and formal political resistance and the movement's successes and struggles in creating both visionary leaders and active constituents (chapter 4); the role of intersectional movement building with similarly marginalized communities, including feminist, LGBT, HIV/AIDS, labor, harm-reduction, and anti-poverty groups (chapter 5); and the movement's key organizing strategies—health and legal services for diverse sex workers, community outreach to advance the notion of sex work as labor in the public imagination, and rights-based law reform efforts to decriminalize sex work (chapter 6).

I also explore the tactics and subsequent harms of political opposition from anti-prostitution activists who champion ineffective and stigmatizing rehabilitation programs targeting sex workers, conservative religious leaders who characterize sex work as both immoral and un-African, and African politicians wielding what I term "political whorephobia," a strategy that seeks to crack down on gender dissidents (chapter 7). The Epilogue highlights African sex worker activists' increasing engagement with the larger global sex workers' rights movement, including their development of innovative South–South collaborations.

I share my on-the-ground observations of sex worker activism in action and provide context and analysis as we explore these themes. But it is the stories of sex workers' journeys into activism collected during my interviews in African cities and small towns that are the book's beating heart. Several of these stories are presented as extended first-person narratives.[39] I chose to include these first-person narratives and spotlight many sex workers' voices by quoting judiciously from my interviews because while I hope I'm considered an ally of the sex worker movement, I'm not a sex worker. And too often non–sex workers take it upon themselves to speak for sex workers when the latter are fully capable of speaking for themselves. By elevating and centering their voices, I hope to both create a platform for them and speak in solidarity with them.

Many of the sex worker activists profiled in this book have experienced horrendous abuse. This reality has often led to the dismissal of sex workers as "broken people" whose voices we can ignore. But people who have experienced abuse are not bereft of agency. A history of personal trauma may—or may not—directly inform people's economic choices, but it should never be used as an excuse to negate their right and ability to speak about the truth of their own lives. There are no broken people in this book. I hope the reader will see the radiating strength of the African sex workers who bring the book to life and who were brave enough to allow me to listen and help bear witness. And I hope that by reading about the deep injustice of the legal and social universe in which African sex workers live, the reader will also come to understand that even those sex workers who aren't "strong," who haven't "overcome" the obstacles of their past or the abuses they currently face, who have no activist stories of triumph to share, are just as deserving of rights by simple virtue of their humanity.

Because the interviews in this study often did reveal extreme instances of abuse, I ensured, by adhering to the following standard when determining whether to feature a particular case in the book, that I didn't include stories simply to elicit an emotional response from the reader: (1) The interviewee's story highlights a recurring theme regarding African sex workers' political and social realities, and (2) it creates knowledge about the link between sex work, human agency, criminalization, and the political struggle for dignity and justice. To include stories that failed to meet this standard would have been to exploit the interviewees by participating in the cynical selling of suffering.

In order to gather the stories for this book, I conducted a wide range of interviews and engaged in participant observation during fieldwork in December 2012, March 2013, June through July 2013, November 2013, and October 2014, focusing on seven countries and twelve field sites in a mix of urban, semi-urban, and semi-rural areas in order to speak with a variety of sex workers in different settings. Urban sites were an important focus because they are hotbeds of sex worker activism. But it was also necessary to focus on non-urban areas to gain an understanding of how the movement is developing across different locations. Sites included Cape Town, South Africa; Windhoek, Namibia; Gaborone, Francistown, and Kazangula in Botswana; Kampala and Mijera in Uganda; Nairobi and Thika in Kenya; Quatre Bornes and Port Louis in Mauritius; and Lagos, Nigeria.

I chose the book's seven focus countries—Botswana, Mauritius, Namibia, and South Africa in southern Africa; Kenya and Uganda in eastern Africa; and Nigeria in western Africa—in order to ensure geographic diversity and to highlight country movements that are at different stages of sex work organizing.[40] Although an in-depth analysis of the focus countries' social and political histories is beyond the scope of this book, the following brief country contexts for several of the field sites may prove useful in framing the developmental trajectory of sex work activism highlighted in this study: Countries like South Africa and Kenya, with vibrant civil societies and rich histories of activism against oppression (in South Africa against the apartheid state, and in Kenya against British colonialism), tend to provide easier launching pads for sex worker–led movements because of deeply ingrained histories of protest in the national psyches. In South Africa, for instance, sex workers I interviewed often had personal backgrounds as anti-apartheid activists and referred to their sex work activism as partly inspired by their previous struggles against the racist apartheid state. In Kenya, there is historical evidence that prostitutes played a role in the Mau Mau uprising against British colonial rule,[41] creating a historical precedent for contemporary grassroots Kenyan sex worker activism. Countries with weaker civil societies and without strong histories of social activism, like Mauritius and Botswana, provide less fertile ground for the fast rise of sex worker–led movements. Sex work activism in countries like Uganda and Nigeria must be understood in the context of their highly publicized and serious legal and social crackdowns against those viewed as gender and sexual deviants.

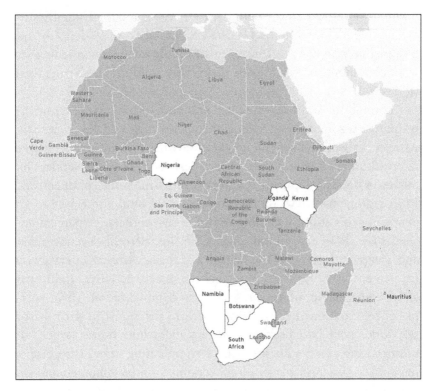

Map of focus countries.

I gained access to sex worker interviewees with the assistance of sex workers' rights organizations such as Sisonke and the Sex Workers Education and Advocacy Taskforce (SWEAT) in South Africa, Sisonke Botswana, the Kenya Sex Workers Alliance (KESWA), Women's Organization Network for Human Rights Advocacy (WONETHA) in Uganda, and Rights Not Rescue Trust (RNRT) and Voices of Hope Trust in Namibia, as well as HIV and harm-reduction organizations such as Chrysalide and *Prévention Information et Lutte contre le Sida* (PILS) in Mauritius. I found that once these organizations had vouched for me, the sex workers they put me in touch with were incredibly open and willing to speak with me about their experiences. These sex workers would then, in turn, introduce me to more sex workers. It also helped that since 2007, as director of a law school–based human rights program, I've worked on projects with well-known sex workers' rights organizations in India, Kenya, South Africa, Malawi, and the United States. When potential interviewees learned of this work, they identified me as someone who has contributed to efforts aimed at strengthening sex work communities, which made them more comfortable sharing their stories with me.

Although the term *sex work* can and does encompass other actors within the sex industry, including porn performers and exotic dancers, African sex workers who are engaged in what is traditionally viewed as prostitution—the in-person physical exchange of sexual services for money or goods—dominate sex worker activism on the continent, and I focused my interviews on this population. In total, I interviewed 211 people for this study, including 163 adult sex workers (75 percent cisgender female, 18 percent transgender female, 7 percent cisgender male, and 4 percent migrant). The majority of the sex worker interviewees (73 percent) were involved in formal sex worker activism, and nearly all were engaged in informal resistance to criminalization. Their workplaces reflected the diversity of the African sex industry: street-based sex work; venue-based sex work in bars, nightclubs, hotels, large-scale brothels, and small-scale brothels often operating under the guise of massage parlors; independent sex work out of private homes; and sex work in border towns. I conducted interviews in various venues, sensitive to comfort and confidentiality for interviewees, including on the streets and in cars, brothels, hotels, restaurants, and the offices of sex workers' rights organizations. I also interviewed 48 UN officials, academics, nongovernmental organization (NGO) workers, lawyers, and health workers who conduct outreach to sex work communities. Many of the interviews were conducted individually, though some were conducted in groups or pairs, and most were digitally recorded with the interviewees' permission.[42] My graduate research assistants and I transcribed the audio recordings.

Along with formal interviews, I observed and participated in sex worker activism in action, including sex worker protest marches and human rights trainings in South Africa and Kenya and health and social outreach to sex workers on the streets and in indoor venues, such as massage parlors and brothels, in Mauritius and South Africa.

I have changed the names of brothels, hotels, massage parlors, and clubs that sex workers reference in their interviews. I have also used pseudonyms for most of the sex worker interviewees. However, high-profile country movement leaders who have already revealed their true identities via national and international media and other public fora, and whose work has been essential to the development of formal African sex worker activism, almost always wanted me to use their real names, which I have done.

Here are just a few of the activists you will meet in the pages that follow: Duduzile Dlamini, a charismatic leader of the South African sex worker movement, deftly convinces members of South Africa's politically powerful national trade union that sex workers are also workers doing the best they can to provide for themselves and their families and are deserving of rights. Mama Africa, the mother of the sex worker movement in Namibia, helps tell the story of setbacks faced by fledgling sex worker organizing in that southern African nation through a remembrance of the short, powerful life and untimely death of Abel Shinana—a lost but unforgotten leader in the Namibia sex worker movement. John Mathenge, a Kenyan activist with a bracing confidence who has become the face and voice of male sex worker activism in the country, stars in a nationally televised documentary illuminating and validating the lives of male sex workers. Daisy Nakato, long a leader in the Ugandan movement, helps tell the story of a severe government crackdown on sex worker organizing that threatens to close a drop-in center that provides health and human rights services to sex workers in Gulu in northern Uganda. She speaks of how Ugandan sex workers fight back against this oppression, and because of their courage, the drop-in center still stands.

The progressive movement of history, the expansive realization of rights, is always, at its heart, a story about ordinary men and women who deeply and unwaveringly believe in the immovable core of their humanity. It is about people who have been relegated to the margins of society righteously claiming the center—an ancient but eternally important endeavor. This book seeks to explore that journey through the fresh lens of sex worker activism in Africa while pushing back against the dangerous notion that all sex workers want to be rescued from sex work.

To Live Freely in This World focuses on the strength and creativity of sex worker activists like Duduzile, Mama Africa, John, and Daisy, the identities of resistance they've formed in response to criminalization and stigma, and the luminous, defiant social movement they're build-ing. Their collective agency will pour through the pages of this book. And I hope in the face of that agency, policymakers, scholars, activists, students, and concerned readers will choose to engage as partners in the struggle for sex workers' rights and not as would-be saviors. This is a book about communities saving themselves by demanding their rights. Ultimately it is a universal story about how those who are most legally and socially ostracized fight back—with dignity and hope.

1

"Our House's Foundation"

Understanding Sex Work in Africa

When we reject the single story and realize there is never a
single story . . . we regain a kind of paradise.
—Chimamanda Ngozi Adichie

Duduzile ("Dudu") Dlamini, a Zulu female sex worker, is small and
round, with piercing, pretty eyes and a powerful energy. Eunice April,
a Coloured and Xhosa transgender female sex worker, is tall and slen-
der, with striking, sharp features and a quiet confidence. They share
the same burning dedication to the health and human rights of their ·
fellow sex workers. December nights in Cape Town, South Africa—
which juts out into the Atlantic, hugging the southernmost western tip
of the continent—can be surprisingly chilly, and on one such night, I'm
chatting with Dudu and Eunice outside the airy meeting space of both
the Sex Workers Education and Advocacy Taskforce (SWEAT), a sex
workers' rights NGO, and Sisonke, the sex worker–led South African
movement that's one of the most active on the continent.[1] They work for
SWEAT and Sisonke's comprehensive mobile outreach peer education
program, which is truly a thing of beauty. Year-round—virtually every
day and night—roving teams of outreach workers seek out sex workers
on the streets and in bars, taverns, clubs, and brothels in Cape Town,
providing them with free sexual health, general health, and human
rights services. Tonight, I'm participating in one of their outreach sessions to street-based sex workers, a jaunt that will last deep into the cold,
windy night.

Around 10 P.M., Dudu, Eunice, and I jump into a large white SWEAT/
Sisonke "mobile wellness clinic" van, overflowing with supplies to hand
out to the sex workers we'll meet tonight: male and female condoms;
personal lubricant, which helps prevent condom breakage; brochures

Eunice April. Cape Town, South Africa. Photograph by author.

about sexual health and hygiene; "know your rights" booklets, including ones focused on police abuse; and contact information for the SWEAT/ Sisonke twenty-four-hour help hotline for sex workers in crisis. In the back of the medically equipped van is a small testing area where sex workers can receive free and confidential rapid fifteen-minute HIV tests, pap smears, and tuberculosis sputum and STI screenings.

The rest of the outreach team joins us in the van, including Buyi, an HIV and tuberculosis counselor, and Tina, a nurse practitioner, as we head out into the blue-black night. Cape Town has a large Coloured population, so most of the sex workers we'll come across tonight are Coloured female sex workers, cisgender and transgender, who've come into town from the impoverished outskirts of central Cape Town. The outreach workers know the areas where sex workers can be found, so we make our first stop on the main road of Cape Town's southern suburb.

Dudu and Eunice spot two women standing on the corner, one of whom they know. We slow down, and Dudu hops out of the van to speak with them. Nelda is in her forties, wearing a long tiger-print bandana, and she's thrilled to see Dudu. "Welcome to Cape Town!" she yells out to me over Dudu's shoulder, her eyes bright, when she learns that I'm visiting from the States. "Would you like to do HIV testing tonight?" Dudu asks Nelda and Elizabeth, the second, younger sex worker standing next to her. "A nurse and counselor are in the wellness van and could give you a rapid fifteen-minute test. They could also do TB testing or STI screening if you'd like."

Nelda proudly reports she's recently been tested on-site at the SWEAT and Sisonke premises we've just arrived from, where weekly testing is provided to supplement the daily mobile outreach work. Elizabeth is visibly nervous at the thought of getting tested. "It's been a long time since I've been tested," she says, moving from side to side, an anxious smile creeping onto her face.

Dudu doesn't pressure her—their program is firmly nonjudgmental and respectful of sex workers' agency. "When you're ready," Dudu says gently, "it's a good thing to keep in mind. Next Wednesday, we'll be doing testing on-site at the SWEAT offices if you change your mind, okay? What about condoms or lube, do you need some?"

Both Nelda and Elizabeth eagerly walk over to the van with us to pick up armfuls of health supplies. They're especially excited by the flavored condoms the outreach team has in stock tonight. And as Nelda grabs her supplies she tells us defiantly, "The cops rarely fuck with me anymore because I know my rights now that I've been going to Sisonke and SWEAT. I tell them that I feed my children! They don't feed my children! This is the confidence I've gotten from SWEAT." Because police abuse of sex workers in Cape Town is rampant, SWEAT and Sisonke educate sex workers about their rights regarding police and provide them with direct legal services in partnership with NGOs like the Women's Legal Centre to back up this rights education.

At our second stop along the main road we approach a young woman named Sana. She has curly dark brown hair down to her chin and sleepy eyes. As Dudu approaches her, a small gray car with a man inside passes by. "Stop, darling," she whispers, reaching out her hand in the air as he slows down briefly and then speeds up. "We saw you the other night when we were doing outreach, do you remember me?" Dudu asks her. Sana smiles and nods in recognition. "Do you want to take a rapid HIV test tonight? I remember last time you weren't sure." As Sana eyes the mobile wellness van parked next to us, she asks, "Will it really only take fifteen minutes?"

"Yes, it's fast, accurate, and confidential, and we have a nurse and counselor with us who will administer the test and answer any of your questions. And they can refer you to medical clinics that are friendly to sex workers for follow-up if necessary," Dudu assures her. Sana pauses for a few seconds, her head tilted slightly to the side, a somewhat wary smile lingering on her face as she decides whether to trust us. "Yes, I'd like to get tested," she finally says and hops quickly into the back of the van with Tina and Buyi while Eunice, Dudu, and I wait outside.

As we wait, a police car slowly and somewhat menacingly circles the block. Sex work is illegal in South Africa. "We sometimes wear t-shirts that say, 'Leave us alone and tackle real crime,'" Eunice says, watching the police cruiser turn the corner and disappear. "Our outreach team hasn't had problems with the cops, but some other teams have experienced police harassment because we're providing services to sex workers," she says incredulously, shaking her head. When Sana emerges from the back of the van in less than fifteen minutes, as Dudu promised, she seems relieved. "Ciao," she says softly with a smile now devoid of suspicion as she walks away.

Rejecting Anti-Prostitution Activists' Single Story of Sex Work

The types of services for sex workers that programs like SWEAT and Sisonke deliver—condoms and personal lubricant to facilitate safe-sex practices, STI and HIV testing, tuberculosis screening, referrals to health clinics, information about rights, legal aid services, sex worker–led organizing, and harm reduction for people who use drugs—have long been celebrated by global health bodies like WHO and UNAIDS as essential to protecting sex workers' health and human rights.[2] Sex worker peer educators like Dudu and Eunice treat every single sex worker who uses their services with kindness, professionalism, respect, and, most important, no judgment, focusing instead on providing sex workers with the tools they need to work safely. Their work mirrors the outreach efforts of many sex worker organizations throughout the world, like the well-known Durbar Mahila Samanwaya Committee (DMSC), comprising thousands of organized sex workers in Sonagachi, the famous red-light district in Kolkata, India.[3]

Anti-prostitution activists would argue that sex workers, or "prostituted women" as they prefer to call them,[4] don't need condoms or "know your rights" workshops—they need rescue from prostitution. Some anti-prostitution activists openly criticize the lifesaving assistance sex workers' rights organizations routinely provide to sex workers.[5] But Indian sex workers in Sonagachi and South African sex workers in Cape Town clearly need this assistance. The reason anti-prostitution activists dismiss outreach programs aimed at sex worker empowerment is that these programs go against the idea that all sex workers are victims of what activists argue is prostitution's inherent violence. Western anti-prostitution activists have long argued that sex work is a form of patriarchal violence against women. Some African reformers have also embraced these anti-prostitution arguments. For instance, Fatoumata Sire Diakite, a Malian activist affiliated with the Coalition against Trafficking in Women (CATW), an influential global anti-prostitution organization, argues, "Prostitution is violence against women and a violation of human rights."[6]

Anti-prostitution activists' insistence on this monolithic narrative exemplifies what the Nigerian novelist Chimamanda Ngozi Adichie refers to as "the danger of a single story." Adichie has argued that when we have a single story about particular people and places it erases the voices and experiences of those who don't fit that universalized narrative.[7] In describing her American college roommate's stereotypes of Africa and Africans, Adichie noted: "Her default position toward me, as an African, was a kind of patronizing, well-meaning pity. My roommate had a single story of Africa: a single story of catastrophe. In this single story there was no possibility of Africans' being similar to her in any way, no possibility of feelings more complex than pity, no possibility of connection as human equals."[8] In the single story of her roommate's imagination, Africa was a continent of people "unable to speak for themselves and waiting to be saved by a kind white foreigner."[9] The danger of a single story, then, is that it makes "one story become the only story."[10]

When I first listened to Adichie's talk, I immediately reflected on how many anti-prostitution activists' arguments exhibit the "danger of a single story" by presenting sex workers as simple objects of pity and potential rescue incapable of speaking for themselves. Because these ideas have penetrated the mainstream, it is difficult for many people to imagine sex workers as capable of consent and agency. This is perhaps why, when I tell people that much of my human rights work is in solidarity with sex workers fighting for their rights, they often interpret that as my saying, "I work on sex trafficking." This is partly because although human trafficking (the movement of individuals through force, threat of force, coercion, or deception into a situation of forced labor)[11] and sex work (the exchange of sexual services as labor between consenting adults) are not the same, anti-prostitution activists have co-opted anti-trafficking language to purposefully conflate the two. They argue that consent in the context of prostitution is impossible and that therefore all sex workers have been forced into sex work—either literally or by circumstance—and our primary focus must be the facilitation of their rescue, not the realization of their rights. They have created a global campaign that, at its core, is not about human trafficking or forced labor but about advancing an anti-prostitution agenda.[12] (There are indeed people within the sex industry—as there are within the agricultural, construction, domestic care, garment trade, and factory industries—who are the victims of trafficking into forced labor. But the conflation of sex work and trafficking does nothing to help survivors of trafficking gain access to the resources and social services they need.)[13] The narrative that people cannot consent to engage in sex work fits squarely into anti-prostitution activists' "single story."

Why is this single story dangerous? Because when we insist that sex workers are "victims" incapable of speaking for themselves, we silence them. When we ignore the multiplicity of sex workers' experiences, we deny them agency. And when we contend that the primary concern for sex workers is *the sex* involved in sex work and not the criminalized and stigmatized nature of their work, not the material conditions of their labor, we fail to acknowledge and address the actual abuses many sex worker communities face.

* * *

At the next stop on the nighttime outreach work I'm observing in Cape Town, Dudu approaches a young woman named Rena who's standing on a corner under a large citrus tree next to a short, rail-thin man who averts his eyes as we approach. At first I'm not sure who he is—all I notice are his hands, a layer of dark soot caked over them, clutching a mobile phone tightly. A minute or so after we arrive and exchange greetings he leaves us to speak with Rena alone, walking away without looking back. Later Dudu says, "Some 'pimps' want the girls to speak to us and will make sure to give them the space to do so. Others won't." Rena is very pretty, spirited right from the beginning of our chat with her, which is intermittently interrupted by her boyfriend, who calls twice to see if she's okay. Her hair is pulled back in a tight ponytail, and she's wearing a white dress with ruffles and dangling red earrings, her hands fluttering excitedly in the air as she speaks: "We need info! The girls don't know their rights! You need to pressure girls to come to Sisonke because they don't know their rights!"

"We have lots of human rights pamphlets with us. Do you want some to pass out to your friends?" Dudu asks. "Yes!" Rena says eagerly. Dudu explains the topics covered by each of the brochures, all specifically created for sex workers, on how to report police abuse, practice safer sex, and safeguard their health. Rena listens carefully and grabs an armful of pamphlets, promising to share them with others as she scuttles off and yells back over her shoulder, "Thank you! Gotta go! Have to make money!"

Still making our way through the southern suburbs, we turn off the main street onto Lansdowne Road, which is darker, lonelier, some of the streetlights missing their bulbs. We see a tall woman in a black shawl standing on the side of the road alone and pull up next to her. She looks at the van curiously and starts to walk away quickly when Dudu steps out of the van. Dudu follows her for a few brief seconds while gently saying, "We only want to talk to you and see if there's anything you need." But the woman doesn't stop, looking over her shoulder as she moves on, so Dudu backs off. "She's not ready," Dudu says calmly as we return to the van. Of the thirty or so sex workers we'll approach over the course of the night, she was the only one who chose not to engage. But the response from the outreach workers was the same—they respect each person's desires. They never apply pressure. They only present options.

We're now going down a main road that is normally busy even at this time of night but is now eerily quiet. We pull up next to a transgender sex worker named Greta. SWEAT and Sisonke host weekly support groups for "female, male, and transgender" sex workers, migrant sex workers, HIV-positive and HIV-negative sex workers, and sex workers struggling with substance addiction. Greta used to attend some of these meetings, but Dudu and Eunice haven't seen her around for some time.

"How are you doing?" Eunice asks her. "Surviving," Greta replies with a smile, elongating the second syllable of the word, a hint of playful mischief in her voice. Her makeup is done impeccably, and she's wearing bright colors—pops of fluorescent pink and green. Her hair is long and auburn. "You look so beautiful tonight," Dudu tells her, and then softly, tenderly, "How come you no longer come to SWEAT and Sisonke? We haven't seen you in a long time."

"Well, since Sasha," Greta says slowly, her eyes falling to the pavement, her voice trailing off until there's only the sound of the wind and a sad, knowing silence between her, Dudu, and Eunice. Sasha was a transgender female sex worker, and two months ago, someone posing as a potential client stabbed her through the heart. She died in the middle of the street, not far from where we're standing now, and the police still haven't found her killer—although it's doubtful they're seriously searching for suspects.

After a few moments pass, Greta starts to speak about the intensified police harassment she's experienced in the past few weeks. "All of my fines are stacking up," she says, worry creeping over her lovely face. "We have paralegals who can accompany you to court to fight the fines and get them dismissed," Eunice reassures her. "If the fines pile up, and we don't fight them, the cops can issue a warrant for your arrest and send you to jail at Pollsmoor the next time they pick you up. So it's better if we help you fight them." "Pollsmoor" is a name that elicits terror on the faces of sex workers in Cape Town. It is an overcrowded, dangerous maximum-security prison where cops sometimes dump sex workers for days. Nelson Mandela spent some of his twenty-seven-year imprisonment there. "I never knew that I could fight the fines," Greta says surprised, assuring them she'll try to start attending SWEAT and Sisonke workshops again. She calls a friend over to come pick up lubricant from the van with her.

Hours later, at our last stop, Dudu comes across two white female sex workers relaxing on the floor of a bank ATM center, soaking in the warmth from the heating system insulating them against the Cape Town cold. Neither has ever heard of SWEAT or Sisonke. They offer Dudu a smoke and begin to chat. Dudu lets them know we have a nurse and counselor with us if they're interested in free health services. "I already know that I'm [HIV] positive," says Alice, one of the women. She is older, maybe in her forties, with short ink-jet black hair and an earthy voice. "But I've never been on ARVs [anti-retroviral medications]," she continues. She points to her friend sitting next to her. "Gina is always encouraging me to get on them, but I've never gotten around to it. I know my CD4 count, and I don't think it's low enough to qualify for ARVs."[14] Dudu explains that she has the wrong information because in South Africa even people with very high CD4 counts are eligible for ARVs. Alice listens intently but says she's not ready. As they continue to talk, she pulls out a small piece of crumpled aluminum foil and a lighter and begins to smoke drugs. "I know that I need to be careful because of my status," she says as she lights the bottom of the foil and inhales. "I might use drugs, but I'm a good person. I don't steal from my clients."

"The police are the main problem," Gina says firmly. She's younger than Alice, in her thirties, with brown wavy hair brushing her shoulders. She seems protective of Alice. "Alice has almost 7,000 rand [$654 USD] worth of police fines stacked up, and the cops are constantly trying to get sexual favors from us," she continues. "They always say they'll let you go if you give them 'something' for free. I won't give them anything without them paying." They're both agitated as they speak about the police and how much they get away with.

Dudu hands them "know your rights" cards about how to deal with the police. "If they give you trouble, hand them one of the cards in this booklet; it explains your rights so they know they can't take advantage of you." Alice and Gina are very interested in the booklet, flipping through it slowly, reading every page and asking Dudu questions. The three of them start to talk about the need for legal reform of the sex industry to prevent these types of abuses. The importance of peer education was so clear—Dudu's being an active sex worker and being able to empathize with some of the problems Alice and Gina face was essential to their opening up. Before we leave, Alice and Gina give Dudu a long, lingering hug.

Months later, I participate in indoor outreach with a different, equally dedicated SWEAT/Sisonke team, this time focused on brothels operating under massage-parlor licenses. The SWEAT and Sisonke mobile outreach program has agreements with many of these indoor agencies, allowing them access to sex workers to provide health and rights services. Past two huge bodyguards hovering outside the Sunset/Sunrise club in Cape Town, in a small room next to the bar where several sex workers are watching television while they wait for potential customers, I meet a white South African woman named Nora. She's sitting on a brown leather couch next to some of the SWEAT and Sisonke outreach workers who have just finished a health presentation. She's in her early thirties, blond hair pulled back in a tight bun, ice-blue eyes, her face warm and open. She started working at Sunset/Sunrise only two weeks ago—her first time working as a sex worker.

"I was working as a personal assistant before, but for personal reasons I recently quit that job," she explains. "I have a young daughter, and while I'm looking for permanent employment I don't want our standard of living to drop. A friend of mine suggested this as an option, so I decided to try it. I only want to do it for two months—I have financial goals that I want to meet, and then I'll move on to another job."

I ask her how the past two weeks have been. "I want to make sure I don't catch anything health-wise during my time here," she confides. "I always try and stay on top of the clients to make sure they're not trying to slip the condoms off."

"What about using female condoms," I suggest, "so that you have more control?" She's very interested and leans in closely: "I've been thinking about that, but how long can I keep the female condom in? I think I can leave it in for eight hours, right?" I quickly call over Gulam Saayman, one of the SWEAT/Sisonke outreach workers, so that she can give Nora information and perhaps a demonstration. Gulam, a Coloured transgender sex worker peer educator, speaks slowly and softly, in long, clear sentences. She radiates cheerfulness. She hands Nora pamphlets and then pulls out a female condom demonstration kit, complete with a plastic vagina. With patience and attention to detail, she shows Nora step-by-step how to insert the female condom and dispose of it. After Gulam finishes the demonstration, a potential client—a stocky man with graying hair—appears at the bar, and the women begin to congregate around him. Nora soon joins them, stuffing the female condoms Gulam gave her into her black purse and sweetly thanking us before she gets up.

Gulam Saayman. Cape Town, South Africa. Photograph by Grace Eunmee Lee.

Coercion, Agency, and African Sex Workers' Lived Experiences of Labor

The South African sex workers who use SWEAT and Sisonke's services have very specific needs. Nora wanted more information about female condoms so that she could have more power over her work's potential health risks—she was not in need of our pity or our judgment or our rescue. Alice, Gina, and Greta wanted assistance and information regarding police abuse and harassment; Rena wanted "know your rights" pamphlets to share with other sex workers; Sana wanted an HIV test that was fast and confidential; Nelda and Elizabeth wanted as many condoms and lubricants as they could carry. Dudu, Eunice, and Gulam trusted that these women, despite difficult circumstances, are agents and experts of their own lives—capable of understanding and articulating what they need to increase their work's safety. And the outreach teams are meeting those needs without judgment—their response is not, nor should it be, "Your work should not exist."

Groups like SWEAT and Sisonke are deeply concerned with abuses of people in the sex industry, so they fight for sex workers' increased access to de-stigmatized health services, fight against rampant police abuse of sex workers, fight for sex workers' increased access to justice when they're the victims of crime, and fight against laws and policies that entrench sex workers' vulnerability.

Moralizing will not stop people from providing sexual services for pay on the streets or in indoor agencies. So, the question must be: How can people involved in the sex industry be safe? How can they have more power over their labor? But first we must acknowledge that there's a multiplicity of sex work experiences, multiple stories; there is no single one.

One of the major themes of anti-prostitution activists' single story of sex work is the idea that all sex work is inherently coercive. They argue that sex workers have highly limited work alternatives, and therefore no sex worker exercises a free choice to participate in the industry.[15] But the real question isn't one of free "choice" but one of human agency. In a world of severe and rising economic inequality under global capitalism, very few workers truly exercise unfettered choice in the modern labor market. But sex workers can and do exhibit human agency—they make rational decisions even amid the limited choices of the harsh economic order. Just as the domestic worker with low levels of education and restricted work opportunities can make a rational decision to engage in domestic work over other options like factory work, sex work, or vegetable vending, so too can the sex worker make a rational decision to engage in sex work over cleaning people's houses or working on the factory line. Or as one Kenyan sex worker activist noted, "Selling tomatoes and cabbages is work, but it pays less than sex work." The role of the African state should be to provide sex workers with economic and social protection for the rational decisions they're making.

African sex workers I interviewed described the provision of sexual services as labor—in almost all my interviews they were engaged in the industry for economic reasons. Single parenthood, financial dependence of extended family members, the need to supplement inadequate earnings through part-time work, and dissatisfaction with other forms of low-wage work can all be economic catalysts for women and men in Africa to work in the sex industry.

Mudiwa, a former migrant sex worker who now organizes sex workers in Cape Town, fled political repression in Zimbabwe in 2007. Soon after losing her job in a Cape Town restaurant, with nine dependents in Zimbabwe relying on the remittances she sends back home, she decided to start sex work: "The point that all the persons who are doing sex work have been forced to do it? No. Some make their own choices. . . . When I couldn't get money, I got so frustrated and stressed . . . and I just thought to myself, should I do sex work, should I not, should I, you know? I had to make a choice because I knew what I wanted. I had family back home [in Zimbabwe] . . . that really depended on me."

Mudiwa was asserting a viewpoint many African sex workers I interviewed emphasized—poverty is often a context for their decisions, as it is for most workers on the continent, but poverty and limited economic opportunities don't negate their agency. If Mudiwa had opted for domestic work instead of sex work, it is highly unlikely anti-prostitution activists would view her choice as her having been "forced" or "coerced" into domestic work, even though domestic workers in Africa, like sex workers, often have limited economic options. In other words, just because someone can't imagine why Mudiwa would make an economic decision to engage in sex work does not mean Mudiwa has not in fact made that decision. To dismiss her as a pawn of the "sex lobby" or a victim of "false consciousness" who has been brainwashed by the patriarchy and unable to recognize her own oppression because of the trauma of sex work—descriptions often given to sex workers who reject the single story of force, coercion, and voiceless victimhood—is to try and silence her.

For other African sex workers who participate in the sex industry, poverty may be one motivating factor, but not the only one. Some appreciate the flexibility and autonomy that sex work provides. "It's an easy way of making cash," says Priscilla, a transgender female sex worker and Sisonke member:

Like, for instance, the people that are earning at the end of the month—takes too long to wait for that period for me. While somebody is waiting for that money at the end of the month, during the month there are a lot of things that I've [already] covered [with the money obtained from sex work]. It's like having my own business. I'm just depending on myself. If

I don't feel like going to work, nobody's going to ask me, nobody's going to say, "Okay fine, you didn't come to work yesterday, now we must see a doctor's certificate."

But neither Mudiwa nor Priscilla would claim universality of their personal experiences in the sex industry. To take any of these stories and universalize them to all sex workers would be both unfair and untrue. Sex workers experience elements of coercion and freedom in their labor on a continuum: There are sex workers in Africa who do view their experience in the sex industry as severely exploitative and want to exit. There are those for whom it is largely liberating because it has given them a significant measure of financial independence. And then there are the majority of people who inhabit the gray area in between, who may at different times and in different ways experience elements of coercion *and* freedom in their work. Debates about whether sex work is solely a source of either exploitation or empowerment are frivolous—the sex workers I interviewed don't view their labor in simplistic and absolute shades of black or white. It is the gray area of the lived experience of labor that I am exploring in this book. Sex workers must be able to highlight the negative aspects of their working conditions without being told that their work should be eradicated. And they should be allowed to acknowledge the liberating elements without being labeled "nonrepresentative."

The one thing that *is* universal is that all sex workers—whatever their diverse experiences in the industry—have human agency. Or as Laura Agustin, a leading international writer and thinker on migration and sex work, astutely argues, "Disadvantaged persons with limited options of how to proceed in life have, until they are actually put in chains, some space to move, negotiate, prefer one option to another."[16]

In order to protect all people in the sex industry, no matter the diversity of their experiences within it, we must remove the stigma and criminal status attached to sex work, view it as a form of labor, and support sex workers who are fighting for their rights. The central tenet of the sex workers' rights movement in Africa and globally is that sex work is work. By understanding sex work as an economic activity and sex workers as laborers deserving of workers' protections, including fair wages, access to health care, and protection from abuse and institutionalized discrimination, we move beyond the tired debates regarding morality and sex work that have resulted in misguided laws and policies that harm sex workers.

African sex workers' understanding and description of sex work as a form of labor, clearly evident throughout my interviews, is not a recent or contemporary development. In a groundbreaking 1990 study of prostitution in colonial Nairobi by historian Luise White, Kenyan women who had worked as prostitutes under British colonial rule challenged White to understand prostitution as they did—as a "reliable means of capital accumulation," not "a despicable fate."[17] In colonial Kenya, prostitutes in Nairobi often sent the money they earned back home to their rural families who had been nearly destroyed by ecological misfortunes and colonial disruption. In doing so, they helped replenish their families' decimated livestock, pay off paternal debts, and provide their brothers with bridewealth cattle. Many other prostitutes, however, used their earnings not to restore their rural patrilineages' economic fortunes but to independently acquire property in Nairobi. They stepped outside traditional gender roles to establish themselves as heads of households and often passed down property to their own children or designated nonfamilial female heirs.[18] Prostitution as labor thus allowed some of these women more control over their familial and individual economic fate and therefore their lives.

Carol Leigh, an American sex worker activist and artist, coined the term *sex work* in 1978.[19] Sex worker activists throughout the world have embraced the term with fierce political devotion. It has resonated in the Global South, including in Africa, where sex work activists so clearly understand entry into the sex industry as largely an economic choice. Social justice movements that have an advanced understanding of their rights and demands realize that language has power.[20] So it's not surprising that African sex worker activists promote the political language of "sex work" in their organizing, which aligns them with the labor movement, and reject the legal designation of "prostitute," with its criminal status and stigmatizing references, and "prostituted people," which suggests passivity and lack of agency.

"It should be acceptable . . . as any other occupation," says Jay, a twenty-three-year-old Namibian gay male sex worker, regarding the idea of sex work as work:

When it feeds hungry stomachs, when it feeds poor families. . . . I started [sex] work . . . when I was staying with my mom and my little brother. She was very sick and she couldn't take care of even herself due to that fact. I was the only one to help out my family, since my brother was young. I would do my [sex] business mainly just to have something on the table. It was not based on money, just based on food actually. Just to, just to meet the basic needs. . . . It's [the Namibian] government's responsibility to take care of vulnerable people and vulnerable kids [but the government doesn't do this]. . . . So I strongly believe, why should we be criminalized if we tend to look after our families, after ourselves?

Rachel, a Namibian transgender female sex worker activist, echoes and builds on Jay's argument:

The reason why I claim and say that sex work is work . . . is because I sent my child to get a proper education [with that money]. . . . You understand? I had to pay my water and electricity. I had to pay my rent, clothing. I mean, if I don't work, what does my child get? My child doesn't get education. . . . But at least if I go on the street, my child won't go hungry. We will at least have a roof on top of our heads. We will have clothing. There will be food. . . . So, there are many different aspects that really make sex work *work*. That makes it a reality. I think ignoring reality within our nation, that is where things happen like violating human rights, abuse of power, and discrimination and stigma—not realizing that sex work is *work*. That it maintains and brings sustenance to certain homes.

I've heard Jay's and Rachel's arguments countless times from African sex workers' rights activists throughout the continent, and its core truth always lingers: The sex worker, the tomato picker, the factory worker, the domestic worker are all doing the best they can—like ordinary people everywhere in often difficult economic circumstances—to provide financially for themselves and their families. They all deserve our solidarity, and the realization and protection of their rights as workers.

That many view the sex worker as fundamentally different from other workers is due to moral hang-ups regarding the exchange of sexual services for money. But what's most important to understand is that our feelings about the moral dimensions of sex work can and do have catastrophic consequences for the lives of people in the sex industry, who often face abuses because of societal stigma and judgment translated into laws and policies that criminalize the industry and make it less safe for those working in it.

In the first-person narratives that follow, Dudu Dlamini, introduced earlier in this chapter, and Mickey Meji, a female South African sex worker activist, speak in detail about the economic circumstances surrounding their entry into sex work and how they understand the concepts of choice, agency, and sex work as labor, as applied to their experiences specifically and sex work generally. In doing so, they provide additional insight into African perspectives on the longstanding feminist debates regarding sex work.

Dudu powerfully recounts how, on behalf of the Sisonke sex worker movement, she gave a speech to the Congress of South African Trade Unions (Cosatu), the influential national South African trade union that represents more than 2 million workers and is one of South Africa's most dominant political forces. Determined to build an alliance between the sex work and labor movements, Dudu believed the Sisonke movement would benefit from convincing potential allies like trade unionists to formally endorse the idea that sex work must be understood through the prism of labor. In describing her entry into and experience of sex work, Mickey demands the recognition of her agency, even amid what some might argue are neoliberal consumerist pressures, and rejects a version of feminism that champions the politics of rescue.

Dudu Dlamini, 37, Cisgender Female Sex Worker and Activist (Cape Town, South Africa)

"It Was Why I Escaped"

I grew up in the townships in Durban. There were five children in my family, and I went to school until standard nine [U.S. high school equivalent of grade 11] when I was sixteen. I came to Cape Town at the end of 2002 to work in a big tavern that a lady in Durban told me about. But when I got here it was not like that. I didn't earn any money, and I was forced to sell drugs and alcohol. I stayed alone until I escaped.

In Durban, I had been involved with a man for almost eight years. It was an abusive relationship, and he was taking advantage of me. Things were not going well, and everything in my head was like, "This man, he is cheating, he beats me. He comes home late and drunk." And things were getting worse and worse. I wasn't finding a job. I was going to interviews for different jobs like government development and hospitals, but then nothing. I was getting afraid that if I got nothing, I would start to steal. And then this lady—we were together in the women's league and she was trying all the time to make peace in my house—advised me, "Why don't you just move to another city? Leave this man because he is going to kill you. I've got a friend in a big tavern in Cape Town. She can help you. Dudu, I know you are very strong, I know you can work there." And then I felt like, "Okay, let me leave Durban."

When I left Durban in 2002, I thought I was going to live and work for three or four months in this big tavern as a cashier collecting the money, and then move out of the tavern and rent a house. That was my thinking. I'm going to rent the house, and then I'm going to find another nice job. But it was a quiet tavern with few people, and they took me to a woman's house that was not the tavern. And on the first day this woman told me, "You're going to clean, and I'm going to pay you 400 [$40 USD]." And I go, "Huh? I've come here a long way from Durban to work for 400 rand at the end of the month?"

Then I told myself, "Okay, it's fine. I will divide this 400 rand into two. I'll give 200 [$20 USD] to my mother in Durban and take 200 for myself for two months. And then I'm going to move into another house." But I didn't move because they cut all the phones, and I couldn't make a phone call. I couldn't contact my mother. I couldn't contact anybody. The lady from Durban called me once, and after that they didn't allow me to talk to her anymore. Things started changing, changing, changing, and after a month I was selling drugs from the house for them without my permission. Sometimes if I refused to do something they'd say, "That's why your man was beating you, because you don't listen." I couldn't even go to town. If I wanted something they would bring it for me. I stayed inside that house for nine months—April, May, June, July, August, September, October, November, and December. It was why I escaped.

"And Then He Was Burning"

I escaped in 2003 with the help of one of the guys who used to come and buy a stock of drugs. He was a gatekeeper. He dropped me somewhere, and then I had to get a place to stay. So I started doing peoples' washing. Washing for food, washing for a place to sleep. Soon after that, I got a boyfriend, and I [became] pregnant. But he was saying, "It's not my child." I was one month pregnant, and I kept the child because I found another boyfriend who was taking care of me, and he's the one who was saying, "No, keep the child. I'll take care of it, I don't have a child." Then when that child was nine months [old], I got pregnant again. I didn't use protection. Because I didn't even know what a condom was at that time. I'd never tried them in my life. I only learned about condoms after I joined the sex business. We lived together in a big shack. And then that boyfriend killed himself. He burned himself to death in the house.

We had gotten into a fight, a quibble. I found him trying to sleep with my sister, who had come to visit Cape Town from Durban, when she was drunk, and that's how the quibble started. I told him, "I'm tired of Cape Town, and I'm tired of you. I'm leaving Cape Town. I want to go home, I don't want Cape Town anymore. I'm going to tell your mother what you've done." And then after I left the house, in not even five minutes, people were shouting, "Dudu, your house is burning! Your house is burning! Fire, fire, fire!" And then when I went back he was screaming inside the house, and I said, "Get out!" He said, "I can't, I'm already burned!" And then he was burning, and he left me with these two kids. He killed himself. I don't know why.

After he burned himself, his family forced me to pay to bury him. A couple of my friends helped me—I got money from two or three of them until the funeral was done. The day after the funeral, his family chased me out. They said, "We don't need you. You killed our son." They knew that I didn't have a place to stay. They knew that I was going to suffer. And then one lady I knew said, "No, Dudu, you can come to my place. I don't have a good place for you to stay, but I've got this small shack that you can use solo." So, I had to send my two kids away. It's when I joined the sex industry.

"I Will Survive and Come Back with Money"

I started sex work in 2004 when I was twenty-seven. I would say although it was not really "choice" because of the limited choices I had at the time, it was *my* choice. I chose it for myself. I was sitting and thinking about it, and I had to choose, so I chose. Because what it's all about is money. And I was thinking, "I don't have money to look for a job in town. I don't have an education or any skills. They will ask for a CV [curriculm vitae], and I don't have money for a CV. What am I gonna eat with my kids? My kids are hungry *now*. I need quick cash. I need a comfortable house." There was no offer for a job. And if somebody says I must go and look for a washing job, nuh-uh, it's not my thing. I had already been in Cape Town cleaning people's fucking bloody houses. I'd done lots of washing for people in different houses. I'd wake up early in the morning and open the windows, clean, cook, make porridge for their children, take their children to school, and do their ironing just for a place to sleep, for a plate of food, and not even a cigarette on top of it. So I was *done* with that. I made my own choice to go [into] the sex industry. I felt, "I will go. I will survive. And I will come back with money. I will buy my own things. I will take care of my kids."

From one night standing in the road, after one hour passes I can get 300 rand [$30 USD], two hours pass I get 700 [$70 USD], and by the morning I've got 1,800 [$181 USD]. So, why wouldn't I think about going back again? When I first started, I was going seven days a week. But now, I'm experienced, and I know Monday there is no money, Tuesday there is money, Wednesday there is no money, and Thursday, Friday, Saturday, and Sunday there's money. So, now, Monday I don't go, it's my off day. That day I do my washing and clean my house. There are times when sex workers do have food, we do have everything, and we're just coming for fun. We go to sit in the pub, and we buy drinks for each other. At the club we'll say, "Eh, I'm not really working today. I'm just taking one or two jumps and then I'll go." We call clients "jumps." We do have budgets, though, and there are other times when it's the end of the month, and things are very tight. Everything is due: rent, groceries, school fees, everything. So I'll stand in the road.

"You Won't Go Anywhere If You're Hiding Yourself"

I'm still working as a sex worker. Like today, I am going. I'm also an organizer with Sisonke and peer educator with SWEAT. Sisonke is a sex worker movement. I'm in the movement, and inside of me it's my goal to one day see sex workers and my movement going forward and for people to understand why we are doing sex work.

Sisonke went to Cosatu [Congress of South African Trade Unions] to support us in calling for the decriminalization of sex work because we believe that what we are doing is work. The main thing was to make Cosatu see sex work as work. Cosatu is very important in South Africa because it's a big union having many babies. Cosatu is the mother-body of all unions, like SATU the teacher's union, NEHAWU for general workers, NUM the mine union, and lots of different labor sectors—they are all children of Cosatu.

In March 2012, Cosatu was having a conference on gender-based violence in Johannesburg. Sisonke chose me to give a speech to Cosatu members at the conference to convince them to support the decriminalization of sex work in a resolution. I'm pretty sure Sisonke chose me to do the presentation because they know that I'm not ashamed of what I'm doing. I'm proud of myself. I'm not a liar. I tell what I know, and what I don't know, I don't know. But if I know, I know, and I'll tell you the truth.

I felt proud Sisonke asked me to do it. I'm a public speaker and I was used to attending meetings, but it was my first time facing a big crowd with lots of black people, cultural people. People who are Zulu, of the same background as me, who believe that a Zulu woman must have one boyfriend and has to get married. They think if you sleep around, you are a bitch, and you are not a lady, all those things. They think when you're doing sex work, you're not taking care of yourself, and you're giving yourself away to men. I was thinking, "After I tell them that I am a sex worker what will they think?" [When I was growing up], my mother would tell me what a Zulu woman should be like, but I'm not those things—the reality is I'm a sex worker, and I want people to respect it. It's my choice. My mother believed in culture. She was a respected person. Me, I was born in her womb, but I am a sex worker. There's something they say in Zulu: "A pastor won't give birth to a pastor." If a pastor has a son, that son won't be like him. My mother was good, with respect and dignity, but in a different way than me. We are not the same. But because I'm a sex worker that doesn't mean that I do not have dignity. My mother and I just did things in different ways. She had her dignity, and I've got my own dignity.

But, still, I knew when I say I'm a sex worker, the Zulu people in Cosatu would be thinking, "What? I know what a Zulu woman is supposed to be like." But I told myself, "If I don't do this, if I'm scared to say things, if I'm scared of my name, if I'm scared of using my face, Sisonke won't go forward. You won't go anywhere if you're hiding yourself." I grew up in a political era, a political location. My brothers were fighters for freedom, so how can I not fight for my colleagues and for what I believe? If I come out, more people will learn and then more sex workers will survive. And maybe some sex workers will be encouraged and think, "If Dudu has done this, then let's all do it." I thought about all the bad things that are happening in the streets because of criminalization. What if my daughter joins the sex industry and these bad things happen to her? If I don't say these things to these people they won't support decriminalization and then what about my daughter?"

These are the things I was thinking before my speech. This is how I was pushing myself, all the things I was saying to encourage myself. Especially the last night, when I knew that the next day I was going to do my presentation in front of lots of Cosatu members. Another thing that was encouraging me was support from Oratile, who was SWEAT's advocacy manager. Ah, that lady encouraged me. She was giving me all respect as a woman. She was saying, "You know, you can do this. You're not doing it for me. You're doing it for yourself and your colleagues. I'm not a sex worker, but I feel your pain, and I feel your colleagues' pain." She was so supportive. She showed me that she believed in me, and I saw that lots of sex workers believed in me. Oratile was the one training me in human rights, and human rights gave me power. I know that sex workers are human beings. I have a right to choose, a right to be treated fairly, a right to be treated with respect, a right to full access to health [care], a right to all those dignities. We need to bring back our dignity. So I told myself that I have to face Cosatu, and if they ask me questions, I will tell them the way I feel, in a good manner, with respect.

I stayed up until 3 A.M. the night before the speech preparing. And sometimes I would say, "No, no, no, I can't do this." And Oratile would say, "No, Dudu, practice, practice, practice, my darling. I know you can do this, I know." And I remember Oratile and me sitting outside, and I smoked maybe twenty cigarettes, and I was thinking, thinking, thinking, "Jesus Christ, tomorrow is the day. And I'm going to do it. I'm going to do it."

"Our House's Foundation"

I gave the speech in the afternoon. I don't remember how many people were in the room, but there were a lot, more than eighty. Shea, a Cosatu member who was announcing the speakers, introduced me. She said, "Our speaker now is Duduzile Dlamini, a sex worker for eight years." I saw the way people reacted—they opened their eyes and were quiet-like. It was *quiet* for my speech. More quiet than for the other speeches. I started by thanking Shea and greeting the Cosatu chairs and delegates on the floor. I told them Sisonke is a movement of sex workers, run by sex workers, for sex workers, and I could see the Sisonke members from Johannesburg standing in the back. And sometimes my eyes were on Oratile's face. And then, I started singing a song in Zulu that Cosatu would know, a song from a long time ago, from the days of apartheid that most people used to sing when I was growing up. The song was *kubi kubi kubi bo siyaya*, my favorite song. It means, "No matter it's bad, no matter they beat us, no matter they rape us, no matter they arrest us, no matter they kill us, we are going forward." I was singing and dancing, and my voice is very powerful, I know this myself. And the whole house stood up and started singing with me. After this, I said, "*Amandla!*" and everyone replied, "*Amandla!*"[21] When I started singing that anti-apartheid song, this gave me power because I freed myself in the space, and I showed them that I am a sex worker, but I am a comrade, too.

I told them, "I'm very comfortable to be here in front of you, comrades, because my brothers are also comrades. My brothers Xorani and Sfiso were ANC [African National Congress] soldiers, a part of Umkhonto we Sizwe, the ones who crossed the country to fight for freedom for blacks.[22] And, me too, today I'm standing in front of you, same like my brothers who were fighting for freedom. I'm fighting for sex workers' freedom that we haven't gotten yet. And I'm proud to stand in front of you."

At the beginning of the speech I talked about the police brutality I have experienced as a sex worker. I told them the following story because I was trying to show them how police are treating us sex workers: If I'm not mistaken it was 2010, and I was standing with my friend on a corner in Bellville in Cape Town working. We saw a police van, and when the two police officers in the van saw us standing there, they turned the van around in the road. My friend ran away, and I ran and hid myself in roof beams in the back of a BP petrol garage. The police parked and searched everywhere, and then they grabbed me in the shack and took me outside. They took off all my clothes and pepper sprayed me in the mouth and eyes. They tried to force me to get into the police van. I didn't want to, and I was fighting and saying, "I'm not going in!" I said to them, "Okay, fine, I respect you, and I won't work today." Although I said that, they kept beating me in public right there in the main road. I couldn't take down the names of the police officers because there were no nametags. There was a number plate on the van, but I couldn't take it down because they had already pepper-sprayed me so I couldn't see anything. They left me with nothing. They took all my clothes, they took my t-shirt, and they took my shoes. They left me with only my bra. After they left, a garage man helped me wash my face, helped me to see. So this is how I started off my speech to Cosatu—with police brutality. I told them everything about police, and I told them my colleagues' stories.

I told them when police confiscate our condoms, when they take condoms from us, they're taking the tools sex workers use to work. And people started saying, "What tools?" And I asked them, "Do you know what our tools are?" And they all said, "No!" I said, "Every worker in South Africa has their tools, like a gardener boy who has a horse pipe or a bricklayer who has a brick and hammer. Sex workers' tools are condoms, dental dams, lubrication."

I was trying to explain to them why we say we are workers. I was counting, step by step, the things all workers do before they go to work and showing them how sex workers do the same things. I told them, "We wake up like you, wash like you, prepare our kids to go to school like you, cook breakfast for our kids like you, put our lipsticks and everything in our bags like you, pack our tools like you, lock our houses like you, take taxis to work like you. When we don't have somebody to take care of our children, we ask neighbors, 'Look after my kids,' the same like you."

I said, "You know how sometimes there are good days when you're working, days that are very nice and very good and you enjoy it, like the days you get paid for overtime? It's the same in the sex industry. We have good times, too, like when we get good clients. Like a client I have who picks me up, takes me to his home, gives me a hot shower, hot food, and pays me even more." When my mother died, it was my clients that helped me. Nothing from my friends—they didn't even come with a bag of potatoes. I told my clients my heart was broken, and they felt what I felt. Instead of giving me 100 rand [$10 USD] or 150 [$15 USD], they'd give me 200 [$20 USD], 300 [$30 USD], some gave me 500 [$50 USD]. Some put money in the bank for me. One bought tickets for my kids, my sister, and me to travel to the funeral. And some of my clients are coming for conversation, only just to sit and go out, and that's all. And then they pay for it. Now when I'm thinking about it, I can say sex work, it's all about time, you pay for time.

I told the Cosatu members what I have gained from sex work. I said, "I used to not have a house for me, my kids, and my sister. I was staying in a shack where if it's raining, it would be full of water, and big rats that could eat you would get in. At night, I couldn't sleep. I had to send my children away. I had to do something, so I joined the sex industry. The first day I did sex work, I told my sister Cindy, 'Today I'm going to work for money to build our house.' And that day I made enough money to put down our house's foundation. And the next day, I told my sister, 'Today I'm going to work for money for the sides of the house.' And the next day, the roof. And the next day, beds for my kids and everything inside the house. I went to the road, and I built my new house within a week with that money. And I was also able to take my kids to pre-school—before they were not in school." I told them this story of building my house through sex work because I wanted to show them, to make it clear to them and open their eyes, that, even us sex workers, our budgets, our plans are there. The money that we get from sex work we do [with] what they do with their money—taking our children to better schools, to get a better education, the same like them. I wanted them to see that there is no difference. If you're a nurse, you're a nurse. If I'm a sex worker, I'm a sex worker. But at the end of the day we are doing the very same thing—we are earning money.

After my speech, the Cosatu members clapped, and they showed me that they enjoyed the speech and that they understand. After all the presentations, I went to the floor, and it was like everyone wanted to grab me. Some people hugged me, some were saying "Oh, we didn't know. And we will try to understand now. You must come to our areas and educate us so we can understand. This criminalization must be over." I was proud and happy and relieved at the end of the speech. And after that speech, Cosatu agreed to support decriminalization in an official resolution.

Mickey Meji, 33, Cisgender Female Sex Worker and Activist (Cape Town, South Africa)

"What's Wrong If Someone Pays You to Do It?"

My mother was married to a man with this surname that I'm using—she is Mrs. Meji. My mother used to be a live-in domestic worker, so I grew up mostly in the backyards of white people here in South Africa. I went to good schools where you didn't find many black children because this was pre-1994, before democracy in South Africa. I remember when I was thirteen years old, my class teacher wouldn't do anything when a white child would tease me. But when I would react the teacher wanted to take action against me. When he reported me to the headmistress, she asked for my mother to come to school. I told her, "My mother will not come to school because the teacher didn't do anything about the discrimination when it happened to me. But now that I'm a black child and I'm reacting to this white child he wants to take action, and I find that to be very discriminatory." So, I have always seen myself as an activist.

After my mother stopped working as a live-in domestic worker we moved back to a township outside of Cape Town, and I've lived there for the past twenty years. I was a street-based sex worker in Cape Town, and in my time doing sex work I used to have a lot of clients. African people have this belief in bewitchment and *mutis*, medicines to draw people to you, and because of this, women never liked to stand with me in the street because they thought I would take all the clients. So most of the time I used to stand on street corners alone.

I began doing sex work in May 2001 when I was twenty-one. I was not introduced to it by anyone. There was one day in Cape Town when I was waiting for a friend from Johannesburg—he was an attorney who had come down to Cape Town for a court case. He couldn't find me that day because he was not familiar with Cape Town so I was waiting for quite some time and just walking up and down Parow Road to keep time. And then this guy approached me in a white car because he thought I was a sex worker. He was Afrikaans and chubby, with whitish hair, and I think he was in his forties. And he smelled very clean, that's the other thing that I noticed.

He stopped and he said, "Are you in business?" I didn't quite understand what he meant, but I didn't have a destination at the time so I didn't mind having a chat with him. And he was not a rude person. I asked him, "What type of business?" Then he said he wanted a blowjob and offered me 350 rand [$33 USD]. The money was an incentive, but I think it was curiosity that got me. I thought, "I've got nothing to lose. He doesn't know me, and I don't know him." And in 2001, we were only seven years into democracy, and we had always had the distinction between white and black. So because he was white and from another city, I thought, "There's no way that I will ever meet him after this."

So I said, "Well, if you show me what it is you need me to do." He asked me to go and buy condoms at a store, and then we went to his guesthouse in the northern suburbs for twenty-five minutes. He dropped me back on Parow Road after paying me. So, I managed to make about 350 rand within thirty minutes. Afterward, I actually didn't feel different from how I felt before because I had already been having sex. I already had two children at that time, my boy who was four years old and my girl who was a couple of months. And even before starting sex work I've never been judgmental of people who sell sex. When I would hear people talking about people who sell sex, I always felt, "We are all having sex, so what's wrong if someone pays you to do it?"

"I Wanted the Much Better Thing"

A couple of months down the line in October 2001, I wanted to buy a Nokia 5110 cellphone, and I remember it was 1,300 rand [$131 USD], which was a lot of money for me at that time. I had an Ericsson phone that a boyfriend had given to me, but I wanted the new Nokia phone that had just [been released]. So I thought, "Okay, where is the best place to look for this money?" So I just went back down that same Parow Road, and I started walking up and down, and I had condoms on me. People started greeting me, and I was able to make that money within a couple of hours of doing sex work. I got that 1,300 rand, and I bought the phone.

I was not in poverty, but my resources were limited. But I had the basic things that every human being needs. I had a roof over my head. I had food on my table. I had electricity. But I have just always been a person who has had an eye for good things. So instead of just having the basic thing, I wanted the much better thing. [I], my mother, my two brothers, and my two children lived in a house together and there was Vaseline for everyone to apply [as lotion] on their bodies, but I didn't just want Vaseline—I wanted Nivea. I didn't want to just send my children to the township schools where I wouldn't have to pay a cent. I wanted to send my children to better, more advanced schools. These are the things that actually motivated me to do sex work. I just wanted better things.

So I chose to do sex work. I've always had alternatives. I've had other opportunities—I've been a waitress, I've been a security officer. After I started doing sex work in October 2001, I also started work with a security firm in December of that same year. At the time they employed people without experience, and they would train you and put you into a position. When I started working with them I had just stopped working as a waitress at a traditional Japanese restaurant in Cape Town. Being a waitress had spoiled me because I had cash all the time, from my tips and stuff. But the restaurant had started getting quiet so there was not a lot of money, and my boss at the time was racist. I was the only black girl working in the front of the restaurant. The rest of the black people were working in the kitchen. So the boss had problems with me, and it was uncomfortable being at work. He used to give me fewer shifts than everyone else—maybe two shifts a week or just one. So I needed to sustain my income, and I wanted to buy that Nokia phone.

I was at the security firm until 2003, and between 2001 and 2008, I also went back to do some waitressing. The work I did as a waitress and sex worker felt the same actually because it's all about the body, about presenting yourself. When it came to being a waitress, to earn more tips I had to look good, the same thing I had to do on the road as a sex worker.

"We Should Respect People's Choices"

Most sex workers I have come across have actually been domestic workers or farm workers. Some of them had opportunities to do basic domestic work in the townships, but they saw fit to do something else. I like to approach it from this point of view: If you offered any farm worker, factory worker, or domestic worker some other job today, maybe they would take that. Would we now come and say being a farm worker or a domestic worker is not a choice? No, it is a choice. But it's a choice that was made out of the limited options that were afforded. A person with a degree, maybe they have many choices. A person whose literacy is very low, they have limited choices. But they still have choices. I could have been a domestic worker. But I didn't want to do domestic work. For starters, I'm just not a house person. Even today I don't cook, and if you went to my room now it's the messiest room that you could ever find because that's how I am. And also the money is not good. I would still have had to sustain it with something else. I'm not looking down on people who want to be domestic workers, let them do it. But for me, I chose sex work.

Yes, sex work is often driven by poverty, but I have a problem with people who look down at the choices that others make or undermine their choices. They think people are not able enough to make choices or decisions, and I find that quite offensive. I think we should respect people's choices. A woman who has not done sex work cannot spend a whole night outside on a cold street looking after herself. But we are able to do this. If we have that kind of ability within ourselves why shouldn't we be able to make our own choices?

"Rescue a Person When They Want to Be Rescued"

I think of myself as a feminist, but maybe we need a definition for what a feminist is. I recently attended the Commission on the Status of Women in America, and I was frustrated for a couple of days because we get to these feminist spaces, and we as women are not equal, our classes are not equal.[23] Transgender women and lesbian and bisexual women are found not to be "woman" enough by the "real" women in these feminist spaces. They think we sex workers aren't "woman" enough. And I find it offensive for women who have been privileged and won't sell sex to impose their choices over other people. These women feel that anyone who chooses to sell sex is being exploited. They think it's not feminist, and that we need to be rescued. But if women are doing things willingly who are you to come and say, "We want to rescue you"? You rescue a person when they want to be rescued. You don't impose your values on the person.

It's actually other women that always have a problem with sex workers. I was reading the newspaper, and there was this story about women who went to a brothel to attack sex workers. These women went to attack other women. They were saying that the sex workers were taking their men. But those sex workers remain in the brothel. Those men come [to us] voluntarily, willingly.

Sex work, in itself, is not a harmful act. It's actually the laws that make sex work harmful, dangerous, and exploitive. In 2001, 2002, and 2003, it was very good doing sex work because police officers were not on our case. I don't know what triggered it, but they started being on our case. So we needed to move to darker and shadier places to avoid the police, who were abusing us, and that's when we started being prey to our clients.

Around 2004, the police started arresting sex workers. Then they started taking money from sex workers. Sometimes they would arrest us and keep our phones and belongings, but when we would go to collect our things the following morning they were not there. Then they moved on to raping sex workers or asking for sexual favors. And then they moved on to pepper-spraying people—I've experienced this. There was a day I was not doing sex work, but I was walking to catch a taxi in a neighborhood where the police would assume you were a sex worker if you walked there. And this female police officer started attacking me. She called me a bitch in Afrikaans. At first I just ignored her and [kept going]. She said, "I'm talking to you!" And I said, "You don't get to call me bitch." Then she slapped me across my face, so I slapped her back, and we started fighting. Her partner got out of the vehicle and pepper-sprayed me, and they arrested me.

Before the police started harassing sex workers I never experienced crime from clients. But after, clients knew that we were afraid. In 2006, there was an incident where I was with a client, and he took me to a really deserted area, very quiet and very dark, because he said he was not comfortable because the police were on our case. So we went to this very deserted area, and that's where he made me do a blowjob at gunpoint, and after that he left me there and told me to just get lost. So, it's not the actual act of being a sex worker that makes it harmful. Like I said, it's the laws.

"South Africa Belongs to All Those Who Live in It"

In the context of South Africa, there's a section of our Constitution that says we have the right to choose freedom, our occupation, trade, or profession.[24] So if I choose to be a sex worker, that right applies to me. If you read our Constitution, the preamble says, "South Africa belongs to all those who live in it." Therefore, there's no one who is greater than anyone else according to the Constitution. So why should people who do sex work not be allowed to do those things?

One thing I tell my children now is let us try and do what is democratically and constitutionally right because it is the humane thing to do. So if you go to school, and a child is hungry, you share your lunch. You should do that because it's the humane thing to do, it's about humanity. In my culture we call it *ubuntu*. So basically for me it's not about people liking sex workers. You just have to respect the choices that people make, and why have a problem with it if we're not infringing on your rights?

2

"In a Dark Place There's No Light"

Criminalization and Human Rights Abuses against
African Sex Workers

We have been sad long enough to make this world either
weep or grow fertile.
—Audre Lorde

All social justice movements begin with pain, birthed by stories of
human suffering—of dreams deferred, lives lost. The African sex workers' rights movement is no different. In my travels throughout the
continent, I heard countless stories chronicling police abuse, client
abuse, lack of access to justice, poor working conditions, health care discrimination, and social stigma. It's eerie how strikingly similar the stories
were. Mauritius was one of the last countries I visited, and as I stood on
the dark streets of Quatre Bornes speaking to Creole sex workers about
the human rights abuses they face, I could not help but think that there I
was in a little-known, tiny dot of a country in the Indian Ocean, and yet
the stories I was hearing were nearly identical to sex workers' stories in
Kenya's bustling metropolises, Botswana's small border towns, and any
number of the other places I'd visited during my fieldwork. The reason
African sex workers' experiences echo one another with such disturbing
consistency, despite their countries' diverse social and political orientations, is that human rights abuses against sex workers originate from
the same source. What ties them together is the fact that in all of these
countries, sex work is criminalized. And it is from sex work's illegality,
as well as deep-seated social stigma, that these abuses flow.[1]

Sex work is criminalized throughout the overwhelming majority of
African countries. Criminalization falls into one of two categories: (1)
Prostitution itself, as well as activities related to prostitution like solicita-
tion, living off the earnings of prostitution, and brothel-keeping, is ex-

plicitly illegal. Or (2) prostitution itself is not technically illegal—that is, the law is silent on the exchange of sex for money between adults—but prostitution-related activities remain illegal, therefore effectively making it impossible to engage in prostitution. In Mauritius, South Africa, and Uganda both prostitution itself and prostitution-related activities are illegal.[2] South Africa's Sexual Offences Act, which criminalizes prostitution, derives from the odious Immorality Act of 1927, which prohibited interracial and same-sex relationships under apartheid.[3] In Uganda, prostitution was generally tolerated in pre-colonial times, as customary law governing crime did not explicitly outlaw it. Criminalized prostitution was introduced in the colonial Penal Code of 1930, which was modeled on England's penal code, and underlying the laws were Victorian notions of female monogamy and chastity.[4] (The fact that many African countries' contemporary anti-prostitution laws were inherited from colonial regulations based on European penal codes shows how anti-prostitution laws are often relics of European imposition of sexual and gender mores.) In Botswana, Kenya, Namibia, and Nigeria, although prostitution itself isn't technically illegal, all prostitution-related activities are criminalized.[5] There is no country in Africa where sex work is decriminalized and afforded the protections of other service professions.[6]

Because it is difficult for police and prosecutors to prove violations of anti-prostitution laws in court, sex workers arrested under these laws often fall into a cycle of jail and release without prosecution. "Section 136 of the Ugandan Penal Code deals with prostitution. It says you can't live off the earnings of prostitution. But that is very hard to prove," notes a lawyer with the Human Rights Awareness and Promotion Forum (HRAPF) in Uganda, which provides sex workers with legal representation. "You need a lot of evidence to prove that. Police won't present evidence or witnesses. They won't even show up in court, so the cases are usually dismissed by the prosecution. It shows that the police are using arrest as a way to extort money from sex workers." State agents often use laws unrelated to sex work to harass and abuse sex workers, including municipal by-laws against loitering, public nuisance, and obscenity.

As one South African activist notes regarding the relentless abuses sex workers experience, "If I'm in a dark place, there's no recourse, there's no light." Ultimately, to begin confronting human rights abuses against people in the African sex industry, we must remove the criminal status attached to sex work and move beyond the tired debates regarding prostitution's supposed inherent violence that result in misguided laws and policies that harm sex workers.

Although Western anti-prostitution reformers originally propagated the notion of prostitution's inherent harm, African anti-prostitution activists have also embraced this idea. Nozizwe Madlala-Routledge, cofounder of Embrace Dignity, a leading anti-prostitution organization based in South Africa, has argued, "Prostitution is the cornerstone of the institution of the system of inequality between the sexes. . . . It is inherently harmful. . . . Prostitution is also deeply degrading and strips people of their dignity, which is why we stand against any attempts to portray it as 'work' or harmless."[7] This focus on prostitution's supposed "inherent harm" is dangerously distracting because the true harm isn't the exchange of sexual services for payment between consenting adults but laws and policies that criminalize sex work and thus make its practice perilous for many sex workers.

The argument that sex has no place in the marketplace because of its presumed innate sacredness is rooted in social anxieties about nonsanctioned female sexual activity that transcend all cultures.[8] African sex workers are acutely aware of how these ideas contribute to the construction of the "deviant sexual woman" and how this othering has translated into anti-prostitution policies aimed at isolating and harming sex workers in the name of rescuing them. Because academics and activists have long focused primarily on debates about whether prostitution is inherently harmful, we've spent less time talking about the abuses that sex workers consistently highlight as their primary areas of concern: police abuse; client violence, which is tied to lack of access to justice; bad working conditions as a result of lack of labor rights; discrimination in health care systems; and the intersection of whorephobia, transphobia, homophobia, xenophobia, and HIV stigma that intensifies discrimination against queer, trans, migrant, and HIV-positive sex workers.

Our fears of the "deviant sexual woman" and our construction and exclusion of the "whore" has led to her criminalization through anti-prostitution laws.[9] Moreover, it is precisely this criminal status that inures us to the harsh realities of criminalization. Criminalization harms sex workers in many ways. The fact that their work is illegal means they're pushed underground and into the shadows with little to no access to labor rights protections, health care services, and other social and economic safety nets. It emboldens police officers and other state agents to use the shield of law as an excuse to take advantage of sex workers. Because police view sex workers as criminals, they rarely provide them with protection of the law when they are the victims of crime. This lack of access to justice emboldens clients with violent inclinations who know that their abuse of sex workers will be met with impunity. It also empowers third-party managers who know that without the benefits of labor protections, including occupational and safety standards, they're free to take advantage of sex workers in brothels, massage parlors, and other indoor venues who may be exposed to dangerous and unfair working conditions. This cycle of violence and impunity involving police, clients, and bosses, coupled with health care discrimination and the underground nature of the work, increases sex workers' vulnerability to HIV and other health issues. And, of course, the social status of people regarded as criminals is very low.

Police Abuse

Mama Africa, a transgender female sex worker in her forties based in sun-swept Namibia, dresses in regal turbans and colorful multi-stranded necklaces befitting a woman affectionately known as the mother of Namibia's sex workers' rights movement. On a night in 2011, she's waiting for clients on Garden Street in the Namibian capital of Windhoek when a pack of officers in the Namibian Defense Forces menacingly approaches her. In a flash of swift rage, they rip her clothes off and begin to sexually assault her by masturbating her in the middle of the street, shining their flashlights all over her naked body as they yell, "How can a man put on a woman's clothes!" Cars pass in the inky blackness, slowing down as drivers gape at the spectacle, their headlights illuminating the horrific scene. Some yell out words of encouragement to the officers as they drive off.

"I have gone through that pain, and I can't forget it," Mama Africa tells me. The past few years had been a particularly brutal period in both Windhoek and Rehoboth, a small town south of the capital, where a slew of transgender sex worker murders remain unsolved. One murdered trans sex worker's bones were found on a main road. Another was buried in a shallow grave without a head. Mama Africa recalls these chilling details as she remembers some of their names: Juanita, Susana, her roommate Phillipa whom they called Spobella. As the officers continue to attack her, all she can think about are these murdered sex workers, wondering if she'll meet their fate on this cruel night.

* * *

Tshepo is originally from a tiny village in central Botswana, but she has a big-city personality—animated, strong, and defiant. She's been a sex worker in Botswana for more than seventeen years, and in August 2012, she too, experiences violence at the hands of state agents. Around 1 A.M., as she exits a bar with a fellow sex worker in Francistown, Botswana's second-largest city, two police officers immediately set upon them. They pull them out into the street by the neck "like donkeys," kicking them with their boots and calling them "bloody, bastard bitches," Tshepo recalls as she shows me her scars. After throwing them into a police car, the officers take them to the central police station, where they lock them in a cell for three days without charge. Tshepo nurses her injuries and is physically unable to work for weeks after her release. She still suffers from residual pain in her lower back where one of the police officers repeatedly stomped on her. And she remembers what bystanders said as they witnessed the police attack, their words like slashes to the skin: "Take them, take them—this is our rubbish."

* * *

Of the many harms tied to criminalization that African sex workers highlighted during my interviews, abuse by police officers and their state proxies, reflected in Mama Africa's and Tshepo's experiences, was often the most ubiquitous and alarming. Anti-prostitution activists rarely speak out against police abuse of sex workers, a curious silence in the face of sex workers' consistent and disturbing assertions.[10] The criminalized status of sex work gives police officers an excuse to use the force of law to marginalize and violate sex workers. They become low-hanging fruit—easy prey—and this abuse normalizes and validates the stigma sex workers experience from the general public. It is unsurprising that when the criminal law characterizes sex work as deviant, police officers don't regard sex workers as members of the society they are meant to protect and serve.

African sex workers report myriad abuses committed by police: physical attacks, sexual assaults (including police demands for sexual favors in exchange for release from detention), verbal harassment, unlawful arrests (such as illegally using noncriminal municipal laws to police sex work), illegal detention (including jailing sex workers without issuing formal charges and not allowing them to plead their cases in court), refusal to investigate claims when sex workers are the victims of violence, the issuance of excessive fines, and extortion in the form of demands for bribes.

In my interviews with African sex workers, they provided only a handful of examples of the police as a positive, protective force. I remember Dumisani, a Zimbabwean migrant sex worker in the northern Botswanan town of Kazangula, recalling an incident in October 2012 when a trucker client had violently chased her out of his truck after she demanded he wear a condom. She reported him to the local police, who actually went with her to confront the trucker, sternly warned him against violence, and told him that in the future he "must agree to what was agreed." Some sex worker organizations, like Keeping Alive Societies' Hope (KASH) in Kenya, have managed to develop constructive relationships with local police forces in a bid to reduce police violence against sex workers. KASH routinely conducts sensitivity trainings for police and has developed a successful peer educator program comprising both police officers and female sex workers who work together to collect data documenting continuing police abuses against sex workers and meet monthly to analyze the data and develop strategies for addressing this abuse. These police officers should be applauded for refusing to participate in the vicious cycle of punishment and control of sex work communities. But unfortunately, the positive themes reflected in Dumisani's story and KASH's experience were more the exception than the rule in my interviews.

More common were stories like these: In Windhoek, Namibia, a police officer confiscates the condoms of Naima, a twenty-one-year-old street-based sex worker and activist, throwing them on the road and driving over them with his car before arresting her and releasing her only after she agrees to have sex with him. In Port Louis, Mauritius, police brutally rape and beat an eight-months' pregnant sex worker. In

Nigeria, Amnesty International has documented widespread rape of sex workers by Nigerian police and has argued that the abuse amounts to torture.[11] In Kampala, Uganda, there's a notorious case of a police officer who has long made grotesque sport of tormenting street-based sex workers in Uganda's congested, throbbing capital. He took great pleasure in arresting sex workers in Kampala's Ntinda neighborhood, stripping them naked, and parading them through town. He told the sex workers he terrorized that if they dared report him to officials, he would shoot them. But despite this intimidation, sex workers filed complaints against him, which resulted only in his transfer to another Kampala police unit, where his harassment of sex workers has intensified. His latest modus operandi is entering the homes of "known" sex workers—some pregnant, others with infants in their arms—and dragging them out by the hair to dump them in the police station.

Because they have more frequent interactions with the police, street-based sex workers often report higher incidents of police violence, but sex workers employed predominantly indoors are not immune to abuse. In South African brothels operating under massage-parlor licenses, police have been known to charge sex workers with violations of the 1957 Sexual Offences Act by misusing entrapment laws. Although under South African entrapment law one can only invite a person to commit an offense— you can neither commit the offense yourself nor persuade a person to actually carry out the crime—officers seeking to entrap sex workers routinely ignore this stipulation.[12] In one commonly reported instance, an officer poses as a client at a brothel; asks a sex worker for oral sex, which he conveniently lets her perform on him; and calls in his fellow officers to arrest her only after he's ejaculated. Customs and immigration officers often raid South African brothels, seizing work permits from foreign sex workers, confiscating condoms, and detaining the women working there. When police violently raid Nigerian brothels, they arrest any sex worker who doesn't shell out a 5,000 naira ($30 USD) bribe to be released. "Police are our biggest problem, more than anyone," noted Gloria, a Nigerian sex worker whose Lagos-based brothel is raided several times a month. "When he puts on the uniform, he thinks he can do whatever he wants."

Confronted with these types of abuses, it is no wonder the vast majority of African sex workers I spoke with don't view the police as a source of access to justice when they're the victims of crime. Sex workers often don't report crimes committed against them to the police because they know they will be met with either indifference or outright hostility.

Client Abuse

Thirty minutes outside of Francistown, in the Botswanan town of Gerald, a twenty-two-year-old female sex worker named Gaone with numerous beauty marks etched like stars all over her striking face experiences a horrific but sadly typical experience of client abuse met by systemic lack of access to justice. In 2012, she meets a client at the Twilight Club in Francistown, and they agree on the nature, scope, and price of her services. As they drive toward what she thinks will be the client's house within the city limits, anxiety grips her chest as he drives down back roads farther away from Francistown. Thirty minutes later they're somewhere near Gerald, hurtling down a gravel road deep into the bush. "Where are you taking me?" Gaone demands, as the client finally stops the car in the dense shrubbery, only his car lights piercing the darkness. "I remembered there was someone in my house, so I had to bring you here," he says, averting his eyes. Gaone is frightened, but she provides the services and he pays her the agreed-upon price. And then, to her shock, he says, "I'm leaving you here. If you want me to give you a ride back to Francistown, you need to give me back the money I just paid you." When Gaone refuses to return the money, he hits her repeatedly in the mouth until her lips swell and split open and then dumps her outside the car before driving off. Stunned and badly beaten, she knows it will take hours for her to walk back to Francistown. And in the dead of night, in the middle of the bush, that would be a dangerous journey. A closer walk would be to the Gerald police station. She's never considered going to the police after a client assaulted her, and she can hear the voices of her sex worker friends echoing in her head, warning her against it: "They'll beat you, Gaone. They'll put you in jail." But tonight she has no choice. She's afraid she'll be killed in the bush.

When she arrives at the police station and reports the attack, the police threaten to imprison her because she was engaged in prostitution at the time of the assault. "But this person, he beat me," Gaone pleads. "He dumped me in the bush. And you're saying I'm doing something that is illegal so you won't help me?"

"We can help you by putting you in a cell," an officer sarcastically retorts. And that's exactly what they do. They leave her in the cell for several hours until a sympathetic middle-aged female officer releases her and agrees to drive her home. She offers Gaone a chilling piece of advice as she drops her off in front of her apartment building in Francistown: "If someone beats you in the future, find help somewhere else. Never with the police. If you go to the police for help all they will do is put you in jail like they did tonight. Never come to us."

* * *

Denial of access to justice makes client abuse of sex workers rampant. Clients who are abusive through rape (including gang rape and non-payment for services), physical assault, and refusal to wear condoms engage in these crimes because they know their actions will be met with impunity because of sex work's illegality. It is important to note, however, that sex workers I interviewed spoke often about good clients as well. In fact, they referred to their "regulars" with a hint of pride, those clients whom they consistently worked with and could trust to adhere to the boundaries of negotiated services and prices without violence or coercion. This is a clear argument against the idea that all sex workers perceive every client exchange as implicitly violent. African sex workers I interviewed articulated and understood their experiences with regulars and good clients as labor, as work: They appreciated a client who stuck to the boundaries of the agreed-upon services, time, and price—that was more money in their pockets to pay for their kids' school fees, buy groceries, and pay the rent. And this is a different question from that of whether they *enjoyed* providing the services. That question seemed irrelevant to most because the reason the majority engaged in sex work was to make money, not to experience pleasure. It is a question that reflects our own assumptions, not sex workers' economic priorities. It is also a question we seldom ask regarding the labor of other workers, particularly low-wage workers—in those circumstances we tend to be concerned primarily with whether the garment worker, factory worker, or domestic worker is safe and has power over her labor, not whether she necessarily finds pleasure in the actual work of sewing clothes, working an assembly line, or scrubbing toilets.

The client experiences African sex workers described as harmful were those in which the client went beyond the boundaries of the agreed-upon time or services and was physically, sexually, or verbally abusive—they did not view these transgressions as "part of the job"; they viewed them as violence. This distinction is terribly important because if we characterize all sex work exchanges as inherently violent, then we blind ourselves to the actual violence sex workers experience. If we say that sex workers are incapable of consenting to the provision of sexual services for pay, and it is all tantamount to paid rape, then a sex worker who is actually raped by a client is invisible. If we insist that a sex worker is "selling her body," when in fact she still retains her body after the exchange and instead is providing a service, then we remove her from the world of labor—with all its potential protections—and banish her to the realm of sexual moralism. Sex workers I interviewed were not preoccupied with good clients. They were concerned with how criminalization empowers clients with criminal tendencies because the client who wants to rape, physically assault, and murder sex workers knows that the likelihood of his being held to account for these crimes is incredibly low. Impunity sends the message that it's open season on sex workers.

Unlike Gaone, who despite her reservations reported to the local police her being assaulted and dumped in the bush by a client, most sex workers I spoke with didn't bother going to the police to report client abuse because they knew nothing would come of it. In April 2012, Boipelo, a thirty-seven-year-old sex worker based in Kazangula, Botswana, was whipped with a belt for an hour straight by a client after he demanded she return the money he'd paid her and she refused: "I was thinking of going [to the police], but I knew the questions they were gonna ask me: 'The money was for what?' That's what they would say." She didn't report the incident because her work is illegal. In the small trucking town of Mijera in Uganda, Jacqueline had a similar experience—a client purposefully went beyond the agreed-upon time for her services and when she demanded he pay her for the additional time, he began to strangle her and eventually took back all of the money he had given her. She didn't report the assault because "police do not decide sex work issues," she said matter-of-factly.

Those who do report client abuse are met with a fate similar to Gaone's when the police locked her in a jail cell and a female officer later advised her that a sex worker who needs help can't actually receive it at the police station. In 2011, a client sexually assaulted Anna, a Namibian street-based sex worker and activist. I can't imagine the courage it took her to report this rape to the police, only to have officers coldly tell her that sex work is illegal in Namibia so they wouldn't help her. I spoke with other sex workers who tried to report rapes by clients to the police, only to be laughed at and told things like, "Come and look at this *marhosa* [whore] trying to open a rape case! She says she gets raped but she is the one that's hunting and selling her body" or simply, and devastatingly, "A prostitute cannot be raped." In 2005, a client stabbed a South African sex worker named Amahle, causing a wound so deep that it required surgery. After all these years, she swears she can still feel the physical pain of the wound, and during that terrifying ordeal she was certain she would die and leave her daughter an orphan. Luckily, Amahle survived the attack and mustered all of her strength to report it to the police. To her surprise, they agreed to accompany her to the attacker's house for what she thought would be a confrontation and arrest. But when they got to the house the police told her that the man could and should lay charges against *her* for engaging in prostitution and encouraged him to do so. Amahle still sees the man who tried to kill her regularly in the neighborhood. This is an example of a recurring theme in which police criminalize the victim. Police are, paradoxically, a ubiquitous presence in sex workers' lives in terms of hyper-criminalizing them, but they are conspicuously absent when sex workers are in need of protection from violence.

"If sex workers are going through all of this, and if people who are supposed to render us protection, more especially the justice system, discriminate against us and stigmatize us for who we are or what we do, where do we go for protection?" asks Rachel, a Namibian sex worker activist. "That's why all these things happen, that's why there's murder, there is rape, there is violence." In this vacuum of justice, some sex workers have taken circumstances into their own hands. A group of sex workers standing on a street corner in Port Louis, Mauritius, proudly told me that when they recently discovered a client robbing and beating a fellow sex worker in a dark alley, five of them came to her rescue, surrounding the client and throwing stones at him until he released their friend and ran off howling and scared.

Lack of Labor Rights

Adaora is a thirty-year-old Nigerian female sex worker who's been employed in a Lagos brothel for almost six years. Her eyes brighten when she learns that both of our families hail from the eastern part of the country, and as she relaxes further in my presence, she draws a detailed portrait of the unfair working conditions that she and other brothel-based Nigerian sex workers endure. She pays the managers of her brothel a weekly house rent of 10,500 naira ($64 USD), but if they lock her out of her rented room for days because of her failure to pay unfair fines (which brothel managers often unjustly levy on workers when clients refuse to pay for services rendered), she has no recourse to tenancy laws that prevent eviction without due process. The brothel fines can be as high as a week's rent, and managers may use the fines to sexually harass and abuse workers—allowing them back into their rooms only if they agree to sex with management. Brothel managers also routinely lock out sick sex workers, who may miss a week's rent because of ill health. For the period a sex worker is locked out of her room, she remains homeless.

Adaora must also pay the brothel managers a monthly "security fee" of 5,000 naira ($30 USD), ostensibly to prevent police raids, even though the authorities still regularly raid her brothel and arrest sex workers. Management never uses the accumulated security fees to secure bail for the workers rounded up during the raids. Adaora pays a monthly "entertainment fee" of 1,000 naira ($6 USD) to contribute money for a deejay meant to entertain clients—a deejay whom the management has never actually hired. On top of all this, management requires Adaora to contribute money for repairs in the brothel, even though management rarely puts the money toward completing the repairs (a broken toilet or a leaky roof often goes overlooked for months). "They make it a thing of the sex workers getting poorer, and they getting richer," Adaora says indignantly.

* * *

It is not only clients and police who take advantage of sex work's illegal status to abuse sex workers. Criminalization also enables bosses, like those in the brothel where Adaora works, to maintain poor and unjust working conditions. This is why prostitution's illegality is so clearly a labor issue—if the state outlaws activity that people are going to engage in anyway, it leaves the workers in that illicit industry vulnerable to abuse by bosses who underpay, overwork, and exploit them in the absence of labor protections. In South African brothels, sometimes brothel owners will force sex workers to work many extra hours without overtime pay, and the workers rarely have any recourse because their work is illegal. In Kenyan bars, bar owners often don't pay overtime to bar hostesses who provide sexual services to patrons. Deejays, security guards, and bar managers sometimes demand that bar hostesses give them free sexual services on threat of being fired. In Nigeria, brothel managers, fearing sex workers will start to collectively organize, often prevent them from holding meetings. Regarding the unequal balance of power between bosses and workers in the sex industry under criminalization, Adaora notes: "Their intimidations are so much on the sex workers . . . and they know that you can't go to anyone and complain." Indeed, the sex industry's illegal status means sex workers lack recourse to labor protections, including employee complaint and grievance procedures, occupational health and safety standards, and employee benefits, which makes it incredibly difficult for sex workers to individually and collectively have control over their own labor.

Social Stigma

Patricia, a fifty-two-year-old Coloured part-time sex worker in Cape Town, South Africa, with a fluttering voice and gentle manner, intimately understands the deep social stigma sex workers face. After she lands a job as a security guard on Robben Island, her employers check her criminal history and discover that in 1989 she'd been arrested and sentenced to six months in jail for violating the apartheid-era Immorality Act by having white men as clients while working as a sex worker. They immediately fire her, and her firing demonstrates how criminal records related to prostitution keep sex workers locked out of other forms of employment, limiting their opportunities.

It is a recent example of discrimination in the long history of stigma Patricia has faced as a sex worker. "Around where you stay, once they know that you are doing sex work, you are not welcome by the community," Patricia says. "They always have that negative stigma, thinking you are dirty, all those things, all those ugly things. . . . You feel isolated. It's like you've got no dignity. When people are saying all those nasty things, you feel down. You feel ashamed." Because of stigma and discrimination, for many years Patricia was unable to open a bank account or rent an apartment. She had her then-boyfriend open an account and rent a flat in his name for her secret use. Once the landlord discovered the arrangement, he evicted her. When she moved to a Cape Town suburb, neighbors who knew she was a sex worker often called the police when they saw any man—whether a client or not—come to her home. She got used to the constant calls that led police officers without search warrants to ransack her house, steal her belongings, and sometimes arrest her.

But perhaps the most heartbreaking example of social stigma she experienced as a sex worker was twenty-five years ago when her now-adult son was five years old. Blond and green-eyed, her son was the product of her relationship with a white man and looked nothing like her. Because of his appearance, the predominantly white community where they lived treated her son well even as they shunned her for being a Coloured sex worker. She suspects it was another call from the suspicious, judgmental community that prompted the police to arrest her and detain her son while they were out buying ice cream one day in the neighborhood: "As we walked to the shop the policeman came and asked me, 'Whose child is this? You couldn't have a child like this.' And he started beating me and dragging me to the van with my child." It haunts her still, the image of her young son sitting with her in the police station, deep fear clouding his eyes: "It is all the hard things that I experienced for being a working girl."

* * *

When the law criminalizes prostitution, it fashions sex workers like Patricia as criminals deserving of punishment, not laborers worthy of rights. Because the law deeply influences how we view one another, and vice-versa, it is not surprising that the law's image of sex workers reinforces and affirms the whorephobia and whore stigma[13] that already exist in African societies. Although there is historical evidence of precolonial prostitution in Africa, some African politicians and religious leaders try to paint sex work as the result of cultural imperialism, as if documentation of prostitutes in pre-colonial West Africa as far back as the seventeenth century were a fiction.[14]

The trope of the deviant sexual woman, the whore, is alive and well, not only in Africa, but in cultures throughout the world. What the law does by criminalizing prostitution is strengthen and affirm our aversion to and fear of her and confirm that we must control women engaged in unsanctioned sexual activity. When anti-prostitution activists in the Global North, echoed by their peers in the South, eagerly paint the sex worker as a victim of prostitution's supposed inherent harm, it is just another bid to rescue women from sex they deem deviant or undesirable. In Africa, media representations of sex workers play less into the narrative of sex worker as "victim" in need of rescue and more into the idea of "whore as aggressor," spreading disease and shame.[15] Both framings seek to control the sex worker and ultimately reinforce stigma by moving her outside the realm of the rational, the ordinary, and the pragmatic. Under the suffocating weight of these limiting narratives she can never be viewed like the rest of us—doing the best she can for herself and her family.

Stigma leads to discrimination against sex workers in African societies, often manifesting itself in the form of verbal and physical attacks; denial of access to bank accounts, rental apartments, and health care; and the stigmatization of sex workers' children. Community members know they can get away with these sorts of abuses because sex workers are criminalized and denigrated by law. In July 2013, as I was meeting with leaders of the Bar Hostess Empowerment Support Program in their offices in Nairobi, Kenya, a group of five or so frantic sex workers arrived with a disturbing story seeking assistance. They all work in a brothel that has existed for many years in a Nairobi suburb, and several months prior a church had been erected near the brothel. Church parishioners preach and protest outside the brothel every Sunday morning, shouting things like, "There are demons in there! The women inside must be brought out and burned to death!" Sex workers often report this type of intense community harassment, and from their stories of stigma, I have learned the word for *whore* in more African languages than I'd ever imagined. The experience and fear of social exclusion mean that many African sex workers don't reveal the nature of their work to even the closest people in their lives, including their own family members.

Health Care Discrimination

As police officers throw Gaone in a Botswanan cell, bleeding, bruised, and scared, it isn't the first time she feels abandoned by state institutions. She remembers her experience at the Gerald public health clinic just a year earlier: A nurse flew into a rage and refused to assist Gaone when she sought follow-up treatment for an STI. "Are you a prostitute?" the nurse asked with disdain, loud enough for other patients to hear. "You see, everyone, this is a prostitute! You are doing something that is not right, and I won't provide you with further treatment until you go and register yourself with the police and let them know that you are a prostitute."

* * *

One would hope that social stigma toward sex workers, reaffirmed and strengthened by criminalization, wouldn't necessarily influence the way health workers, who should provide nonjudgmental services to all people, deliver care to individual sex workers. Unfortunately for Gaone and many others, this isn't the case. Stigma frequently leads to overt discrimination against sex workers when they try to access health care services. Like many in the public, health workers often view sex workers as "vectors of disease." Sex workers report various abuses from health workers, including outright denial of services, verbal attacks, breaches of confidentiality, and demands that they identify and bring in sexual partners for STI treatment, a requirement impossible for sex workers to fulfill because of the nature of their work. This mistreatment, along with the fear of arrest if their work is revealed, drives sex workers away from health facilities.

It was disheartening to hear the stories of sex workers who'd found the courage to go to health centers seeking medical advice and assistance only to face discrimination: A nurse outs an HIV-positive sex worker to other patients as the sex worker is picking up her ARVs. A male sex worker reports that health workers turn away his sex worker friends who have been beaten and raped, coldly telling them, "You are the reason why this happened to you." Angeline DeBruin, a South African sex worker and longtime activist based in Cape Town, remembers going to a health center to obtain free condoms only to have a nurse at the recep-

Angeline DeBruin. Cape Town, South Africa.
Photograph by author.

tion say in front of all of the other patients, "She is a prostitute, prostitute! That's why she comes looking for condoms at this time of night." "You don't even know how to face those people afterwards," Angeline says.

The stigma and discrimination sex workers experience at health centers have prompted the creation of notable health clinics on the continent that cater specifically to sex workers' health needs, including the University of Manitoba's sex worker health clinics in Nairobi and the University of Witwatersrand's sex worker health project in Johannesburg, as well as many health outreach programs run by African sex workers' rights groups.[16] These programs provide sex workers with de-stigmatized, accessible health services. However, the fact that they are so desperately needed is an indictment of public health systems that generally fail many on the continent but exhibit a particularly intense level of discrimination toward sex workers and other marginalized groups.

Abuses chronicled in this chapter—discrimination in health care services and violence at the hands of police and clients—are all tied to stigma and the illegal status of the sex industry, which drives sex workers underground and away from needed health prevention and treatment services. This makes African sex workers more vulnerable to HIV/AIDS, which has long afflicted the continent. As has been stressed by UNAIDS and WHO, it is impossible to get to zero HIV infections if vulnerable groups like sex workers experience violence and discrimination as a result of their illegal status.[17] Criminalization in the face of the African AIDS epidemic is particularly egregious. In a frank conversation I had with doctors, health workers, and policymakers at the National AIDS Secretariat in Mauritius, they openly expressed concern that criminalization of sex work impedes their work by stigmatizing sex workers and making them afraid to approach clinics for preventative services and HIV and STI treatment. Stigma and criminalization also lead to bad health policies in the fight against HIV, as countries like Uganda misguidedly seek to pass laws that will make HIV testing compulsory for people arrested on prostitution charges.[18] Coercive measures like mandatory HIV testing for already stigmatized groups like sex workers lead to bad public health outcomes by further alienating at-risk groups.[19]

Anti-prostitution laws have nothing to do with honest concerns about sex workers' lives. If we're truly concerned about sex workers' safety, then we must support sex workers in advocating for action on the issues they highlight as most pressing in their lives. And we must also acknowledge how other laws and stigmas work in conjunction with anti-prostitution laws to compound the specific suffering of queer and trans sex workers, migrant sex workers, and HIV-positive sex workers, a topic I explore in the next chapter.

3

Out of the Shadows

Multiple Stigmas against African Transgender, Queer, Migrant, and HIV-Positive Sex Workers

Intersectionality simply came from the idea that if you're
standing in the path of multiple forms of exclusion, you are
likely to get hit by both.
—Kimberlé Crenshaw

African sex workers intimately understand the dehumanization involved in the denial of an individual's or a group's reality. It is in this spirit that the movement has nurtured inclusivity by illuminating the stories of a diverse range of African sex workers. The previous chapter highlighted the abuses that all African sex workers face because of stigma and sex work's criminalized status. But the harmful effects of sex work's illegality also intersect with transphobia, homophobia, xenophobia, conflation of sex work and trafficking, HIV discrimination, and associated discriminatory laws, rendering African transgender, queer, migrant, and HIV-positive sex workers vulnerable to multiple overlapping stigmas.

Although the majority of African sex workers are cisgender women, it's not only straight cisgender women who engage in sex work. To dismiss those who don't fit that paradigm as anomalies unworthy of sustained and serious attention only deepens their susceptibility to abuse. Transphobia and homophobia are harmful to transgender sex workers, queer sex workers, and male sex workers of diverse sexual orientations who are often perceived to be gay. Legal discrimination against LGBT people in Africa is widespread: In thirty-eight African countries, homosexuality is illegal, including six of the seven countries in this study.[1] Authorities often identify and denigrate transgender female sex workers as "cross-dressers" tied to illegal homosexuality. Thus, trans and queer sex workers experience a double stigma because of their criminalized status as both sex workers and people who are or who are perceived to be LGBT.

African migrant sex workers also experience double stigma because of both their criminalized status as sex workers and their lack of legal status as migrants. And because migrant sex workers are too often wrongly labeled as victims of human trafficking, the abuses they face as economic migrants who voluntarily cross borders to work in the sex industry receive little attention. Often ignored as well is the double stigma experienced by HIV-positive sex workers in Africa. The discrimination they face as both sex workers and as people living with HIV underscores the need for HIV prevention, care and treatment policies, and interventions that veer strongly away from fear-mongering.

The stories of transgender, queer, migrant, and HIV-positive sex workers explored in this chapter show how one must look at the entire legal and social status of sex workers and how intersections of discrimination increase susceptibility to abuse.

Transgender Female Sex Workers

Few interviews were as heartwrenching as my talks with African transgender female sex workers and the stories they told of brutal abuses they face because of whorephobia and transphobia. It is often a struggle for trans sex workers just to be seen as human beings, the most basic level of acceptance. Many African political and religious leaders have tried to undermine the African LGBT rights movement by propagating the idea that Africans who identify as LGBT are "un-African" and exist in stark contradiction to cultural norms.[2] To speak of static and monolithic African cultures is reductionist and misleading, but political and religious leaders successfully use this argument to place African LGBT people outside the cultural mainstream. This othering creates and reinforces stigma against transgender sex workers.

African cisgender female sex workers often have access to other types of work outside of the sex industry if they so choose, including domestic work, waitressing, hairdressing, and security work. For transgender female sex workers, however, employment opportunities outside of sex work are often almost nonexistent. "Homelessness among trans women in South Africa is extreme," says Netta, a trans sex worker activist based in Cape Town. "It's because they're being discriminated [against], stigmatized, can't find jobs. . . . Because their IDs say they're men they have to dress up as men. . . . They [people who discriminate against trans women] will always say, 'He is a man, why is he always dressing up every time [like a woman]?'" Rejection from family members, homelessness, inability to have their chosen gender reflected on their identity documents, and nonexistent job opportunities because of pervasive discrimination mean that trans women often choose to work in the sex industry as a result of painfully limited options.

The human rights abuses that transgender female sex workers face in the industry must be viewed through the lens of their illegal status as both sex workers and LGBT people in Africa. They are viciously murdered as a result of *both* whorephobia and transphobia. Police officers pepper them with transphobic insults, publicly strip them, and purposefully place them in jail cells with men whom they encourage to physically and sexually abuse them. I remember one particular story in which police officers forced a trans sex worker in a Cape Town jail to perform oral sex on both officers and male inmates. Trans female sex workers also report being profiled as sex workers by police even when they aren't working or when they are in the company of other transgender people who are not sex workers. Their gender identity marks them as perennial targets for policing. They face additional discrimination in health facilities because health workers are often ignorant of their specific health needs and stigmatize them for engaging in illegal sexual acts like anal sex.

I met Beyonce Karungi, a Ugandan trans female sex worker and activist, in the summer of 2013 in Kampala. She had just returned from a conference in Istanbul, and when she entered the gates of Uganda's leading sex workers' rights organization's offices, away from the prying eyes of the public street, she immediately removed her wool hat, and her long braided hair flew out. In the safe space of the sex workers' rights office she could be herself without fear. In the past few years she has blossomed into her activism, despite how dangerous things have become for LGBT people in Uganda, which became notorious recently for a draconian anti-gay law.[3] Although the law focused on anti-homosexuality measures, transgender people in Africa are often incorrectly viewed through the lens of sexual orientation, so anti-gay efforts are inevitably

Beyonce Karungi. Kampala, Uganda. Photograph by author.

anti-trans efforts as well. Beyonce's story, told in her own words in the first-person narrative that follows, clearly captures the stories I heard from many African transgender female sex workers about the abuses they face from police, clients, and the society at large because of their gender identity, perceived sexual orientation, and illegal status as sex workers and LGBT people.

Beyonce Karungi, 33, Transgender Female Sex Worker and Activist (Kampala, Uganda)

"People Are Saying You Are a Curse"

I am from a small, rural village in the midwestern part of Uganda. From childhood, starting when I was five years old, I always felt like I was a girl. My mother had passed away when I was a little kid, and in a family of seven, I was the only boy so I grew up with my sisters. I used to love putting on their dresses, playing with dolls, and cooking. Going to school was a challenge because I didn't like to play with boys. So whenever my dad took me to school, he would tell the teachers, "This boy fears boys." He didn't have a problem with me at that time—he thought I was the way I was because I was growing up with all my sisters.

In my teens, I felt even more like a woman, so I changed my dress code and began growing long hair. And then people began insulting my dad and saying it was a problem. They would say, "How come you have a useless son? He is a curse. How can you keep such a thing in your family? That one will never give you grandchildren. Throw that thing away." My dad got upset, and after these people began insulting him, he changed and rejected me. My dad told me, "People are saying you are a curse. I can't keep you. You're a useless thing." It was a small town, and people are ignorant about trans issues. I was sixteen years old then, and I couldn't stay in the village because people were so hostile to me. So I had to leave. My sisters loved me and were very sad.

I moved to Kampala and stayed with three girls living in a hostel. I used to see them go out and come back with money. They were giving me accommodation and food, but I needed to sustain myself. I always wondered where the girls were getting the money so I finally asked one of them and she said they were doing sex work in clubs, bars, and hotels. She said, "You should come and also get people to take you out." So, this is how because of misery I began doing sex work. I was from a poor background. I needed to survive. I didn't have any source of income because it's very difficult for transgender people to get jobs. We are born and feel like women, and it doesn't matter how much education you have, [we] can never get a job because people reject us and don't take us seriously. Nobody gives [us] a job. So lots of trans women engage in sex work. That's the only thing that can sustain us. What was good about it was [that] I was able to get money to go back to school, purchase school supplies, and pay for my school fees. But I faced a lot of violations from people on the streets and the police.

"God Is Going to Burn Our Nation"

One time the police humiliated me in public. I think it was 2003. Around nine o'clock in the morning, I was [returning] from doing sex work at the Palm Tree Hotel in Kampala and walking to my home. Five police officers stopped me and said, "Are you a man or a woman? You're confusing us." They arrested me, and then they stripped me completely naked, beat me up, and took scissors and cut off my hair. They took everything I had—my shoes, my bag, and my money. They were calling out to people on the street and saying, "Come and look at this homosexual!" Some of the people who came had solidarity with me, but others began beating me up. They were screaming, "Kill that thing! That thing is spoiling our nation. God is going to burn our nation because of that thing." It was a very big mess for me. I felt very small.

They took me to the police station. They gave me back my clothes, but I found that all my other things, including my bag and shoes, were missing. They put me in a cell with men who also began beating me up. When my sex worker friends found out that I was missing they began looking for me everywhere, including in all the jails in Kampala. They bailed me out when they found me.

At bars where I've done sex work, people have poured booze on me, burnt me with cigarettes, and bounced me out of the pubs. You can still see the scars on my face, hands, everywhere. I hadn't caused any harm—I would just be dancing, having a drink, and looking for clients and money. And from nowhere people would begin insulting me. These hostile people would say, "Which kind of thing is this person? Why do you allow this thing in here?" There is persecution because transgender sex workers are mistaken to be gay, so we are unacceptable. We are criminalized as being sex workers and being homosexuals. Another problem is "corrective rape." If people get a transgender sex worker, they will gang-rape her and then say [they did so] because "those are men pretending to be women."

In 2004, one time a client who looked rich took me to his place in Kampala. He knew I was transgender. I provided him sexual services, but he used the fact that I'm trans to refuse to pay me. He took out a pistol and said he wanted to kill me. He screamed, "What are you doing here in my house! Get out of my house!" I was very scared. I just put on my jeans and ran out of the house. I forgot my shoes. I forgot to even put on my top and my jacket. It was three o'clock in the morning, and I sat outside of the gate in the cold, crying. It traumatized my life. Other transgender sex workers have complained about the same thing—clients throwing them out and not paying them their money. They throw them out, and then call people and say, "See, I found a man pretending to be a woman."

We are facing a lot of abuses, including murder and hate crimes. We've lost a lot of transgender sex workers, and I want justice. One of them who was murdered, we used to do sex work together. Her body was found in

Kampala outside a hotel. Her name was Udiara; she was a trans sex worker of Indian descent. There was another one called Bony; she was also murdered. And there was Patience; she was murdered, too. And there was Shirina. They were all found in different places. I think it is now eight years since they have all been gone. Their murders haven't been solved and there's been no police investigation. Nothing at all. So there are a lot of violations, and this is why I came out—to raise awareness. We are trying to sensitize people so they realize who we are.

"I Am Someone Who Is Not Useless"

I've faced a lot of violations, but I kept moving on because I needed money to survive at the end of the day. I've persevered and continued doing sex work, and it helped me. I was able to continue my O level [equivalent of U.S. high school], attending at least three times a week. And if I had not gone to school, I wouldn't even be speaking English today. I have also reunited with my dad because of sex work. My dad was very sick in 2005 with diabetes and high blood pressure, and one of my sisters called me and told me they didn't have any money for his hospital bills. I went back home and was able to pay all the bills. My dad saw my importance, and when he got better he told me, "My child, I love you, forgive me. You are always welcome back home." I told him, "Dad, I was born male but I feel female." And he said, "Oh, so this is the little boy-girl I used to see." He was ignorant before, but now we are back together. He accepts me the way I am. Now people in the village see that I have grown up and that when I go back I do good things for my father. People say that I am useless because I am transgender, but I wanted to show them that I am someone who is not useless.

I became an activist six years ago. I was working with WONETHA, an organization of mainly female sex worker activists. When the landlord of the building where the WONETHA office was located saw us doing sex work activism on TV that included transgender sex workers like me, she said, "I didn't know you were promoting these people." She felt we were gay and WONETHA was promoting homosexuality. So because of her hate, the landlord threw WONETHA out. She doubled their rent, so they had to leave. I started Transgender Equality Uganda in April 2011 to advocate for trans and sex work issues. I created this space to talk about the violations we face. We are still working as partners and allies with female sex workers because we are all facing challenges—being stigmatized and discriminated against and being harassed by the police. I have always heard about religious leaders in Uganda being very abusive and preaching hate, talking about how religion and culture [don't] accept sex work and LGBT, that if we allow such activity, God is going to burn our country. People say sex workers promote immorality, that they snatch husbands, that religion doesn't accept them. We'll go to hell. God will punish our souls. Those are the kinds of things I hear. So we need to work together to fight for our rights. We need to raise our voices together.

Queer Male Sex Workers

Like openly transgender female sex workers, African queer male sex workers who identify as gay, bisexual, or as men who have sex with men (MSM) also face abuses because of sex workers' and LGBT people's criminalized status. Homophobia is often a central basis of abuse against queer male sex workers. Clients may use the threat of outing them as a way to avoid paying for sexual services, and they report experiencing stigma at health clinics both because they are gay and because they are sex workers. Violence from police officers against queer male sex workers is also often tinged with homophobia. If we view sex work solely through the lens of the cisgender female sex worker, and if we don't acknowledge the existence of queer male sex workers and the way in which both the illegality of sex work and homosexuality fosters abuses against them, then we marginalize their voices and experiences.

During my second trip to Nairobi, I met Jafred Okoyana, an openly gay sex worker and then a leading activist with Healthy Options for Young Men on HIV, AIDS, and STIs (HOYMAS), a Kenyan NGO that advocates on behalf of both MSM (men who have sex with men) and male sex workers. Because of HOYMAS's advocacy, the presence of male sex workers in Kenya, the majority of whom are queer-identified, is more visible than in other African countries. Jafred is tall and striking, with a beautifully chiseled face and an air of gracefulness about him, and I was deeply moved by his personal story. Jafred overcame a difficult childhood—it is a part of his story I briefly repeat here—not because he believes these childhood experiences were the catalyst for his later entry into sex work but because he, like others I interviewed, is confident that overcoming these childhood obstacles directly contributed to the resil-

Jafred Okoyana. Nairobi, Kenya. Photograph by
author.

iency, fortitude, and leadership he has showcased as an activist on behalf
of male sex workers. (Indeed, although it is a commonly held notion
that sex workers enter the industry because of childhood trauma, my
interviews revealed that African sex workers have a diversity of childhood experiences.) More important, the full story of the abuses Jafred
has experienced reveals how the illegal status of sex work and homosexuality intersects with and increases African queer male sex workers'
vulnerability.

Jafred was born in 1971 in a small village in the western part of Kenya,
among the Luhya people, the second-largest ethnic group in Kenya. His
parents were small-scale farmers, and theirs was a deeply troubled marriage, scarred by domestic violence. When Jafred was five years old his
father abandoned the family. For a year, his mother struggled to provide
for her four young sons by selling clay pots in village markets, and then,
one day, she too disappeared. Jafred was six years old at the time, and
when he and his brother, who was eight, arrived home from school they
found that their mother and two youngest brothers had vanished, and

all that was left in the house was one wilting plant and a bag of flour. Bewildered and afraid, Jafred and his brother continued to go to school, hoping their mother would return. They cooked one meal of porridge to share between them every day, "without sugar, without taste." It's been more than thirty-five years, yet Jafred still remembers that his mother left on a Tuesday. It wasn't until Saturday, after five days of living alone, that Jafred and his brother decided to search for their mother.

They had no idea where she could be, but they remembered that their grandparents lived in a nearby village. Maybe their mothers' parents would know where she was? So they began to walk, uncertain they were heading in the right direction, until a kind neighbor on a bicycle who recognized the boys and was startled to see them walking on the road alone near dark asked them where they were going. "We are looking for our mother," they said, eyeing the fresh milk in the man's bicycle basket. "If you can help us find our mother's parents we will be very happy." He sat both of the boys on his bicycle near the handlebars and took them to their grandparents' village. It was there they learned that their mother, desperate to make more money to support her family, had taken their two younger brothers to a small town where she was doing small goods trading and planning on sending money back to their grandmother for their school fees. Jafred stayed with his grandparents for some time, but he ached for his lost family. "We were missing our farm. We were missing our father. We were missing our mother," Jafred remembers. "Sometimes we would be happy, just being young boys and playing. But in the evenings, we felt something in us was not complete."

After leaving his grandparents' village Jafred worked on his aunt's farm, where he did the fieldwork of someone twice his age. He spent school vacations with his mother, and she often become verbally abusive. "You should leave me alone!" she would shout. "Leave my home life!" It was during this time, when he was around ten years old, that Jafred first realized he was gay: "[W]hen I was in school I had these feelings. . . . I wanted to have someone close to me who was not of the opposite sex." It was also during this time that he began to develop the leadership abilities he would later exhibit as an activist: He attended a two-year vocational school that he paid for himself by harvesting cotton, onions, and chilies and was often in charge of organizing school events. He also took on leadership roles in his church youth organization.

In 1998, when Jafred was twenty-five years old, he could no longer deny the intimate feelings he had felt toward other men since he was young, so he decided to move to Nairobi with 50,000 Kenyan shillings ($575 USD) saved from working in carpentry and flower shops to look for "someone to love." One day he went into a public restroom and was confused when he found men standing idly in the facilities and exchanging furtive glances with whoever entered and exited. He did not realize it was a "hot spot" frequented by men looking for paid sex, but there was something about the scene that sent feelings of attraction shooting through his body as he left the washroom. A man from the restroom followed him. "I like you," the man said. "Want to visit my place?" It was the first day Jafred engaged in sex work.

His primary motivation for entering sex work was not at first economic. It was initially about the rush of finally finding other men who loved men like him, but it soon became financially necessary when his cousin kicked him out of the apartment they shared, rendering him homeless and, like many economically and socially marginalized LGBT people, dependent on sex work to support himself financially. Jafred has been engaged in sex work now for more than seventeen years. He advocates for the rights of MSM and male sex workers and understands many of the psychological and physical abuses they face because of the grinding stigma attached to both sex work and homosexuality. An experience he had in Nairobi is a perfect illustration of the dangerous ramifications of this double stigma.

Jafred once had a client who was a priest affiliated with a politically connected Catholic church, and although initially Jafred just provided the priest with sexual services, their working relationship had also blossomed into a romantic liaison. He would often visit the priest in the church offices, which soon aroused the church staff's suspicions. One day after Jafred visited the priest, police officers immediately arrested him and pushed him into a car with tinted windows, wrapping a scarf around his face as they sped off to an unknown location. For eight hours the police interrogated Jafred in the car, until he revealed the nature of his working and romantic relationship with the priest. Without issuing formal charges, they put him in a jail cell for six days where he became ill because of the horrible conditions. They denied him medical attention except for one night when a kind police officer clandestinely snuck him out to receive treatment at a Catholic health clinic. After his release, they drove him to the Kenya–Uganda border, where they confiscated his identification papers and warned him never to return to Kenya. Jafred was able to come home only because of the kindness of a Ugandan immigration officer of Luhya descent, who because of their shared ethnic affiliation took pity on him and allowed him to cross the border back into Kenya. He hid in the seaside town of Mombasa and relatives' homes for months, terrified and traumatized by the experience.

Jafred was targeted based on the suspicion that he was a sex worker and gay man, both criminalized statuses, and after this horrific experience, he became an activist working with male, mostly queer-identified, sex workers. "It gave me the power to become an activist," Jafred says. "I'm from a poor family. I've lived as a parentless child. I've lived on the streets. I wanted to come out and teach young men that they need to take care of themselves, that life is not going to be easy, but you have to make decisions for your own life."

Queer Women, Trans Men, and Gender Nonconforming Sex Workers

Cisgender women, transgender women, and queer men are the most highly visible communities within the African sex work industry. Openly queer women, trans men, and gender nonconforming people are less visible in their work—this, of course, does not mean that they do not exist.[4] Because of this lack of visibility, however, I did not interview any openly trans male sex workers or gender nonconforming sex workers. I did interview several openly bisexual and lesbian female sex workers who spoke of the overlapping stigmas of whorephobia and homophobia in the lives of queer women in the African sex industry. In one example, the infamous Ugandan tabloid the *Red Pepper*, which harasses both sex workers and LGBT people by "outing" them as "top homosexuals" in its pages, targeted Daisy Nakato, a leading Ugandan sex worker activist who openly identifies as bisexual.

Recognizing these intersectional stigmas, some activists are trying to increase queer women's visibility within the African movement. When Julie Katongole, a Ugandan sex worker activist, founded the sex workers' rights organization Crested Crane Lighters, she focused much of her outreach efforts on female sex workers who identify as lesbian, bisexual, or "women who have sex with women" because she felt this was a large but invisible and neglected population within the Ugandan sex worker movement. Crested Crane Lighters is cultivating a dynamic space in which queer women in the sex industry are seeking support and solidarity.

In Lagos, Nigeria, I met Serenity, a sex worker who exclusively has romantic relationships with other women and has come out to family members and close friends. When I interviewed her, she had recently joined the Women of Power Initiative (WOPI), the only sex worker–led organization in Nigeria, where she hopes to be a bridge between the larger Nigerian sex worker activist community and the hidden population of queer female sex workers. "I know a lot of people like me who like women and are sex workers, but they hide it," says Serenity. "There are many of us, but we are in Nigeria, so they don't like to open up." In January 2014, Nigeria passed a harsh anti-gay law, leading to public crackdowns against those suspected of being LGBT.[5] Pat Abraham, a prominent Nigerian sex worker activist and WOPI founder, recruited Serenity into WOPI to help extend the organization's outreach to the queer female community of sex workers in Lagos, especially in light of the intensified discrimination they face under the new law. "We need to include them in our programs and training," Pat said adamantly about WOPI's new outreach efforts. "We know that they're there, but they are not comfortable coming out and saying it. People are afraid. People need a touch." The encouraging example of outreach efforts undertaken by organizations like Crested Crane Lighters and WOPI will hopefully inspire other African sex work activists to create and nurture more spaces that reach out to queer women, as well as trans men and gender nonconforming people who may be experiencing multiple stigmas.

Migrant Sex Workers

In the same way that characterizing African sex workers as being only cisgender straight females obscures the abuses faced by transgender and queer sex workers, so too does insisting that we view all migrant sex workers through the lens of human trafficking. Human trafficking involves the movement of people (oftentimes across borders) through force, deception, or coercion into situations of forced labor in factories, agriculture work, domestic work, prostitution, and other industries. Although trafficking occurs in many different industries, anti-prostitution activists have commandeered the anti–human trafficking movement in an attempt to make all sex work synonymous with trafficking.[6] This conflation has resulted in a growing international focus on trafficking into forced prostitution, commonly referred to as "sex trafficking," from the general public, governments, and the media which often assume that all sex workers, specifically foreign sex workers, have been forced into prostitution.[7]

This conflation is damaging in several ways. It discourages societies from tackling the poverty, strict immigration policies, and unprotected labor sectors that make economic migrants vulnerable to trafficking,[8] and it ignores the experience of migrants who freely emigrate to engage in sex work but nonetheless experience abuses because of xenophobia, sex work's illegality, and their frequent lack of legal status as migrants. Human trafficking is indeed a reality in many parts of the world, including Africa, but the extent of the problem is often overblown as a result of trafficking research of highly questionable methodology that lacks reliable figures.[9] Although the scope of trafficking into forced prostitution in Africa is hard to determine without reliable studies, I interviewed sex workers who acknowledged the existence of trafficked people in the African sex industry. In South Africa, for instance, sex workers noted that they had met women from poor villages in countries like the Democratic Republic of Congo who had been promised jobs in South Africa by traffickers, only to find themselves forced to work in brothels when they arrived. In Nigeria, sex workers spoke of people who may initially agree to have a "fixer" provide the fake documents and travel expenses that will allow them safe passage to Europe, knowing that they will be involved in prostitution when they arrive as a way to pay off their debt to the fixer. However, at their destination, they may find themselves in a situation of unbearable forced labor that meets the definition of trafficking.[10] At the same time, Nigerian sex workers I interviewed also stressed that they knew many Nigerian women who have moved to Europe to work in the sex industry, have not experienced conditions of trafficking, and have done well financially, sending money back home to care for members of their extended families. In general, sex workers I interviewed, while acknowledging the existence and horror of trafficking, expressed frustration at how the trafficking narrative is applied to far too many situations of economic migration involving the sex industry and how this situation has served to discount the concerns of foreign sex workers who haven't been trafficked.

The migrant sex workers I met had compelling reasons for migrating from their home countries to engage in sex work abroad. In July 2013, in the wintertime in Botswana when wilting Mophani trees line the barren landscape, I drove north to the border trucking town of Kazangula outside of the safari-tourist town of Kasane, known as the "four corners" of Africa where Botswana, Zambia, Zimbabwe, and Namibia meet. Because of this interesting geography Kasane-Kazangula is home to many migrant sex workers, and I wanted to hear their stories. There was Maria from Zimbabwe, who left her country in 2007 to migrate to Botswana. She is the sole breadwinner for six children—two of her own as well as her deceased sisters' four children. Zimbabwe was in a severe political and economic downturn at that time: "There was nothing in the shops," Maria says. "Nothing whatsoever. No bread, no mielie-meal [porridge], nothing. The shops were empty so you couldn't buy anything. So looking for food we have to cross to Botswana or some were crossing to Zambia. Some were going to Mozambique." She was thirty-four years old when she arrived in Kazangula and decided to try sex work in order to provide for her large family back in Zimbabwe, a decision she admits was a very difficult one. At first she felt ashamed doing sex work, but within a week she was able to send rice, clothes, and money back to her family. She has continued to provide for them adequately, a fact that makes her proud.

The migrant sex workers I met in Kazangula were all from Zimbabwe and had similar stories. Some had been sex workers back in their home countries, and others, like Maria, had begun sex work only after they had migrated. They were all sole breadwinners for extended families back home and easily made more money doing sex work than in other jobs. Former migrant domestic workers who turned to sex work spoke of the low pay and often harsh conditions of domestic work. They were routinely underpaid and underfed ("Sometimes we won't eat. Sometimes maybe just drink tea in the morning, tea in the afternoon, tea in the evening," remembered one migrant), and they had to beg for time off to visit their families in Zimbabwe. Former hairstylists and domestic workers reported making on average 400 Botswana pula ($44 USD) a month after they migrated and discovered that by doing sex work they could earn between 600 and 1,000 pula ($66 and $110 USD, respectively) a month. The higher rate of pay, combined with the many people back home depending on them, made their decision to engage in the sex industry economically rational. People like Maria and the other migrant sex workers I met in Kazangula who migrate voluntarily to engage in the sex industry are as deserving of rights as those who have been trafficked into forced prostitution.

In South Africa, where migrant sex workers from all over Africa, including Zimbabwe, Zambia, Malawi, Nigeria, Tanzania, and elsewhere, abound, I interviewed Mudiwa, a migrant former sex worker from Zimbabwe and organizer of migrant sex workers in South Africa with an effervescent, youthful personality. Like the sex workers I met in Kazangula, she too had left Zimbabwe searching for greener pastures. She was a sex worker in South Africa for several years until she achieved her financial goals and was able to adequately support her nine dependents in Zimbabwe and the son who lives with her in Cape Town. But even after she left the industry and transitioned to other pursuits, she could not forget the many migrant sex workers she had worked alongside and the specific abuses they suffer because of xenophobia and prostitution's illegality.

Because of foreign sex workers' often two-fold illegal status as sex workers and undocumented migrants, clients may refuse to pay migrant sex workers for their services, asserting, they "won't give money to foreigners." They may also physically and sexually abuse them, knowing that someone who is both a sex worker and an undocumented migrant has two reasons for not reporting this abuse to the police. Mudiwa explains:

> A lot of the ladies, they don't have papers [legal immigration documentation]. . . . So if you go to the police and they know you are a foreigner, the first question they ask you is, "Where are your papers?" They leave the other case you're there for, and they arrest you because you don't have papers. So you would rather keep quiet than to go to the police and get arrested. Even if foreign sex workers get raped, they can't go and report it

because who would you report it to? Instead of [the police] dealing with your case, they throw you into prison. [They'll say,] "You don't have papers and now you come and tell us your nonsense of being raped."

Mudiwa encourages the many migrant sex workers she engages in her outreach efforts to pursue official migration status or to keep their documents up to date so that they don't fall prey to the actions of police and clients as well as those of third-party managers who will sometimes use a foreign sex worker's lack of official migration status to get away with abuses.

But it is difficult for Mudiwa and other migrant sex worker organizers to advocate for their rights when people insist on viewing all of their experiences through the lens of trafficking. In my time interviewing sex workers in Africa, I did not meet one sex worker who believed that anyone should be forced into prostitution. They were all uniformly against trafficking, and some sex worker organizations, like SWEAT in South Africa, help connect victims of trafficking they meet in their outreach work with social development organizations. (The repeal of anti-prostitution laws would provide a more conducive environment for community-based sex worker organizations to help identify victims of exploitation and link them with necessary social services.) But sex workers' resentment of the trafficking label's being erroneously applied to their own lives, despite the diverse circumstances of people who enter the sex industry, was clear—it robbed them of agency and made it difficult to discuss the issues actually affecting their lives. "Even the locals, if you're talking to them they'll tell you, 'Oh, you foreigners are all being trafficked, oh shame. That's why you're doing all these pathetic things,'" Mudiwa says. "But not everyone who's in South Africa has been trafficked." So, instead of discussing xenophobic and whorephobic violence against them or how it is difficult to secure and maintain legal migration status, foreign sex workers are stuck attempting to prove their self-determination and reject labels like "trafficking victim" that obscure the true issues they deal with.

HIV-Positive Sex Workers

Like transgender, queer, and migrant sex workers, HIV-positive African sex workers also face double stigma. Their vulnerability is due to their illegal status as sex workers and the grinding stigma and discrimination they experience as people living with HIV. One out of every twenty adults in sub-Saharan Africa is HIV-positive, and Africa has long been the continent hardest hit by the epidemic, constituting 70 percent of people living with HIV worldwide.[11] HIV prevalence among cisgender female sex workers is 45 percent in Kenya, 24 percent in Nigeria, 59 percent in South Africa, and 35 percent in Uganda.[12] Unfortunately, statistics of HIV prevalence among transgender and male sex workers rarely exist. Sexual and physical abuse, the underground nature of the sex industry, and discrimination at health care centers make sex workers a group deeply affected by the epidemic. Yet, all too often, they are viewed as drivers of the epidemic or "vectors of disease," rather than as people highly vulnerable to HIV because of the human rights abuses they face.

The combination of whorephobia and HIV stigma has led to harmful governmental policies and laws targeting sex workers. For instance, in Uganda, human rights and HIV/AIDS activists have long fought a bill in Parliament requiring forced HIV testing of people charged with prostitution offenses. Those sex workers who test positive would then be additionally charged with the felony of intentionally attempting to transmit HIV.[13] Coercive measures like forced HIV testing and the criminalization of HIV transmission violate rights by breaching medical confidentiality and facilitating stigma and discrimination against HIV-positive people, therefore discouraging vulnerable groups from seeking out voluntary and confidential counseling, testing, and treatment, which can successfully stem the tide of HIV transmission. Unimpeded, de-stigmatized HIV treatment access for sex workers is necessary for the sake of their own health and the health of the public and is in the spirit of equity, because sex workers as a group are highly vulnerable to HIV.[14] A person with HIV who consistently adheres to a treatment regimen can lead a relatively healthy life and drastically minimize the chances of passing on the virus to sexual partners.[15] But bad policies like forced HIV testing, as well as the discrimination and breaches of medical confidentiality that African sex workers experience in health care clinics where their HIV and sex work status is often openly revealed can drive sex workers away from HIV treatment programs.[16]

Because of the abuses they face as a result of both sex work's illegality and persistent HIV-related stigma, African sex workers have begun to create support groups for HIV-positive sex workers. These groups are crucial in helping HIV-positive sex workers deal with the psychological effects of stigma, and this support helps them adhere to their HIV treatment regimens. "We come together," says Carol, an HIV-positive Kenyan sex worker who is a founder of Warembo Sasa, which organizes HIV-positive sex workers and roughly translates to "we are beautiful" in Kiswahili:

> If I am HIV positive, and I don't have another person to encourage me to continue with my adherence [to HIV treatment], continue with my good feeding, to have good diet, then that means that I will ignore life and feel like I am in an empty world, that I am the only human being that is existing. . . . I cannot think anymore. I cannot do anything else and I only decide I am not going to adhere again. I would rather die and vanish from this empty space. But together, with these groups of positive sex workers, we have seen it have a very good impact.

I was also lucky to meet Lucy, an HIV-positive sex worker and another founding member of Warembo Sasa. I had heard about Lucy long before I arrived in Nairobi. Two of my graduate research assistants had been in Nairobi for several months designing and conducting human rights workshops, and they often mentioned Lucy, who was a motherly protector over them in the fast-paced Kenyan capital. When I met Lucy, I was also struck by her sweetness and maternal nature. She's originally from Embu, near Mount Kenya, in the eastern part of the country. When she was twenty-two years old, and by then a young single mother, she was introduced to sex work by a friend and saw it as a way out of Embu and a way to feed her daughter. When she started sex work, she was completely uneducated about HIV, as were many people in her village, and she didn't know that condoms could impede its spread. She remembers hearing of a sickness in her village that people referred to as *mukimo* and *mukingo*, meaning "the killing" in the Embu language. People who were stricken with "the killing" were rarely touched, and when they died the villagers didn't bury them in coffins. They wrapped them in nylon and placed them directly in the ground. It was only later Lucy realized that the villagers who had died of "the killing" had in fact died of AIDS.

Lucy learned she was HIV-positive in 2002, when she went to a sex worker health clinic in Nairobi to get tested. By then, ARV medication was widely available, but it was still a devastating diagnosis: "I cry for two hours, three hours. I cry, I cry, I cry, I cry, I cry," Lucy says. Because she was in a clinic for sex workers, the doctor was exceedingly kind and gave Lucy hopeful and informative counseling about living with HIV. "She talk to me, she talk to me good," Lucy remembers gratefully. "And after that, I relax my heart."

Lucy is now thirty-six, works part-time as a sex worker, and has been living with HIV for more than a decade. She "lives positively"—strictly adhering to her HIV regimen, consistently using condoms, minding her nutrition, and dedicating herself to assisting other HIV-positive sex workers through the work of Warembo Sasa and by volunteering as a sex worker peer educator. She speaks of the crushing stigma they experience as HIV-positive people in general: "No somebody love you. Everybody talk bad to you. No somebody trust you. Even the cup you drink tea, or plate or spoon you using, no somebody can using that with you." This stigma also comes from non–sex workers who are themselves HIV-positive but see themselves as fundamentally different from HIV-positive sex workers, blaming them for spreading HIV—a perfect example of the intersection of whorephobia and HIV stigma. "They say it is the sex worker who bring sickness," Lucy says. In fact, reputable research has debunked the myth that sex workers are the main drivers of the HIV epidemic in Africa.[17]

Collecting the many stories chronicled in the past two chapters of the police abuse, client abuse, lack of access to justice, health care discrimination, and social stigma that affect all sex workers because of sex work's illegality and stigma, as well as the stories exploring the specific ways that trans, queer, migrant, and HIV-positive sex workers are made vulnerable because of intersecting stigmas, was difficult. It was like listening to an unending chorus of suffering. But out of the ashes of all these stories of abuse something remarkable has arisen—the birth and growth of the African sex workers' rights movement.

4

"Each Other's Keepers"

The Birth of Sex Worker Organizing in Africa

If I cannot air this pain and alter it, I will surely die of it.
That's the beginning of social protest.
—Audre Lorde

The supreme intolerability of injustice sparks social justice movements.
So in some ways it is unsurprising that despite the challenges a criminalized environment presents for activism, chronic human rights abuses
tied to sex work's stigma and illegality have created a political consciousness among sex workers that has ignited the sex workers' rights
movement in Africa. Sex worker organizing exists in all seven of the
diverse countries covered in this book—Botswana, Kenya, Mauritius,
Namibia, Nigeria, South Africa, and Uganda. And in the past several
years there has also been evidence of formal sex worker organizing in
Benin, Cameroon, Cote d'Ivoire, the Democratic Republic of Congo,
Ethiopia, Lesotho, Madagascar, Malawi, Mali, Mozambique, Sierra
Leone, Tanzania, Togo, Zambia, and Zimbabwe.[1] These organizations
join a global sex workers' rights movement that has existed for more
than forty years.

This chapter explores the birth of African sex worker organizing,
including both informal and formal political resistance, through case
studies of country movements at different developmental stages of sex
worker organizing, including South Africa, Kenya, Namibia, and Mauritius. The origins of the sex workers' rights movements in South Africa
and Kenya, the most vibrant and active on the continent, trace back to
the 1990s. They are Africa's oldest sex worker movements[2] and present
two different but equally compelling models of sex worker movement
building. The fledgling movement in Namibia and a remembrance of
the brief, inspiring life and tragic death of one of its young leaders pro-

vide important lessons learned about the cultivation of leadership as sex worker movements grow. The island nation of Mauritius is an example of a country at the early stages of sex worker organizing that is urgently exploring and beginning to succeed in igniting a truly sex worker–led movement.

South Africa: A Bigger Voice

The sex workers' rights movement in South Africa, the most well known on the continent, is the oldest movement in the southern African region. In November 1994, Shane Petzer, a South African university student and part-time sex worker; Use Pauw, a clinical psychologist; and Dr. Gordon Isaacs founded the Sex Workers Education and Advocacy Task Force (SWEAT) in Cape Town, the country's first sex workers' rights organization. Initially affiliated with the Triangle Project, an LGBT rights organization then known as the AIDS Support and Education Trust, SWEAT branched out on its own in 1996.[3] With government and private funding, they began conducting activities primarily focused on sex workers' health needs, such as the distribution of condoms. According to a SWEAT advocate, they soon realized that a human rights approach was also essential: "There was a focus from the early days [on] looking at health needs. . . . As the program developed, we recognized that the [distribution] of condoms was just merely an access point to sex workers—they would then begin to relate their stories of human rights abuse, the lack of facilities, certainly stigma, and when they were confronted with abuse from health care professionals. We then decided as a SWEAT team that this program would begin to feed the human rights approach."

SWEAT, whose activities have expanded to encompass rights-based legal reform advocacy; legal, social, and health support and services; and media activism, was the launching pad for the formal creation of the South African sex worker–led movement known as Sisonke, founded in 2003 in Cape Town by South African sex workers during a SWEAT-organized conference. SWEAT invited a diverse group of seventy sex workers from seven of the country's nine provinces to the conference and was able to gain their trust by respecting confidentiality, because many sex workers hide their occupation from their families, and emphasizing the human rights–based approach to sex work—the idea that sex workers must be allowed to realize their right to work, to gain access to health care, to migrate, and to live lives of dignity free from violence and discrimination. During the conference, the sex workers in attendance came to the realization that although SWEAT's work as an NGO is invaluable, it isn't led by sex workers, and the movement would truly advance only if sex workers themselves raised their voices in defense of their rights. "We were tired of being abused. Tired of hiding. We wanted to have a bigger voice," says Kholi Buthelezi, a forty-one-year-old female sex worker and the current head of Sisonke, who along with longtime sex worker activists like Angeline DeBruin and Joyce Mali is one of its founding members. They agreed to name their movement Sisonke because it means "togetherness" in Zulu and has a similar meaning in the South African languages of Xhosa and Ndebele. The seventy sex workers in attendance at Sisonke's founding returned to their provinces to spread the word about the movement's emergence.

In Sisonke's early years, from 2003 to 2008, SWEAT continued to provide useful human rights trainings in Cape Town to Sisonke representatives from different provinces. Kholi Buthelezi took the initiative to independently distribute the rights information she received from SWEAT to other sex workers in her home province:

> In order for them to understand that they do have rights . . . I would use an example of high-profile people, that the rights they have are the same as ours. . . . I used [to] say to them, I would always tell them, that we all have rights, just like our president, that my rights are the same as his. . . . Regardless of the profession that we do, that does not mean we don't have rights. . . . Some were not sure if it was true, some did not believe me, but some they did. And every time I came back, they wanted to listen more.

But despite the importance of SWEAT's trainings, without consistent and strong sex worker leadership and without a more widespread and formalized peer education model that would give sex workers a sense of ownership over the movement, organizing stalled during Sisonke's early years.

The Sisonke movement really began to gain steam in 2008 when Kholi took over as the head of Sisonke and began working with SWEAT as a development and outreach worker. There, she helped establish a formalized peer education program through which sex workers receive training on health and human rights and then go out to educate other street-based and indoor sex workers on these issues. I first met Kholi in 2012 in New York City, on her way to the International AIDS Conference in Washington, D.C. When I first saw her speak about Sisonke's growth and her own activism, I remember her saying that when she was younger, she had dreamed of becoming a singer, and how she felt that through her advocacy she was fulfilling that dream by singing for the rights of sex workers in South Africa. I was struck by her quiet confidence, and during my subsequent trips to Cape Town to meet with Sisonke members I was not surprised that many of them partly credit her humble and unwavering leadership and her insistence on cultivating everyone's development as leaders and activists, not just her own, for the growth and visibility of formal sex work organizing in South Africa. "Kholi is a true leader," they would tell me.

Even before Kholi began engaging in formal organizing as head of the Sisonke movement, for many years prior she had already been informally organizing sex workers in brothels in Johannesburg. Informal organizing includes the diverse ways in which, outside of formal structures like NGOs and other accredited organizations, sex workers try to increase their safety collectively, safeguard their health, and financially and emotionally support one another. Informal organizing is a form of resistance to criminalization and stigma. "Kholi was already organizing a movement before she came to SWEAT," notes a SWEAT advocate. "She was organizing women in the brothels and taking sick sex workers to the hospital. A movement starts then. There is a place for all this informal movement building. . . . NGOs have a role, but the NGO is not a movement."

Indeed, although sex worker activists have proven they can still maintain a radical agenda even when they formalize their activism into NGOs,[4] Kholi's informal organizing before she took the helm of Sisonke is a testament to the importance and centrality of everyday informal resistance in the birth of sex worker movement building. Kholi began working in brothels in 2002, and after being discriminated against at a public hospital in Johannesburg based on her sex work status, she began to attend a sex worker–friendly health clinic then known as the Repro-

Kholi Buthelezi. Cape Town, South Africa. Photograph by author.

ductive Health Research Unit (RHRU).[5] She soon began recruiting other sex workers in need of accessible and de-stigmatized health care to take advantage of the RHRU clinic's services, even personally escorting sex workers in her brothel to the clinic. She also set up a referral system in the brothel in which a specific sex worker designated as the health care point person would organize treatment access for sick sex workers. Uncomfortable with the dirty and run-down environment of the brothel she was working in, Kholi also informally organized her brothel co-workers to create and maintain a clean and healthy work environment by collectively buying new bedding for their rooms, purchasing kettles so they could take warm baths, filling their spaces with fresh flowers, and instilling a sense of professionalism and pride in their work. She encouraged her co-workers to save their money wisely and use some of it to put their children into daycare. The sex workers she lived and worked with affectionately nicknamed her "Mother."

It may be tempting to view movement building solely through the lens of the creation of formal organizations like SWEAT and Sisonke, but instances of sex workers' informally organizing and finding everyday ways to support one another, as Kholi did with her fellow sex workers in their Johannesburg brothel, abound in Africa. Sex workers I interviewed provided numerous examples of how they employ methods to look out for one another and improve their working conditions. They share safety information on harmful clients and police officers, keep track of one another via text messages, and often work together to enhance their security. They combine their money to purchase safe-sex supplies like condoms, refer one another to sex worker–friendly health clinics, and share medical information in order to protect their health. They take turns looking after one another's children during working hours in order to provide the social support lacking in their communities. They lend one another money during lean times and sometimes agree on set prices for services in order to lessen competition and increase their economic viability. They also find interesting ways to maximize their money jointly. For example, *motshelo* is a traditional communal financial savings system in Botswana that many Botswanan sex workers utilize. Every month the members of a *motshelo* must all contribute an agreed-upon sum to a joint account, and each month a different *motshelo* member receives the accumulated money. Sometimes to build on their capital, the *motshelo* members will lend the month's money to a nonmember who must pay it back with interest. Informal organizing among sex workers also has historical resonance: Oral histories of Kenyan women who worked as prostitutes in Nairobi under colonial rule reveal that they shared living quarters and working spaces, helped pay one another's fines, and sometimes designated one another as female heirs of their individual property.[6] These contemporary and historical examples of everyday ways in which sex workers in Africa help one another outside the support of NGOs and other formalized structures create a foundation for movement building by engendering a sense of community that can become the springboard for mass action. Through these informal structures, sex workers continue to prove themselves a positive resource for one another. It is a reminder of the innate power that lies within all of them and can be used to ignite and sustain a movement.

Officials at the RHRU clinic where Kholi would often take sex workers for treatment soon took notice of the informal organizing she was engaged in. They invited Kholi to be trained formally as an RHRU peer educator, and it was this training combined with the human rights train- ing she received at SWEAT, all buttressed by the informal organizing she was already engaged in on her own, that put her in a great position to lead Sisonke. With Kholi came the formal establishment of the SWEAT and Sisonke peer education model in 2008, which gave sex workers a more significant role in the development of the sex workers' rights movement in South Africa. Soon, every day, sex worker peer educators trained by SWEAT and Sisonke were taking to the streets and educating other sex workers on health issues like breast cancer, cervical cancer, and STIs and HIV and human rights issues like police and client abuse.[7]

In addition to the establishment of the formal peer education model, the Sisonke movement also grew stronger with the 2009 introduction of a workshop mechanism called "Creative Space," which had success- fully been used as an empowerment tool for former prisoners reentering society. Sisonke and SWEAT, with the initial help of advocate Richard September, designed and used the Creative Space methodology to create a safe physical and emotional space for sex workers to meet to discuss the issues they face, brainstorm innovative ideas of how to handle their problems, and receive vital information from invited outside educators on health, safety, finances, and human rights. In Creative Space, they often use artistic means, including painting, drawing, drama, dance, and singing, to explore relevant issues.[8] Creative Space first started in Cape Town, and in the very early stages Sisonke members would often con- duct "mobile creative spaces," impromptu workshops in a well-known sex worker's living quarters or areas of a township where sex workers were known to congregate. Soon SWEAT provided Sisonke with physi- cal space at its offices to conduct weekly Creative Spaces to which they would invite sex workers in Cape Town to participate. This soon ex- panded to other provinces in the country, where Sisonke members would appeal to host organizations to provide them with the physical space needed to conduct consistent Creative Space workshops with sex workers.

Creative Space serves as an important way of both building commu- nity as well as planting the seeds of political consciousness among its participants and watching them bloom into powerful and persuasive human rights demands regarding sex work as labor. Creative Space also became an important tool for identifying and recruiting potential leaders of the Sisonke movement—particularly, active and dedicated Creative Space participants, who would receive skills development and peer education training. Kholi describes Creative Space as a way of "building space for sex workers within themselves. Because if I don't accept myself as a sex worker with rights, no one will understand and respect that." This idea of building a "movement within" is fundamentally about fighting against the internal stigma so many sex workers feel because of the external abuse and stigma they experience. It is impossible to build a movement for change without this political reorientation.

An adviser to Sisonke and former SWEAT outreach coordinator who was an integral part of introducing the Creative Space methodology remembers the space "opening up" because sex workers also began to view it as a practical place from which to address their pressing needs: "It became a viable space, there was something happening in the space for them. . . . [For instance, there was a sex worker] who had just lost a child and I remember being overwhelmed at the response of the other women because here was a sex worker who had nothing, who had just lost a child that she had to bury, and the women pulled together and helped her bury the child. These are the things we began talking about in Creative Space, and eventually the sex workers just took it over." Creative Space and the peer education model now take place in all seven provinces where Sisonke is active in South Africa: Eastern Cape, Western Cape, Guateng, KwaZulu-Natal, Limpopo, Mpumalanga, and the North West. Other sex worker movements in Africa have successfully replicated the Creative Space methodology.

As Sisonke continues to grow, it is balancing direct service work addressing the practical, everyday problems that sex workers face, including lack of legal recourse, lack of access to de-stigmatized health care, and rampant physical and sexual abuse at the hands of police, while also maintaining a radical posture regarding sex work law and policy reform.[9] SWEAT and Sisonke's outreach services focus on sex workers of all backgrounds, something I witnessed as I accompanied sex worker peer educators on street and brothel outreach to black, white, and Coloured sex workers. (So far, racial collaboration in South African sex work activism has escaped some of the overt racial tensions on display within the South African LGBT movement, where in 2012, for instance, white LGBT activists physically attacked black lesbian activists at the Johannesburg Gay Pride Parade.)[10] They are meeting diverse sex workers' needs at the grassroots and embracing a sex workers' rights ethos that rejects criminalization and stigma.

Kenya: One Another's Keepers

The sex workers' rights movement in Kenya, also one of the oldest on the continent, is a striking example of bottom-up organizing, a truly grassroots movement. Informal and formal organizing has rapidly mushroomed throughout the country, totaling more than seventy active groups led by sex workers. The first formal rights-based sex worker group in Kenya, and in the whole east African region, was the Bar Hostess Empowerment and Support Program (BHESP), formed in 1998 by Kenyan women who worked in bars in the Kasarani neighborhood of Nairobi. They founded the organization as a direct result of the deep violence they were experiencing as bar hostesses and venue-based sex workers from police officers, city council *askaris*, and clients: Police officers put them in the trunks of cars as punishment for refusing to provide sexual services; clients beat them unconscious and dumped them at the roadside; bar patrons used guns to threaten and intimidate them. Women working in five bars in Kasarani came together to brainstorm ideas about how to begin to address this unrelenting abuse. They launched BHESP as an organization that would welcome all affected populations—those who identified as sex workers as well as bar hostesses who, because of stigma, didn't necessarily view themselves as sex workers but who nevertheless provided sexual services for pay in addition to their "regular" work at the bars.

I met Peninah Mwangi, a forty-three-year-old sex worker activist, one of BHESP's founding members, and one of the midwives of Kenya's sex worker–led movement, in Kasarani, where the Kenyan sex worker movement was born. As BHESP's executive director, she's still one of Kenya's leading sex worker organizers, and younger activists engage her with abiding respect and fondness. Peninah graduated from Kenyatta University in 1995 with a bachelor's degree in sociology, and soon after leaving the grinding reality of a postgraduate job working on a factory line she began managing a family-owned bar in Kasarani. It was there that she first began engaging in sex work and felt deep solidarity with

Peninah Mwangi. Nairobi, Kenya. Photograph by author.

the bar hostesses and venue-based sex workers who were also providing sexual services in the bar and facing constant abuse. "We were just all girls going through the same hassles, and so we came together and said now what can we do? What can happen?" Peninah recalls. "We didn't even see it as organizing at that time. We just saw it as a way of addressing [the police about the violence], and you couldn't do it alone."

They began organizing in Kasarani at the peak of the HIV/AIDS epidemic in Kenya when HIV infection rates in Kenyan adults hovered around 10 percent.[11] Long before health experts began to highlight the dire effects of HIV in the country, sex workers and bar hostesses were seeing its effects on the bar scene as their co-workers, as well as clients and bar owners, began dying. The Kasarani sex workers formally registered BHESP and appealed to the government to provide free condoms and send HIV educators into the bars to teach sex workers, bar hostesses, and clients about HIV prevention, testing, and treatment. But even though women working in the bars were living in the shadow of HIV, they often viewed the violence they were experiencing from police and clients as a more pressing issue. "We would go to a bar to talk about HIV, and the women would tell us . . . three of their girls were already in the cells and there was a girl who was murdered yesterday or beaten unconscious by a client or policeman," Peninah remembers of those early days of activism. "There's an interesting conversation we held with a lady who told us, 'HIV, I can live with it for the next ten years, but [from] the violence I will die tomorrow. . . . So even as we address HIV, can we find a way to deal with this [the violence]?'" In one of BHESP's first formal activities after its founding, sex workers went en masse to the police officer in charge of the Kasarani area and declared that they would no longer suffer in silence at the hands of police officers.

By 2009, the determination of people in the Kenyan sex industry to no longer simply accept the violence in their daily lives had spread from its birthplace in Kasarani. In addition to BHESP, several formal sex workers' rights organizations had emerged, including Healthy Options for Young Men on HIV, AIDS, and STIs (HOYMAS) in Nairobi; Keeping Alive Societies' Hope (KASH) in Kisumu; and Survivors in Busia, although these groups worked separately in different parts of the country, and the movement was far from a cohesive one. The movement's real blossoming began in 2009 when activists affiliated with these organizations, including Daughtie Ogutu, Peninah Mwangi, Phelister Abdalla, John Mathenge, Velven Joviese, Caroline Kemunto, and Grace Kamau, attended the first continent-wide gathering of African sex worker activists hosted by SWEAT in Cape Town. This gathering would eventually lead to the official launch of the continent-wide African Sex Worker Alliance (ASWA), which continues to provide a platform for sex workers in Africa to network and strengthen their respective countrywide and regional movements. (During this time, activists also benefited from a workshop aimed at African sex workers in the east African region convened by the women's rights organization Akina Mama wa Afrika.)[12] The Kenyan activists returned from the conference invigorated and determined to accelerate the movement in their own country. That same year, they formed the Kenya Sex Workers Alliance (KESWA), an umbrella organization that would help strengthen their joint efforts.

With seed money from ASWA and out of their own pockets, the dynamic activists who helped found KESWA did something remarkable— they began to methodically and systematically go from town to town, meeting with fellow sex workers, listening to their stories, providing them with training to understand through a human rights lens the abuses they face, and helping them establish informal and formal sex workers' rights groups throughout the country. In the first-person narrative that follows, Phelister Abdalla, KESWA's national coordinator and a leading, fierce voice for sex workers' rights in the country, tells the story of the feat of grassroots activism that led to the explosion of sex workers' rights groups in Kenya and the intensely personal story of her own birth into activism.

Phelister Abdalla, 33, Cisgender Female Sex Worker and Activist (Nairobi, Kenya)

"They Have a Story That Nobody Else Can Tell"

There were a few organizations that had done fabulous work with sex workers in the country, like Bar Hostess [BHESP], KASH, and Survivors, but we wanted to start small groups in other parts of the country to empower more sex workers, so the voices of sex workers would be heard all over the country. We went from town to town throughout Kenya to start conversations with our fellow sex workers. We went to Mombasa, Malindi, Changamwe, and Ukunda in the east. We went to Kisumu, Busia, and Eldoret in the west and Thika in the center. The first thing we did when we visited such places was to befriend our fellow sex workers. We used Creative Space, which we learned in South Africa, in order to create a safe space where they could tell their stories and share their experiences. And they shared stories that showed they had no knowledge about their human rights. They only knew that they are "criminals." When they're beaten, they just keep quiet. When they're arrested, they just see a way of bribing the police so that they can go back home to their children. They used to [think of] themselves as if they are not human beings because of the way the community was [treating] them. The religious leaders used to [say] bad things about the sex workers and abuse them in the community. They had no peace. And this was not only toward sex workers but even toward their children. People have hated sex workers so much until sex workers have no one to trust, no one to run to. They only trust themselves. Some trust drugs, some trust alcohol, you see? But, inside them, they are different. They are human beings that you cannot sell. I say sex workers are brilliant because if you confess to suffering all this violence, neglect, and abuse, and yet you are still a parent who gives love to somebody else, the love that you're not getting, then you are a brilliant person.

So many sex workers were talking while crying because it was so painful for them to tell their stories. It was so emotional. They really needed a space, which they didn't have before, to just come and pour everything out. They needed somebody to come and sit there and listen to them. Often, we were supposed to go to a place for only two days, but as they kept on talking we knew that a few days was not enough, and we would extend our time. We just sat and kept on listening to them. Because of listening to all these different stories we came to know what the needs of the community were. We used to talk to them about human rights because we wanted the sex workers to know what their rights are. We wanted them to understand that they are human beings, and they're supposed to be enjoying what is theirs in their community.

After listening to their stories in Creative Space, we would ask them, "What benefits do you think would come if we work together as a team, form small groups, and are a family? Can we be each other's keepers? It is upon you—if you want to be your sister's or brother's keeper, then you need to stand up. Nobody will come to be your keeper. But you can be each other's keepers. We can move forward as a group but not as individuals." At first, few believed it was possible. Initially, some sex workers were afraid to organize—they feared the government, feared the community, feared to come out as sex workers. But soon, they liked the idea. They knew if we form a group then we will be sharing our experiences and talking about our challenges and seeing how to overcome them. We told them, "One thing that sex workers are lacking is each other."

"We Own This Space"

Before they started their own groups, we referred so many of the sex workers we met with to organizations like Bar Hostess [BHESP], KASH, and Survivors so they could learn from them, be mentored by them, and be trained by them on human rights and as paralegals so they would have basic knowledge about the law. So they would be empowered to support their own rights and speak on their own behalf. We also provided capacity-building from the Kenya Sex Workers Alliance. The sex workers who got this knowledge felt like they were more empowered, and they wanted to start their own small sex worker groups. The knowledge that we gave to the sex worker community, they kept on passing on this knowledge to other sex workers. From this process, we now have over seventy-four sex workers' rights groups in Kenya. They keep on calling me to say, "We have a new one!" They keep on forming them all the time.

Many of the groups are specialized, like for male sex workers or women sex workers who are HIV-positive. Some are formally registered as Community-Based Organizations [CBOs], self-help groups, and peer educator groups. And we also have many groups that are not formally registered as organizations because if a group tries to register and "sex worker" is part of the name of the group, local government officials just send a letter that says, "We cannot register this group." But still these informal groups meet and discuss their issues. It was even difficult for us as the Kenya Sex Workers Alliance to register—we had to officially change the name to Key Affected Population Health and Human Rights Alliance in order to get a chance to register KESWA. But I think it is important to have both registered and unregistered, formal and informal groups, in the movement because they are all important. All of these seventy-four sex worker groups are part of KESWA.

This is not the same community that we had before 2009. This is a different community, an empowered community. It is a real movement. Now if somebody violates sex workers, all the sex workers in Kenya will come up and say, "No, that is not right. We don't want this." Like in the town of Thika when they were murdering sex workers. The sex workers in Thika told us they needed us to come there and support them. And so hundreds of sex workers from different parts of Kenya went to protest in Thika. We wanted to say to the community in Thika, "You guys are killing us, but we are human beings like you. You have no right to kill us." So we went there, and we had the biggest crowd. We had this beautiful march, moving all over Thika. Our fellow sisters had been killed, and enough was enough. We said no more killing in Thika. I would say it is a grassroots movement because we own this space. We the sex workers drive the movement. . . . We own it. We sing it. We shout loudly for everybody to hear.

"To Live Freely in This World"

I will tell you the story of why I myself became an activist. One day when my son was five months old, I went to do sex work on the streets in Mombasa, and five street children started running after me. I felt they were going to do something bad to me so I ran, and as I was running away from them, I saw lights on a police car. And I said to myself, "Thank you, Jesus, I have been rescued." So the street children ran away from the police, and the police rescued me. There were five policemen and they carried me away in their car. But when I entered the car, they started harassing me. "What were you doing there? Are you a sex worker?" they asked. And then they started shouting, "What is this you are wearing!" And I felt like, what is this? These are supposed to be my saviors. But you would not believe that these policemen took me to their police cubes where they live and these guys, they all raped me. They locked me inside there for three days. They just kept on coming and sleeping with me. They didn't even give me water to drink. They didn't give me food. The last policeman that slept with me said, "I think I'm the last person to sleep with this lady and then she dies."

Later I heard somebody come to the door. And I didn't even have the power to look because I just knew that it was one of them coming to sleep with me again. Or even to shoot and kill me. Because I had heard them say before, "If she doesn't die today, let's just shoot her, then dump her somewhere." But it wasn't the officers at the door. Instead it was the older woman who does their washing. She said to me, "There were some other girls like you here, and they were all killed and dumped. So these guys are going to kill you." That woman took me out of that place. I could barely walk, so she helped me to the roadside. She brought me milk to drink, but I vomited all the milk. Then she brought me water to drink and some food to eat so I would get a little strength to be able to walk back home. I still remember her voice. Before she left me at the roadside, she told me, "You have to be strong. Because if you are not strong, they will find you here and they will kill you. Just like they killed the others. This is your surviving chance." I remember that voice came with love. That was out of love, you see? She looked at me, and she saw a daughter in me. She was risking her life because the policemen would definitely know that this woman was the one who took me away from there. I never really got to know who that woman was because I was too weak to know her. And I couldn't go back to look for her. But today I am alive because of her.

I gave myself strength and said that I'm not going to die. I am a very strong woman. I will go home to my baby. So I walked and walked until I reached my place. But when I reached home, I was so down. I wanted to die, and I just drank poison. But I didn't die. My friends came and rushed me to the hospital. It was so painful for me, and there was a time I couldn't even speak about it, and I had to undergo counseling. This is why I have this passion for working and fighting for the rights of sex workers. Because it has not been easy for me. It is not easy for them. When I found myself alive, I said to myself, enough is enough. I want to be an activist. I want to talk about my story. I want to share this so that everybody can know what sex workers experience. I tell my fellow sex workers—if you want to be somebody, stand up, pay attention to yourself. Enough is enough. It is high time we come out and tell people that we are sex workers. It is not easy to be where we are. They will point. They will call you a thief. They will spoil your name all over. But, it is about us as a community. We need to live freely in this world.

* * *

When I first listened to Phelister's haunting story, I was floored by her courage. This woman, so close to being killed, transformed her trauma into activism on behalf of sex workers' rights. She is now one of the most well-known leaders of the sex workers' rights movement in Kenya and as Peninah Mwangi has been for her generation, Phelister has become an inspiration to the next generation of Kenyan sex worker activists. Phelister found the strength to evade her captors, and it was this same strength that pushed her to travel throughout the country with her fellow activists, encouraging sex workers to be one another's keepers, to find power within themselves and one another.

KESWA and groups like BHESP continue to provide capacity-building and mentoring for the ever growing number of sex worker organizations in the country, creating a movement that is truly grassroots and organized from the bottom up. And yet despite this inspiring growth, they still know they must ensure that even more sex workers are given platforms, opportunities, and support. For instance, they acknowledge that although the growth of the Kenyan movement has remarkably reached roughly half the country geographically, they still haven't made much headway in reaching out to and organizing sex workers in rural and semi-rural areas. They are determined not to allow their organizing to fall into the trap that erroneously sees all sex work as an urban phenomenon.

South Africa and Kenya: Two Models of Sex Work Movement Building

The history of sex work organizing in South Africa and Kenya presents two different models of sex worker movement building on the continent. South Africa is an example of a movement sparked by the relationship between a funded outside service provider and sex worker leaders, while Kenya presents a model of grassroots mutual aid among sex workers absent a highly funded partner. Both models have their strengths and weaknesses.

Similar to South Africa, there are other movements on the continent in which the launch of formal sex worker organizing was aided by top-down support from committed service providers that are not sex worker–led. The Sisonke movement bolstered by SWEAT has been immensely successful and has its advantages, including the capacity-building and resources that come with a funded partner NGO that can help launch a nascent movement. But this sort of top-down movement building isn't without its faults. For example, the outsider NGO must ensure that it avoids tokenizing sex workers in its advocacy. "We have the responsibility to provide support, but SWEAT cannot try and control Sisonke," noted a SWEAT advocate, reflecting on the delicate balance of SWEAT and Sisonke's relationship. As the years have gone by, Sisonke has continued to value and develop its long-term relationship with SWEAT while also trying to become more politically and economically autonomous in order to ensure that the movement remains sex worker–driven in determining programs and goals.

In the absence of the type of consistent in-house support that Sisonke has received from SWEAT, some movements like the vibrant Kenyan movement have taken on a more grassroots character. Without the support of a highly funded outside partner, Kenyan sex workers may have been more motivated out of necessity to draw on their own resources and initiative in organizing and building a movement. This is the potential strength of the grassroots mutual aid model. Its limitation is that the lack of a highly funded outside partner can prove challenging because funding remains a crucial and recurring issue in sex worker movement building.

There is extremely limited funding for sex worker organizing outside of the HIV/AIDS realm.[13] (And even within the HIV/AIDS funding arena, African sex worker organizations are sidelined by policies such as the "anti-prostitution pledge," a U.S. federal law that requires foreign NGOs receiving U.S. government AIDS funding to adopt policies opposing prostitution.[14]) A 2014 survey of 200 sex worker organizations around the world found that it is difficult for them to receive funding for policy and advocacy, legal services, research, and organizational development.[15] This poses a serious and continued obstacle to sustained sex worker movement building.

Namibia: Losing Abel, Leadership, and Lessons Learned

The South African and Kenyan movements remain the most advanced in Africa in terms of visibility, influence, and activity, in part because they experienced some of the earliest formal sex worker organizing on the continent. Other country movements, like the one in Namibia, are in a middle stage of sex worker organizing, and as their sex worker activist communities continue to coalesce and demand their rights there are lessons to be learned in their advances and setbacks. The story of the life and death of Abel Shinana, a young emerging leader of the Namibian sex worker movement, provides a relevant case study regarding the cultivation of leadership in sex worker organizing and how movements can be stalled when resources and training are largely invested in a few individuals—however deserving and talented—and not extended to the movement at large.

Abel Shinana was a twenty-nine-year-old gay male sex worker from a sleepy sheep-farming town in southern Namibia who experienced a difficult, peripatetic childhood and the double stigma of being both gay and a sex worker and yet had managed to put himself through school and financially care for his extended family. So, he came to the sex workers' rights movement, as many of its activists do, with a quiet, unwavering inner strength. In 2012, he was chosen as the co-chair of the Namibian country chapter of ASWA and was housed in the offices of the AIDS and Rights Alliance of Southern Africa (ARASA), where the staff helped him develop his leadership and professional skills. He was initially regarded as somewhat shy and quiet, and perhaps lacking in confidence, but as he participated in more meetings with stakeholders from different organizations and UN agencies, it became increasingly clear that he had an impressive level of commitment to sex worker organizing and to strengthening his own skills as an advocate. Because of the steady dedication he showed to the movement through his work ethic, sense of responsibility, and trustworthiness, he was given and took advantage of numerous opportunities to build his leadership capacity—attending regional trainings and international conferences, conducting important qualitative research on sex work in Namibia, helping devise a prostitution legal reform agenda in Namibia, and developing strong relationships with allies of the sex worker movement in the NGO and intergovernmental field, as well as with fellow sex worker activists like the longtime advocate Mama Africa, the mother of the Namibian sex worker movement and director of the Rights Not Rescue Trust (RNRT), with whom Abel developed a warm and trusting relationship.

Abel had always known in his gut that the way sex workers are treated is fundamentally unjust, but the training he received on how these wrongs are violations of sex workers' human rights gave him powerful language to attach to his innate sense of justice. There had always been people like the ever-dedicated Mama Africa who'd been involved in the political leadership of the sex workers' rights movement in Namibia, but Abel's determination brought a new level of national attention to the movement. In only the span of a year in his role as the head of ASWA Namibia, he helped jumpstart and advance the movement in numerous ways. He was recruited by UNAIDS and UNFPA to help lead and carry out important qualitative research that would for the first time systematically expose the realities faced by Namibian sex workers at the intersection of HIV, health, and human rights through a mapping exercise of sex work in five Namibian towns.[16] Abel helped train sex workers who were actively involved in conducting the research and presenting the findings at a national meeting, which underscored the idea that sex workers must be engaged as partners, not as subjects. Abel didn't fear expressing his frustration at the sometimes patronizing attitudes exhibited by NGOs working with sex workers, and he was very vocal about the need for stakeholders to treat sex workers as equals in outreach and advocacy efforts.

He also helped ease tensions that had existed within the sex worker activist community. Prior to his leadership, the movement had rival factions that allowed personal issues and organizational politics in terms of competition for resources to eclipse the forward movement of their formal organizing. Abel used his diplomatic skills to encourage his fellow activists to come together and try to iron out their differences. He also became a mentor for many Namibian young people who found themselves in the sex trade. Many of my interviewees expressed the need to develop strategies that address the issues which make certain youth vulnerable to entry into the sex trade as well as respond to the self-identified needs of youth who are currently in the industry in terms of access to housing, health care, and job opportunities. It pained Abel to see teenagers engaged in the sex industry, but he understood that it is important to work with youth in the sex trade respectfully and without judgment and to empower them by listening to what it is they feel they need in order to live safe, healthy, fulfilled lives. He developed a project reaching out to street-based youth in the sex trade and organized a group of twenty such youths who were trained on how to do a mapping exercise to determine the extent of youth in the sex industry. This project would result in the development of community interventions to help support these young people. Through this work, he garnered a devoted following among young people engaged in the street-based economy who saw him as a father figure.

Through all of these activities, Abel helped build a young Namibian movement that was filled with hope and potential. And then in April 2012, in the early morning hours of a public holiday, everything changed. Abel had been returning from a party with three friends in a car that was going too fast. "They were bending a curve," remembers one of Abel's friends and colleagues. "There was a witness there who said they were flying. So then they just flew over the bridge and into the railway [underneath]. . . . It was terrible, terrible, I can tell you. Young person with so much potential. . . . He was growing and then, just like that." Mama Africa; Tomas Zapata, then with UNFPA in Namibia; and Linda Baumann, a leading Namibian LGBT activist, all went to the mortuary to identify his body.

"What was really true in the case of Abel was that he died at a time when he was just starting to shine in a way," says Felicita Hikuam, an advocate with ARASA who had mentored Abel. "He was really embracing who he was and the opportunities and finding his voice. . . . He was becoming more assertive about this passion around protecting human dignity and human rights and understanding what human rights are and how they're applied to sex workers."

LGBT and sex workers' rights activists traveled 450 miles south of the capital to bury Abel in his hometown. They laid him to rest in a t-shirt that read "Sex Workers' Rights = Human Rights" and draped a rainbow flag and red umbrella flag over his coffin. They refused to remove the flags even after church officials demanded they do so. In response, Mama Africa calmly walked up to the church lectern and said, "This is what this man who's in this coffin lived his life for. Why not bury him the way he wants to be buried?" All the young people he had worked so hard to provide assistance, guidance, and support to sat in the pews weeping.

Abel's passing was followed by an incredibly frustrating time in the Namibian sex worker movement. When he died, all of the momentum that had been built in the movement disappeared, and for more than a year, the movement was at a standstill. "I don't think any of us really realized the repercussions of what his death would mean for the coalition and the movement at the time," noted Felicita. "I think it was only weeks or months later that we started to reflect and think, 'Wow, there are all these things that have not moved since Abel's death.' A lot stood still when Abel died. And then you realize what his energy meant for the movement."

The quieting of the movement immediately after Abel's death provoked an honest reflection on the part of his fellow sex worker activists as well as their allies on the pitfalls of investing too much capacity-building in one person. Part of the heartbreak of all movements for change is that along the way, you will lose people to tragedy. Movements must be built to guarantee their continued survival and growth beyond the individuals who lead them. In a meeting I had with some of the most vocal sex worker activists in Namibia, they all echoed a similar refrain: There must be a leadership structure in place in which opportunities to engage in advocacy are dispersed among many different people so that everyone can build his or her skills and so that the movement isn't dependent on only a few individuals. So that it can survive inevitable heartbreaking losses.

There can be a tendency in sex worker organizing to declare leaders and continue to give the same people opportunities. In a way, this happened unconsciously with Abel. He was universally praised as humble, not power hungry, and deeply dedicated to the cause—his determination, growth, and visibility made people naturally gravitate towards him. It wasn't necessarily a strategic decision on the part of people in the movement to invest so much in Abel at the expense of others' development, but in essence, that is what happened. At the time, this was a clear benefit to the movement because he was one of the engines driving it forward, but when he passed away and the movement faltered, the fact that there was so much focus on this one individual proved a detriment to the movement. And one thing that was clear to me interviewing dedicated sex worker activists all over the continent is that because their activism is controversial, being a vocal and visible leader requires a lot of heavy emotional lifting that is best dispersed among many leaders in the movement.

After meeting with sex worker leaders in Namibia I was heartened that, although still affected by Abel's death, they are emerging from the winter of his passing dedicated to carrying the movement forward in a way that builds leadership potential and skills in many of them. In South Africa, part of the success and longevity of the Sisonke movement has been the fact that they are very sensitive to the leadership question and have consciously spread the wealth to a broad array of sex workers who are active in the movement in terms of leadership development and advocacy opportunities. For instance, when they choose activists to represent the movement at national and international fora, they do so through a bottom-up, democratic process wherein sex workers active in the movement themselves choose who will represent them at any given time, bearing in mind that they must ensure that many people showing dedication to the movement are given a chance to grow and develop as leaders.

After Abel's tragic loss, Namibian sex worker activists internalized these lessons about the cultivation of leadership that all movements on the continent should be mindful of, and the Namibian movement is regaining its footing and coming alive once again. In October 2012, for instance, in a feat of inspired collective advocacy, Namibian sex worker activists from different regions met with the UN Special Rapporteur on extreme poverty and human rights during her country visit to Namibia in order to raise the numerous issues affecting their communities. The result of their powerful testimony and joint advocacy was evident in the Rapporteur's final report to the UN Human Rights Council, which strongly ties criminalization to the abuses sex workers face in the country.[17]

These important lessons for nascent sex worker organizing are the main reason I wanted to tell Abel's story. But I have also included this narrative in order to honor the memory of a great advocate who was just coming into his own. "In our movement people die and they never get recognized," lamented an activist as she remembered Abel and all he did to amplify the voices of Namibian sex workers. Everyone I spoke with in Namibia about Abel was thoughtful in reflecting on lessons learned about leadership and movement building when they realized the effect his loss had on the movement. But more than anything, they seemed incredibly eager to speak about Abel's legacy in order simply to honor him, to remember him, in sweet determination that he not be forgotten.

Mauritius: Beginnings

One of the smallest countries in the world, the Francophone African island nation of Mauritius lies more than a thousand miles off the southeastern coast of Africa, with a small countrywide population of a little over a million people. There, too, the sex industry is criminalized, leading to the same types of rampant abuses that sex workers experience wherever criminalization, married to stigma, reigns. And yet even there, in a little-known, remote, beautiful island of sugar cane fields and looming mountains, I learned there was evidence of a sex workers' rights movement, one of the newest in Africa, grappling with the urgent and important question: What ingredients are necessary to ensure that sex workers themselves are at the heart and helm of an emerging movement in the fight for sex workers' rights?

I traveled to Mauritius in November 2013 to try and understand the roots and challenges of this nascent organizing. What I quickly learned was that the movement, although earnest and rights-based, was not necessarily being led by sex workers at that time. Mauritius has the second-highest opiate consumption of any country in the world, and since 2009, several Mauritian harm-reduction organizations working with people who use drugs and HIV/AIDS organizations such as Chrysalide, PILS,

Lacaze A, and *Collectif Urgence Toxida* (CUT) have promoted the rights of sex workers because of an overlap in populations of people who use drugs, the sex work community, and people at risk of HIV. Through working with sex workers addicted to drugs in harm-reduction work and hearing the stories of the abuses they experience, these advocates began to realize that introduction of a sex workers' rights ethos was necessary in order to address the totality of the challenges many of their sex worker clients were facing.

Since 2010, advocates working at Chrysalide have held an annual march on December 17 to mark the International Day to End Violence against Sex Workers. Mauritian sex worker allies are rightly proud of these highly visible demonstrations that proclaim sex workers' rights, but they realize that in order to have a true sex worker movement it must be sex worker–led. Understanding this importance, Chrysalide has moved toward that goal by seeking out active sex workers to assume leadership roles in the movement. In March 2014, Chrysalide formally launched an outreach and advocacy program whereby sex workers who join Chrysalide's red umbrella group, *Parapli Rouz*, help design empowerment activities and recruit new members. But, getting sex workers involved at the forefront of the movement is not without its challenges. One of the difficulties of identifying and nurturing sex worker leaders in any early movement is the fact that an environment of criminalization makes it difficult for individual sex workers to risk admitting publicly that they are engaging in sex work. To do so in many environments of criminalization is to admit to breaking the law. In addition, the possibility of experiencing public stigma, discrimination, and condemnation discourages many sex workers from engaging in advocacy. So I was unsurprised when I learned that many Mauritian sex workers feared simply identifying as sex workers, let alone doing so in the public manner that activism requires.

In the face of these challenges, how does a movement that is truly sex worker–led take flight? Mining and reflecting on the South African, Kenyan, and Namibian examples presents several key ingredients to ignite sex worker–led organizing: (1) harnessing the power of informal organizing and consciousness raising among sex workers, (2) creating spaces for sex workers to air their grievances and brainstorm solutions, (3) tying a rights-based framework to abuses that sex workers face, (4) creating consistent outreach services that directly respond to sex work-ers' everyday experiences of abuse, and (5) developing democratic lead-ership that seeks to build the professional capacity of many sex workers as activists.

One of the many things that made me hopeful for the future of sex worker–led movement building in Mauritius is how much informal organizing I learned is taking place among street-based sex workers, those working in massage parlors, and housewives providing part-time sexual services out of their homes. They spoke of helping one another increase their security and fight the everyday violence they face: In Qua-tres Bornes, for instance, transgender female street-based sex workers spoke of keeping meticulous track of license plate numbers when their friends get in cars with clients and keeping tabs on one another through phone calls and text messages. In Port Louis, a female street-based sex worker spoke of sex workers who have physically rescued one another from violent clients when hearing their colleagues' screams. Mauritian sex workers also provide health support to one another. In one reported instance, when a PILS mobile outreach caravan that provides condoms and lubricants to sex workers was uncharacteristically unable to deliver them in the Bambous neighborhood one night, the sex workers in Bam-bous pooled their funds together to purchase and distribute condoms themselves in order to ensure that sex workers in the neighborhood had safe-sex supplies. Housewives engaged in sex work, a growing popula-tion of the Mauritian sex industry, and sex workers working in massage parlors give one another financial and emotional support. Housewives will often provide one another with child care to facilitate their sex work, and if a sex worker in a massage parlor is having a particularly slow night, some of her colleagues may share a portion of their night's earn-ings with her.

In speaking to Mauritian sex workers it was evident that there are many ways, as proven in the foregoing examples, that they're already informally organizing, but it was also clear they didn't necessarily un-derstand that there's power within these everyday collaborations and expressions of community. Interestingly, when I asked Mauritian sex workers, "Do you help one another?" they initially tended to focus in-stead on ways in which they compete with one another for clients or how tension, distrust, and friction manifest within sex work communities. But those same sex workers would then go on to, in fact, name many ways they show solidarity with one another. The reasons these acts of solidarity are not at the forefront of their minds is that they don't necessarily give value to or place political significance on the many informal, everyday ways they try to keep one another safe and improve their living and working conditions. They didn't realize that by engaging in these activities they are already organizing, creating identities of resistance to the harms of criminalization and stigma, operating within existing networks, proving themselves as leaders, engaging in consciousness raising, and laying the foundation for movement building.

They needed opportunities to come together and become aware of the power and value of the solidarity they already exhibit and how these efforts can coalesce into a movement for change. They needed a Mauritian version of Creative Space, and the *Parapli Rouz* outreach group is an encouraging and exciting start. A sex worker–led steering committee has been elected, and the committee members continue to identify areas for the development of empowerment activities. Mauritian sex workers I interviewed echoed the need to cultivate these spaces and opportunities. As Dalale, a sex worker in Beau Bassin, said, "Sex workers must come together to talk about problems and issues that they face. We want to speak together and share. We all face the same problems." They also stressed the importance of confidentiality as a core tenet of any of these gatherings, in order to guarantee that more sex workers will be willing to participate.

Parapli Rouz has provided fertile ground to embed rights-based ideology regarding sex work into the political consciousness of Mauritian sex workers. Public proclamations of rights-based appeals regarding sex work have already begun with the annual marches organized by Chrysalide that take place in Port Louis. In Quatre Bornes, a female sex worker who had attended the previous year's march, spoke of the effect it had on her own understanding of her rights: "The march is effective in spreading awareness. . . . For instance, the police don't treat us like human beings, and after the march, an officer slapped and arrested me. In court, I [pleaded] not guilty and was released on bail. Before I used to always just plead guilty. I learned from the march [that] I don't have to."

I met articulate sex workers on the streets of Mauritius who exhibited glimmers of leadership potential and who, with resources and continued support, could harness their experiences of informal organizing to begin a sex worker–led movement in earnest. In fact, it's already happening—at the end of 2014, Mauritian sex workers who have been active in the *Parapli Rouz* outreach group began the process of formally registering it as a sex worker–led NGO. Mauritian sex workers also continue to have the firm support of partners in the harm-reduction and HIV/AIDS communities, and as will be explored in depth in the next chapter, the support and dedication of allies has played a significant role in the development of sex worker movements in Africa.

5

Solidarity Is Beautiful

Intersectionality of Sex Worker, Feminist, HIV, LGBT,
and Social Justice Organizing

A sister can be seen as someone who is both ourselves and
very much not ourselves, a special kind of double.
—Toni Morrison

It is March 2013, and I'm back in Cape Town observing a Creative Space workshop in SWEAT and Sisonke's cavernous communal meeting space. The organizers tell me that today's will be a special session. I know many of the sex worker activists present, although I notice a group of women clustered in the back whom I don't recognize and who I assume are sex workers new to the organization. To formally open the Creative Space, the group starts singing a rousing medley of old anti-apartheid songs in Xhosa and new songs about their Sisonke sex worker movement ("All around, all around, Sisonke is rolling!" they sing in unison). Then a petite, middle-aged woman in a vibrant blue blouse and matching head-dress from the group of women gathered in the back walks to the front of the room and begins an impromptu solo performance: "Who can sing a song?" she croons, and everyone quickly joins in, dancing and clapping in a circle.

I soon learn that the woman in blue and her friends are not sex workers but members of an organization that collectively organizes South African female farm workers. So, today's Creative Space session does indeed end up being special—a joint workshop of sex worker and farm worker activists who are part of two marginalized communities that routinely experience violations of their labor, health, and human rights. They engage in a robust discussion about what it means to be allies in a society wherein they face economic marginalization as low-wage workers and how to build political bridges between the two movements. After the session is over, as the farm worker and sex worker activists dance and sing together once more, I think, "Solidarity is beautiful."

The story of the advent of sex worker organizing in Africa is also a tale of intersectional movement building, of the conscious and continued cultivation of solidarity between sex workers and other marginalized groups whose communities are fighting against multiple, intersecting oppressions. This chapter highlights the role that intersectional activism with feminist organizers in Uganda and HIV organizers in Botswana played in the birth of sex worker movements in those countries, as well as the foundations and contours of the acute solidarity that exists between African sex worker and LGBT activists. It will also reflect on unique opportunities for inclusive movement building between African sex workers and human rights, labor, anti-poverty, and harm-reduction advocates. Solidarity is beautiful—essential, really—but it is also complicated, as alliance building is never without power and class tensions. Thus, this chapter will examine the continuing challenges of these partnerships.

Feminist and Sex Worker Intersectional Organizing

Sex workers' rights are rarely an agenda item in African women's rights circles, although there are a few glowing exceptions, like the work of Ugandan feminist legal scholar Sylvia Tamale, who has been a strong ally of the sex worker movement in Uganda. She's faced public rebuke for her vocal support of sex workers and the LGBT community: When she was elected dean of the Faculty of Law at Makerere University in Uganda in 2004, the national Ugandan newspaper *New Vision* published a cartoon that depicted "prostitutes and homosexuals" romping after her into the dean's office. *New Vision*'s conservative readers later voted her "Worst Woman of the Year." In addition to Sylvia Tamale, a handful of other prominent African feminists have publicly embraced sex workers' rights, including Hope Chigudu, Solome Nakaweesi-Kimbugwe, Zawadi Nyong'o, and Leila Sheikh. But African feminist scholarship remains largely silent on the issue, particularly in terms of advocating for the idea of sex work as labor, and African women's rights organizations rarely take on sex workers' rights as a mainstream gender issue.

Although African feminisms have long focused on political and economic areas such as gender-based violence, gender and the law, the feminization of both poverty and HIV, and the devaluation of gendered labor—all areas related to sex work—these African feminist preoccupations have rarely included a sex workers' rights analysis. "The reaction of African feminists is oftentimes very much steeped in religion and morality. The sex work debate is difficult to break through with feminists here," an African feminist scholar and sex workers' rights advocate told me. Feminist solidarity calls for women's rights groups to greet the daily attacks on sex workers with the same outrage as when "ordinary women" are targets of abuse. Unfortunately, this is rarely the case, as exhibited by the following brief yet instructive example from Zimbabwe.

"You can't go to the shops after 8 P.M. because they assume everyone is a hooker. It is plain harassment, simple," said a frustrated female resident of Harare, Zimbabwe, complaining about the government's 2013 No to Loitering campaign, a police crackdown ostensibly aimed at prostitution that had spilled beyond the surprise raids on sex workers in bars and nightclubs into the lives of women at large, harassed for infractions like simply walking unaccompanied down the street.[1] The No to Loitering campaign was preceded by previous organized efforts to "clean up the streets" that included crackdowns on sex workers, including Operation Chinyavada ("Scorpion") in the early 1980s immediately following Zimbabwe's independence, and Operation Chipo Chiroorwa ("Girl Get Married"), Operation Chengetedza Hunhu ("Maintain Your Dignity"), and Operation Murambatsvina ("Drive Out the Trash") in the decades that followed.[2]

These crackdowns, however, were never limited to the public punishment of Zimbabwean sex workers. The government has used these tactics as a cover to publicly humiliate, harass, and control all women they deem to be behaving in ways that don't conform to gendered notions of virtue (e.g., dressing a particular way; being out in public after a certain time; showing independence in their public movements). It is the manifestation of whore stigma on the political stage—the government uses these campaigns to attack all women they believe are acting like "whores," both sex worker and non–sex worker alike. This behavior is reminiscent of similar efforts by the British colonial administration in Zimbabwe, which cited the "immorality and prostitution of native women" in their bid to repress women living under colonial rule by re-stricting women's public movement.[3]

Zimbabwean women living under British rule boycotted these mea-sures, and so have Zimbabwean women who have faced public harass-ment since the launch of the No to Loitering campaign. But women's groups who have protested against the No to Loitering crackdowns did so only when "ordinary women" began to feel the effects of the cam-paign in their daily lives, not because sex workers are also targets of abuse. They filed a formal petition with the Ministry of Home Affairs protesting the harassment that women who are not sex workers have faced as a result of the government crackdown on prostitution. The peti-tion reads: "Zimbabwean women are outraged by the continuation and escalation of the arbitrary arrests and harassment of women in Zimba-bwe on grounds of loitering, soliciting and prostitution, whilst going on with their daily business during the day or evening."[4] As highlighted by the Sexual Rights Centre, a sex workers' rights organization based in Bu-lawayo, Zimbabwe: "Notably, these protests are against the indiscrimi-nate nature of arrests[,] and the protests have accordingly not articulated women's right to engage in sex work or shown solidarity with the plight of sex workers."[5]

Zimbabwean mainstream women's rights organizations have never filed formal petitions or led protests regarding the fact that Zimbabwean sex workers, who are disproportionately women, routinely face harass-ment, extortion, and assault from police officers. In one survey, 85 per-cent of Zimbabwean sex workers reported being extorted by the police.[6] The women's groups object to the government's treating women who are not sex workers "like they are prostitutes" by harassing them as they independently go about their business. And although women's groups have filed a positive constitutional challenge to the criminal code's so-licitation law,[7] the motivating factor was again its effects on "ordinary women," not necessarily its effects on sex workers. This absence of ex-plicit solidarity with sex workers among some feminist activists can have dire consequences for sex work communities: "[S]o long as there are women who are called whores, there will be women who are trained to believe it is next to death to be one or to be mistaken for one," writes author Melissa Gira Grant. "And so long as that is, men will feel they can leave whores for dead with impunity."[8]

The indifference toward and disregard for sex workers' rights among some women's rights advocates is, of course, not limited to this recent example from Zimbabwe. But in East Africa, particularly between 2008 and 2011, there was a surprising, magical, and ultimately fleeting period in which, because of the vision of key individual feminists and select women's rights organizations, the mainstream women's movement embraced sex workers' rights as a pressing human rights issue. Ugandan sex worker activists still readily acknowledge that African feminists played a central role in launching sex worker organizing there. In the early years of Ugandan sex work activism, budding sex worker activists nurtured personal connections with mainstream feminist organizers in order to build their capacity as movement leaders. The Uganda example presents a compelling narrative regarding intersectional movement building between feminist and sex worker organizing.

In 2008, the African women's rights organization Akina Mama wa Afrika (AMwA), then led by Ugandan gender activist Solome Nakaweesi-Kimbugwe, began to invite sex workers to their women's rights workshops (as early as 2001 AMwA also began providing support to the budding East African LGBT rights movement and mainstreaming queer issues into their gender advocacy).[9] AMwA's inclusion of sex workers and LGBT people into its women's rights agenda proved a radical shift in mainstream feminist priorities at the time. In an AMwA publication, Solome noted: "[AMwA] started its journey into sexual rights and body politics with groundbreaking interventions working with 'women's human rights defenders on the periphery.' Internal refocusing of our work . . . [meant] gender identity, social class, or lifestyle choices . . . redefining women's empowerment and what it means to be African [women] fighting patriarchy, rejecting repressive body politics systems, control and exclusion. And above all, restoring African women's agency and personhood to constantly engage with and negotiate the harder issues."[10]

They were courageously rejecting the idea that prostitution is the ultimate symbol of patriarchy and embracing the notion that sex workers' exclusion from mainstream women's rights concerns is itself a *symptom* of patriarchy. AMwA was asserting that the separation of women into "good women" and "bad women" serves only as a method of exerting social and sexual control over all women. They began to understand that one's feelings about the morality of sex work are irrelevant in light of the denial of sex workers' basic human rights. And by underscoring the notion of agency, they were rejecting the politics of othering—sex worker as symbol, sex worker as idea, sex worker as passive and voiceless victim—and embracing sex worker as sister. "No 'good' woman ever made History/HerStory or changed the world," noted Solome,[11] in acknowledgment of the fact that it has always been women on the margins willing to challenge dominant narratives who have tried to push mainstream feminisms toward a more inclusive and intersectional posture.

Despite their transition to an embrace of sex workers' rights, AMwA's first early attempts to integrate sex workers into mainstream feminist spaces through workshops that brought diverse groups of women together in 2008 proved difficult. "When we would get up to speak about our issues, some of the other women were very uncomfortable," noted a former Ugandan sex worker who was involved in these initial efforts. "Some people got up and left because they didn't want to hear sex workers speak. Some were saying that the women's movement was losing track if prostitutes and lesbians were involved."

It was this early resistance that made Solome and AMwA realize that in order for sex workers to explore openly the pressing issues affecting their communities and develop a political agenda, they needed a safe space where they could incubate their ideas and put fire under their activism. So in March 2008, AMwA decided to organize a workshop in Kampala, Uganda, targeting budding sex worker activists that specifically focused on sex worker issues, including human rights, sexual and reproductive health, and organizing tactics. The workshop was set to take place at a Kampala hotel, but once Ugandan government officials got wind of the plans, which had been leaked to the press, the Ugandan Minister of Ethics and Integrity promptly banned the workshop, and journalists soon descended on the AMwA office to harass activists. Undeterred, AMwA moved the workshop to Mombasa, Kenya, where they trained an initial cohort of eight sex worker activists.

After this March 2008 gathering, the breakthrough moment of intersectional movement building between feminist and sex worker organizing came in June 2009, when AMwA, along with the Open Society Foundations, Hivos, and Urgent Action Fund–Africa, launched a one-week African Women's Leadership Institute (AWLI) for East African sex workers in Mombasa, Kenya, that built on the initial 2008 workshop and brought together twenty-one female sex worker activists from Uganda, Kenya, and Tanzania, under the theme "Breaking Boundaries: Collective Organising for a Just Society." Key African feminists served as organizers, facilitators, or consultants.

Through plenary sessions, role plays, songs, walking meditations, women's circles, and other exercises, the AWLI created a space for sex workers' rights activists to enhance their leadership skills and gain "critical information and skills in communication, negotiation, financial planning and management, risk management and reduction, sexual and reproductive health, information and technology, human rights, women's rights, organizational development, and feminist movement building."[12] Through the institute, feminist leaders themselves acknowledged that they had learned about "sisterhood, self care, sustainability, personal relationships with money, the power of negotiation, safety, security, sexual autonomy, bodily integrity, and choice" from the sex workers in attendance.[13]

The gathering also resulted in the publication of the booklet *When I Dare to Be Powerful: On the Road to a Sexual Rights Movement in Africa*, in which African sex workers who participated in the AWLI spoke of their lives and work in groundbreaking first-person narratives. At the end of the workshop, the sex worker activists made the following public pledge: "I am a human being. I am a sex worker. I deserve respect. I deserve to be protected by the police. I deserve to vote. I deserve to be protected by my government. I have the right to go to church. I have the right to walk on the streets. I have the right to free medical care. I have the right to say no to rape. And today I stand here and say I am free!"[14]

Many of the sex workers involved in this pivotal institute remain leading sex worker activists in their home countries to this day, and it proved particularly essential in launching the sex workers' rights movement in Uganda. Before the AWLI workshop, there had been some formal organizing among sex workers in Uganda, but it lacked direction, focus, and capacity. Daisy Nakato, Macklean Kyomya, and Katherine Namakembe were Ugandan sex workers who had formed the sex workers' rights organization Women's Organization Network for Human Rights Advocacy (WONETHA) in 2008. In those early years they dreamed of turning the sex industry into one dedicated to upholding the rights of sex workers, but they struggled to transform these ideas into concrete activism. They had passion but very little experience on how to run a professional activist organization aimed at effecting change. The Ugandan and East African women's movement, on the other hand, had deep roots and knowledge to impart about the potentials and pitfalls of movement building. Several members from WONETHA attended the AWLI workshop and received essential training on leadership, teamwork, and how to manage organizational finances and apply for grants.

The WONETHA members returned to Kampala from Mombasa invigorated and immediately put what they'd learned at the institute into action with the continued early support of feminist activists. Daisy, now thirty-one years old and head of WONETHA, which has become the leading sex workers' rights organization in Uganda, remembers with tenderness the effect the AWLI workshop had on nurturing solidarity among budding East African sex worker activists:

> It was the first time sex workers were in one space. . . . We got to know what our sisters in different countries face. How hard or how easy is it to organize? What should be the issues we organize about? What kind of noise do we want to make? What kind of change do we want to see happening in our countries? We were guiding each other. It was really a moment of cleansing ourselves. . . . It was something to bond the sex worker movement in East Africa and kind of launch it because from there people went back with a lot of fire in them and started working. In Tanzania, the movement is there now. In Kenya, it is huge. And in Uganda, we did the same thing. . . . That was the point we became black sisters. . . . So it helped us to create a voice and also to bond us.

She also remembers what it meant at the time, as they emerged from the shadows to demand their rights, to have key figures in the women's rights movement standing beside them:

> For me, having their support made me even more stronger and work harder. And each time I'm losing morale, I'm like, What about the people who fight on our behalf when they've never sold sex? You know, seeing these women, they have their husbands, they have their families, coming out in the media talking about sex work. You know, including us in

Daisy Nakato. Kampala, Uganda. Photograph by author.

spaces that we didn't belong to. . . . They were fighting to bring us there [into feminist spaces]. If these women will stand up for [sex workers], then what about me who is selling sex? Why can't I stand up on my own behalf? So they gave us a space, they provided us a space to stand up and talk about our issues.

The solidarity among sex worker and feminist activists in Uganda continued in the initial years after the AWLI workshop. Sex workers became a fixture in meetings of the Ugandan Feminist Forum, not as women who needed to be rescued and rehabilitated but as partners in the longstanding fight against patriarchy, and their inclusion in these feminist spaces provided them with further opportunities to develop their organizing skills. When WONETHA was kicked out of its offices in 2009 after the landlord discovered it was a sex workers' rights organization, the Uganda Association of Women Lawyers (FIDA-Uganda) generously housed WONETHA rent-free for more than a year in its offices as a show of solidarity. Press releases and joint statements signed by both sex worker organizations and mainstream women's rights groups strengthened WONETHA's activist hand.

The Uganda case study is a strong example of direct African feminist involvement in the launch of a sex worker movement by building sex workers' capacity to advocate on their own behalf while also mainstreaming sex workers' rights into the larger women's movement. What happened in Uganda was stunning—it would have been the equivalent of mainstream feminist activists' serving as midwives to the birth of the prostitutes' rights movement in the United States in the 1970s, something that would have been unthinkable. "I think they did some extraordinary work," Daisy reflects, in reference to the individual feminist activists who helped launch the Ugandan sex worker movement. "Elsewhere in the world, it is not common that the sex work movement is close to the women's movement. There's always that big gap. They feel they're more 'women' than sex workers. They feel they're more 'holy,' which is not the case." This early history of sex worker and feminist solidarity and intersectional movement building in Uganda and East Africa should serve as an example for other burgeoning sex work movements.

Despite this inspiring history, the Ugandan feminist movement's early vocal dedication to sex worker issues has cooled somewhat in the past several years. Sex workers' rights and women's rights activists whom I interviewed in Kampala noted with pride the central role of women's rights organizing in the birth of sex worker activism in the country, but they also acknowledged that the relationship has weakened as well-known feminist figures who embraced sex workers' rights have moved on from leadership roles in mainstream women's organizations, including Solome's departure from AMwA. It has led some to surmise that the true engine behind the early solidarity between feminist and sex worker organizing in Uganda was the presence of key personalities in feminist spaces, and perhaps the idea that sex workers' rights have a home in women's organizing had not penetrated all the way to the roots of mainstream feminist thinking. It is also possibly a result of what's been acknowledged as a general overall weakening of the women's rights movement in Uganda, perhaps because of the increasing professionalization of movement leaders at the expense of political activism aimed at concrete change.[15]

It is unfortunate that more newly formed sex worker groups in Uganda, like the dynamic Crested Crane Lighters, missed the heyday of sex worker and feminist intersectional movement building in the country. Julie Katongole, a twenty-eight-year-old sex worker who leads Crested Crane Lighters, notes, "Actually we've not yet managed to work with women's rights organizations in Uganda. . . . The first thing that you get from there is discrimination, the stigma. And that has kept us behind, fearing to go to them." This statement would have been unheard of in 2009 when feminist activists and women's organizations were openly helping cultivate sex workers' leadership potential and publicly railing against the government for banning sex workers' rights workshops. One note of hope, however, is that even though the broader women's rights movement in Uganda may have cooled on sex workers' rights, the individual African feminist activists who helped nurture intersectional movement building between sex workers and women's groups in Uganda and elsewhere in East Africa, who believed fervently that a feminist space without sex workers or queer people is no feminist space at all, are still out there, championing these messages. The Solomes and Hopes and Sylvias still exist and should be a shining example for feminists throughout Africa and the world.

HIV and Sex Worker Intersectional Organizing

"There's been resistance—they've never really taken on sex worker issues in the gender agenda," a longtime Botswanan advocate with the HIV/AIDS organization Botswana Network on Ethics, Law and HIV/AIDS (BONELA) tells me, referring to the nonexistent relationship between sex workers' and mainstream women's movements in Botswana. "They see it as a form of abuse against women—it is totally misunderstood, totally misrepresented." In Botswana, the formal sex workers' rights movement was birthed not from progressive feminist activism like in Uganda but in HIV/AIDS organizing and outreach. It is impossible to examine the origins of sex worker movements in Africa without exploring how alliances with the HIV movement opened doors of opportunity for sex workers to organize. Botswana's leading sex workers' rights organization, Sisonke Botswana, was formed following BONELA-led HIV/AIDS peer education training for sex workers in 2009 and is housed within the BONELA offices. Both sex worker and HIV activists in Botswana readily acknowledge how HIV/AIDS, specifically a health and human rights approach to the epidemic, created a space for sex workers to raise their issues publicly. A BONELA activist contends: "HIV really catalyzed formation and mobilization on sex workers' rights. Though their issues are not just centered on HIV, they're diverse, but . . . sex workers saw this as a very concrete reason to organize, a very concrete reason to gather to support each other. They've seen their mates, their friends dying, not having any support. . . . And human rights should be given credit for mobilizing around sex work [as well]—sex workers learning their rights and people with a human rights perspective saying, 'Wait a minute, sex workers have rights as well.'" But as much as Botswanan activists acknowledge the degree to which HIV organizing helped launch formal sex worker organizing, regrets and frustrations also accompany this solidarity. Botswana provides a case study of the potentials and pitfalls of intersectional movement building between HIV and sex worker organizing.

BONELA began its outreach to sex workers in Botswana in 2007 after acknowledging the need to include marginalized populations in its HIV/AIDS work. Although Botswanan sex workers had long been informally organizing, by, for instance, financially assisting one another through the traditional group savings mechanism known as *motshelo*, at the time there was no formal sex workers' rights organization through which BONELA could directly reach sex workers. Its initial outreach to sex workers was through the Nkalikela Youth Organization, which was then the only organization that had direct access to large numbers of sex workers and whose goal is to "rehabilitate" them. When BONELA completed its first HIV/AIDS workshops with sex workers identified through Nkalikela, it quickly realized that rehabilitation was anathema to what sex workers really needed—a human rights approach to empower, not shame, them.

Following these initial outreach workshops and a subsequent situational analysis BONELA conducted on the status of sex work and HIV in several Botswanan towns and cities, it documented the severe stigma and discrimination sex workers in Botswana experience in the health care setting as well as a low level of knowledge about HIV transmission and treatment among sex worker populations. Through these initial efforts BONELA also soon realized that reaching out to sex workers was simply not enough—sex worker–led organizing focused on HIV/AIDS and other issues affecting their lives, including police abuse and social stigma, was necessary. An activist who was involved with BONELA's initial outreach to sex workers reflects on the lessons the organization quickly learned as HIV/AIDS advocates wading into the new terrain of sex workers' rights:

> We knew we had to get sex workers involved in the response to HIV/ AIDS. By 2007 we were having workshops with sex workers, and we were talking about mandatory testing, confidentiality, if they were experiencing discrimination in healthcare. The sex workers were saying that although these issues were very important they weren't the only issues they were facing. It was then we realized that we had skipped a step—sex worker organizing itself. Because there was no sex worker leadership at the time laying out what they needed and wanted. It became clear to us that if we were going to have a sustainable response, there needed to be sex worker organizing and not just us checking off a box to say yes we've had sex workers involved.

Tosh Legoreng, one of the leading sex worker activists in Botswana and head of Sisonke Botswana, vividly remembers these early workshops: "[They were] always talking about HIV interventions. And I was like . . . it's not [just] about HIV. We face a lot of abuse from our clients. We face a lot of abuse from police officers. . . . And we *never* talk about these things."

The BONELA advocates learned one of the essential lessons about the struggle against HIV/AIDS: It is about power—who has it, and who doesn't. The highest rates of HIV are often seen in groups that have the least amount of power: the people and communities relegated to the shadows of our societies. You can't adequately address HIV in sex worker populations without facing head-on the police who confiscate their condoms, the police and clients who rape them because they know they will never face justice for doing so, the health care workers who openly discriminate against them and drive them away from prevention and treatment services, the laws that push them underground and further away from health services. This is why it is impossible to talk about HIV/AIDS in a meaningful way without talking about human rights.

By 2008, armed with the knowledge that HIV could be an entry point for rights-based sex worker–led organizing, BONELA began to mobilize sex workers in the town of Kasane in northern Botswana, near the Zimbabwean and Zambian borders, an area populated by sex worker communities and other mobile populations. BONELA trained an initial group of fifteen sex workers to be peer educators who would then train other sex workers on human rights and health interventions. They also arranged an exchange visit with sex worker activists from Sisonke in South Africa to educate Botswanan sex workers about outreach, mobilization, and movement building.

But BONELA's determination that outreach to sex workers be rooted in a rights-based approach soon clashed with the mandates of government and development organizations intent on using health interventions as another way of controlling sex workers. BONELA activists admit they were naïve during this early period: After they initially trained the Kasane sex worker peer educators, they partnered them with development groups like the organization Tebelopele and the local district AIDS council to continue the training, wrongly assuming that these actors would embrace the human rights approach to health interventions targeting sex workers. But the district AIDS council and development groups embraced a rehabilitation approach, believing that any intervention that centered on sex workers' human rights would amount to official encouragement of prostitution. Their determination to use health interventions as a way to control sex workers is indicative of many governmental views of sex workers as vectors of disease from which they must protect the general population. Some sex worker groups on the continent had in fact been originally formed by government ministries of health that sought to mobilize sex worker populations in an effort to enforce regular and coercive STI treatment and monitoring—the complete opposite of a human rights approach.

As BONELA worked on nursing its relationship with the Kasane sex workers back to health following the difficult experience with the district AIDS councils, they held tight to the lessons learned from their missteps: Developing partnerships between sex worker groups and government officials in an environment in which all actors aren't on board with a human rights approach can be damaging and a way of simply reinforcing stigma. BONELA put these hard lessons into practice as they helped to build communities of sex worker activists in the capital, Gaborone.

Despite these bumpy origins, HIV activism has been crucial in forging a path for sex worker organizing. In Botswana, high-level politicians, like former President Festus Mogae, have publicly called for the decriminalization of sex work in order to fight the HIV/AIDS epidemic in Botswana,[16] no doubt influenced by nascent sex worker organizing buttressed by HIV/AIDS activism in the country. But intersectional movement building between sex worker and HIV/AIDS activist communities requires a delicate balance of priorities. On the one hand, attempts to seriously downplay HIV within sex worker organizing ignore the devastating effects HIV/AIDS has had on sex workers in the Global South—no sex worker communities anywhere in the world have suffered more because of HIV than those in Africa, where prevalence rates among sex workers are extremely high. On the other hand, sole or predominant emphasis on HIV in sex worker organizing can potentially limit society's broader understanding of the myriad abuses sex workers face.

Sex worker and HIV activists in Botswana, though pleased that some high-level politicians highlight criminalization as an impediment to HIV/AIDS efforts, also express discomfort that these same politicians don't call for decriminalization when the conversation is not centered on HIV. These politicians don't, for instance, champion decriminalization of sex work as a method of ensuring labor rights. If the framework isn't HIV, somehow sex workers disappear from the public conversation in Botswana, as if that is the only context in which they exist. Discussing sex work only in relation to HIV may cause further stigmatization by giving credence to the idea that sex workers are inextricably linked to HIV. In reflecting on the fine balance of intersectional movement building in sex work and HIV organizing, an epidemiologist and HIV researcher who has worked extensively in Africa told me:

> I think actually the extent to which HIV/AIDS has opened the door for the organizing of sex workers (and other marginalized groups) cannot be underestimated. Certainly a lot of the groups I have worked with would not have gained the visibility and support if it were not for HIV funding. This is not without problems, of course—sex worker groups being railroaded into a very narrow approach, or being funded only to talk about HIV. Sex workers being frustrated that the platforms and opportunities

for them to talk, such as national AIDS meetings, won't hear the bigger picture as they are not designed to do so.

Indeed, while sex worker groups have been somewhat successful in getting funding for HIV/AIDS outreach, garnering financial support for broader movement building, or for activities that, for instance, focus on police abuse or law reform, continues to prove incredibly difficult.

In addition to trying to avoid being pigeonholed into a sole HIV/AIDS focus that obscures all other issues, sex workers have to consider how those in the AIDS industry understand the cohesiveness of their diverse communities. The epidemiologist further noted: "Partly because of the success of civil society pushing the idea of vulnerable communities there is now this tendency on the part of decision makers to essentialize groups as communities when in fact they are not really cohesive. . . . Often what they have in common is the fact of being an epidemiological category! But now in many countries you will find AIDS administrators effectively demanding that sex workers be some neat, organized democracy with a single mouthpiece." Regarding the essentialization of groups in AIDS advocacy, sexual and reproductive health law scholar Aziza Ahmed has argued that identity politics in HIV/AIDS organizing that has helped spawn the idea of "key populations," though successful in mobilizing resources for marginalized groups in the AIDS response, may also inadvertently exclude people who don't easily align with identity-based movements but are nonetheless vulnerable to HIV/AIDS.[17] There are many people in Africa and elsewhere, for instance, who engage in transactional sex but don't identity as sex workers because of stigma, though they remain equally vulnerable to HIV. Sex work and HIV/AIDS organizing that stubbornly relies on fixed and monolithic categories, or AIDS industry people who demand them, will necessarily overlook those in need of outreach who fall into the cracks because they don't align with neat categories of identity politics.

So the challenge of this brand of intersectional movement building remains how to be both focused and broad—how to acknowledge and address the devastating effect of HIV/AIDS on African sex worker communities without HIV/AIDS becoming the only thing on the agenda, how to use identity politics to mobilize HIV/AIDS and other resources without ignoring those who can't be squeezed into a narrow epidemiological box.

LGBT and Sex Worker Intersectional Organizing

Some of the most visible forms of intersectional movement building in Africa are occurring between sex worker and LGBT organizing. In Kenya, sex worker and LGBT activists are fixtures at each other's public street protests, have begun joint strategy sessions aimed at the decriminalization of sex work and homosexuality, and in 2007 both communities came out in a public show of force and solidarity when Kenya hosted the World Social Forum. LGBT organizations are welcome as member organizations of KESWA, and sex worker organizations are active members of the Gay and Lesbian Coalition of Kenya (GALK). In Uganda, sex worker and LGBT activists worked together in a formal civil society coalition to protest Uganda's draconian Anti-Homosexuality Act. And in Namibia, these two activist communities have an almost symbiotic relationship, with leading sex worker and LGBT organizations sharing office space in the country's capital.

In the past several years there's been increased international media attention on the plight of LGBT communities in Africa, including the introduction of stringent anti-gay legislation in Nigeria and Uganda and the public persecution of LGBT people in countries like Cameroon and Senegal.[18] What has received less notice, however, is the continued strengthening of an indigenous African LGBT rights movement. African LGBT rights activists are publicly condemning institutionalized homophobia, filing lawsuits arguing for the recognition of LGBT rights and taking their grievances directly to government officials.[19] It was largely in the 1990s, the same decade that witnessed the birth of formal sex worker organizing in East, Southern, and West Africa, that African LGBT rights activists also began to build nascent social justice movements. Young LGBT rights activists in East Africa in the 1990s and 2000s received the same support from progressive feminist activists and organizations that sex worker organizers encountered during those early years of formation.[20] Political attacks against the LGBT community expressed by government leaders in Namibia in the 1990s had the unintended effect of launching the Namibian LGBT rights movement.[21] And the LGBT rights movement in South Africa reaches as far back as the 1980s, when it grew alongside the anti-apartheid movement.[22]

Intersectional movement building between African sex worker and LGBT organizing is rooted in many factors. There's the strategic reason of strength in numbers, but there is also an emotional solidarity that has formed between two communities that have been othered and oftentimes discarded by their societies, a camaraderie among those who have fought against the notion that their lives don't matter, that they aren't worthy of rights, respect, and dignity. There are other important reasons for intersectional organizing among sex work and LGBT communities: (1) Many people in the African sex worker community are queer-identified; (2) politicians and religious leaders often characterize and attack both sex workers and LGBT people as gender, sexual, and cultural outlaws; (3) abuse and marginalization have led to devastating rates of HIV in both communities; and (4) the effects of the criminalization of sex work and homosexuality have nurtured legal solidarity.

There is a strong presence of people who identify as LGBT in the African sex worker community. "A lot of LGBT people are thrown out of their homes [by family members] and end up in the sex industry," noted a Namibian LGBT rights organizer who works closely with sex worker activists. "The sex worker movement in Namibia is actually being led by LGBT people who are sex workers. So we had to [ask] why we have intersections, and we said we can't leave each other behind." Indeed, many people within the African LGBT community have engaged in some form of sex work or survival sex because of homelessness and limited economic opportunities resulting from homophobic and transphobic discrimination.[23]

The fact that sex worker and LGBT communities have been the targets of state-sponsored abuse, discrimination, and violence has also been a rallying point for intersectional movement building. Government leaders have painted sex workers and LGBT people as un-African, immoral, sexual deviants and examples of Western corruption. Since 2008, for instance, Ugandan government leaders have shut down sex worker human rights workshops; used the police to raid sex worker and LGBT meeting spaces; and passed the Anti-Pornography Act, which bans "indecent" dressing, and the Anti-Homosexuality Act (a Ugandan court later overturned the law on narrow procedural grounds; the Parliament could easily revive it).[24] Religious leaders in both Kenya and Uganda openly preach against both the sex worker and LGBT communities as examples of the "moral decay" of their nations, adding to the cloud of stigma and discrimination hovering over them.

The toll that HIV has taken on both the sex worker and the LGBT communities has also provided solid ground upon which to organize collectively. Stigma in the form of homophobia, transphobia, and whorephobia and the criminalization of sex work and homosexuality have created a social and legal atmosphere that puts the sex worker and LGBT community at heightened risk of HIV. For instance, HIV prevalence rates among MSM rest at 43.6 percent in South Africa and 43 percent in Kenya, while HIV prevalence rates among cisgender female sex workers in these countries are also high—59 percent in South Africa and 45 percent in Kenya.[25] Collective organizing in the face of these dire statistics has raised the voices of marginalized groups within national AIDS frameworks and strengthened their hand in insisting that governments include their communities in robust and de-stigmatized prevention and treatment programs.

Legal solidarity remains an important point of intersection for these communities. The criminalization of sex work and homosexuality, in addition to impeding HIV/AIDS efforts by making it difficult for these groups to gain access to STI and HIV prevention and treatment programs, also severely limits the groups' employment opportunities. A known sex worker with criminal convictions for prostitution may find it difficult to secure work outside the sex industry, and legal discrimination against LGBT people creates severe employment barriers.

These points of commonality have created a beautiful solidarity between sex worker and LGBT communities in many African countries, one in which they have sought to build each other's capacities and strengthen each other's voices. However, this solidarity isn't without its complications or identity and class tensions. LGBT activism, for instance, isn't immune to whorephobia. Denis, a twenty-eight-year-old gay Kenyan journalist who engages in online sex work, is a leading voice for gay rights in Kenya and a vocal proponent of and activist for sex workers' rights. Having come up in Kenya's gay rights movement, he's been an important bridge between the country's LGBT and sex worker movements. But he's open about what he sees as the tensions that exist between these movements, despite the overall political solidarity that's evident: "There are gay people who will never identify as sex workers, even though they do sex work. . . . When I started [a news service focusing on LGBTI and sex work issues], I came from [an LGBT organization] where it was very gay there and there wasn't a lot [of talk about] sex work and suddenly I was mixing LGBT and sex work, and I got a lot of flack. People were saying, even to this day, 'Why are you mixing LGBT issues with sex work issues?'" Transgender sex worker activist Beyonce Karungi bemoans the fact that trans sex workers in Uganda have found it difficult to be accepted into non–sex worker trans groups, some of which feel that inclusion of sex workers will "taint" their advocacy. Some mainstream African LGBT organizations' resistance to exploring these intersections may be an unfortunate embrace of the politics of respectability—the LGBT community has been branded with so many negative social markers that some LGBT activists may be reluctant to assert the sex work linkage as an additional marker that could further ostracize the LGBT community. In addition, because of the deep shame attached to sex work, it may be difficult for people within the LGBT community who have engaged in sex work or survival sex to acknowledge these experiences openly. Sex worker activism, on the other hand, isn't completely free of homophobia or transphobia. Beyonce also speaks frankly about how it took some time for trans sex workers to gain acceptance from cisgender female sex workers in the Uganda movement whom they had to educate on trans and gender identity issues.

So although, on the whole, there is strong solidarity among these groups in many African countries, and this must be celebrated, there are pockets of resistance that these movements must address and overcome. In their article on sex worker and LGBT joint organizing in East Africa, Solome Nakaweesi-Kimbugwe and Hope Chigudu state that, in addition to paying attention to power dynamics and identity issues that can derail intersectional movement building, sex worker and LGBT communities should continue to pursue other key priorities for joint organizing, including cultivating relationships with activists in broad-based social justice movements.[26] Indeed, there are increasing, exciting, and varied opportunities for sex worker groups to reach out and develop partnerships with human rights, labor, and class-based anti-poverty movements.

Building Linkages with Human Rights, Labor, and Class-Based Anti-Poverty Movements

Some of the most interesting instances of intersectional movement building involve partnerships that African sex worker groups are developing beyond the important but more common targets of feminist, HIV, and LGBT groups. Their pursuit of alliances with human rights, labor rights, harm-reduction, and anti-poverty activists and organizations signals a welcome and necessary broadening of the sex worker rights agenda.

Just as influential international human rights organizations like Human Rights Watch have come to the inevitable conclusion that an anti–sex work stance is anathema to human rights, mainstream African human rights groups are in some instances beginning to take on sex workers' rights as a broad-based human rights issue, lending their services and expertise to sex worker movement building. One example of an African human rights organization working in solidarity with sex workers' rights activists is the Human Rights Awareness and Promotion Forum (HRAPF) in Uganda. In 2010, HRAPF started to work in partnership with WONETHA and Crested Crane Lighters, providing sex workers with legal advice, legal representation, and paralegal training and conducting sex workers' rights awareness sessions. HRAPF lawyers whom I interviewed noted that they often experience stigma from police, judges, and other lawyers because they've mainstreamed sex workers' rights issues into their human rights work. "Someone I went to law school with, when he heard I represent sex workers and LGBT people, told me, 'Your head and their heads should be cut off,'" noted an HRAPF legal officer. "But I have passion for the people who are most marginalized."

Sex worker activists have also been developing partnerships with labor organizers and harm-reduction groups. In chapter 1, South African sex worker activist Duduzile Dlamini's first-person narrative related how South African sex workers have successfully gained recognition from the country's politically powerful national labor union, an effort to ensconce sex worker activism firmly in a labor rights framework that should be emulated throughout the continent. And as I explored in the previous chapter, harm-reduction organizations working with people who use drugs in Mauritius are playing a leading role in nurturing nascent sex worker organizing there, after it became abundantly clear that many of the participants in their drug harm-reduction programs also engage in sex work. Their intersectional approach is important. As researcher Melissa Hope Ditmore has argued, few organizations cater to people who both use drugs and are involved in the sex industry, even though these populations can overlap and both experience increased vulnerability to violence as a result of their existing in similar environments of criminalization.[27]

In Kenya, sex workers have joined an anti-poverty movement known as Bunge la Mwananchi, also called the "People's Parliament," a class-based movement of street vendors, street families, *matatu* [minibus] drivers, sex workers, LGBT people, and other street-based communities that face harassment and physical abuse from *askaris* and protest against significant government increases in the taxation of basic commodities that hit the poor the hardest. Kenyan sex worker groups have aligned themselves with this broader class-based struggle, joining in Bunge la Mwananchi street protests and other actions, even as they continue to confront the whorephobia, homophobia, and transphobia that exist in segments of the movement.

As sex worker organizers in Africa grow their movement, they understand the need to continue broadening their outreach to more communities with which their issues intersect. They realize that in a world of multiple intersecting oppressions, solidarity just might save us all.

6

Watering the Soil

Key Organizing Strategies and Law Reform

This chapter examines the key strategies of sex worker organizing in Africa, including: (1) service provision to diverse sex workers through health outreach, legal assistance, and the strengthening of sex workers' financial literacy and professionalism; (2) public outreach to foster the recognition within African communities of sex work as work through protests, community sensitization, sex worker–led community theater, and media advocacy; and (3) law reform campaigns to decriminalize sex work. The heart of the chapter is the story of South African activists' daring grassroots campaign to decriminalize sex work through legislative reform. The chapter highlights scenes of sex workers entering the halls of the South African Parliament for sessions with lawmakers, sitting face-to-face with some of the most powerful people in the country, and boldly demanding a sex industry free of criminal penalties. In the wake of this ambitious legal advocacy, African sex worker activists should begin to grapple with complex post-decriminalization questions, including how existing and newly crafted progressive laws and policies can advance a labor rights framework promoting sex workers' rights.

Service Provision as the Foundation for Advocacy: Health Outreach, Legal Assistance, and Professionalism Services

African sex workers' rights organizations understand that rights and justice advocacy devoid of sustained dedication to the provision of direct services addressing African sex workers' desperate needs is meaningless. Service provision most often takes the form of health outreach, legal assistance, and training in professionalism, including financial management. Direct services address sex workers' daily needs and create a door through which many sex workers take their first steps into activism.

Health outreach remains African sex workers' rights organizations' most common form of service provision. In chapter 1, I introduced SWEAT and Sisonke's health outreach program in Cape Town, one of the most advanced sex worker health outreach programs on the continent, if not in the world. The program is outfitted with peer educators, mobile wellness vans, nurses, medical counselors, and paralegals doing day and evening outreach six days a week throughout the year to street- and venue-based sex workers. Their goal is to provide services to 80 percent of known sex workers in Cape Town and its surrounding environs within five years. In addition to condom and lubricant distribution, rapid HIV testing, and TB testing, SWEAT and Sisonke's outreach and on-site health work also provides sex workers with access to a general wellness program that includes diabetes, blood pressure, and weight management; sexual and reproductive health (including breast, vaginal, penile, and anal health and family planning); a harm-reduction support program for people who use drugs; an HIV-positive support group; an HIV-negative wellness group that seeks to help sex workers maintain practices supporting their HIV-negative status; a twenty-four-hour helpline providing emergency medical and legal advice; and referrals to sex worker–friendly health clinics for follow-up care.

SWEAT and Sisonke run a highly sophisticated health outfit, but nearly all of the sex workers' rights organizations whose members I interviewed were engaged in some form of health outreach, even if on a smaller scale. Groups under the KESWA umbrella in Kenya have completed peer health outreach to more than 4,000 street- and venue-based sex workers in Nairobi. HOYMAS has introduced a home-based care program that provides health assistance to Kenyan male sex workers too ill to leave their homes. Crested Crane Lighters in Uganda runs monthly meetings for its service users with HIV counselors. It, like other organizations, is also trying to expand its services beyond HIV prevention and treatment to include family planning to help sex workers avoid unwanted pregnancies. As sex worker organizations grow their health services programs, the need for access to safe abortion will also likely become a more pressing issue.

Organizations are also translating their experiences with health outreach into policy by advocating for the visibility of sex workers in national health strategies. Sex work organizations in Kenya, for instance,

were essential in convincing the Kenyan government to officially recognize sex workers in its HIV/AIDS policy as one of the most at-risk
populations, a designation that has helped spur the development of government policies for the prevention and treatment of HIV/AIDS within
the sex work community.[1]

Legal assistance is another essential form of service provision that African sex workers' rights organizations offer to their constituents. The
importance of legal assistance and advocacy in sex workers' rights activism can't be overstated, because criminalization constantly puts sex
workers in direct conflict with the law. Sex worker groups often partner
with legal services organizations to offer legal assistance and court representation to sex workers when they are the victims of arbitrary arrest
and detention. They also help them negotiate bail applications, contest
police-issued fines associated with municipal by-laws, and provide advice
and legal counsel in noncriminal cases where sex work stigma leads to
violation of sex workers' legal rights—for instance, in family law matters.
In one such example, BHESP in Kenya worked with the legal assistance
organization Centre for Rights Education and Awareness (CREAW) to
represent a sex worker whose parental rights were blatantly abused when
her twin babies were taken away from her in the hospital and sent to a
children's home because she's a sex worker. BHESP and CREAW helped
her obtain a court order mandating that the children be returned.

SWEAT and Sisonke in South Africa have ingeniously paired their
legal assistance and health programs. Paralegals accompany health outreach workers to the field in mobile wellness vans and provide legal assistance when needed. The Women's Legal Centre (WLC) in Cape Town
works in partnership with SWEAT and Sisonke to implement this innovative legal services program. WLC trains former and current sex workers as paralegals who, in addition to their mobile outreach work, run
weekly legal assistance workshops for sex workers in SWEAT's offices.
They also accompany sex workers to court, run human rights training
workshops for Sisonke members, and staff a weekly toll-free hotline
that sex workers can call for legal advice. Sex workers with more complex legal assistance needs, such as brothel-based sex workers charged
with violations of the 1957 Sexual Offenses Act through the illegal use
of entrapment, are referred to WLC's full-time attorney, Stacey-Leigh
Manoek, who oversees the work of the SWEAT and Sisonke paralegals.

Soft-spoken and unassuming, with a deep passion for women's rights and an authoritative knowledge of South African law, Stacey-Leigh is a strong ally of the sex workers' rights movement in South Africa who for years has provided individual sex workers with legal assistance as well as engaged in high-stakes impact litigation and other legal advocacy to uphold sex workers' rights. Impact litigation is an important part of Stacey-Leigh's docket, and her work presents several examples of what this type of advocacy can and does look like in the African context. Prior to joining WLC in 2009, Stacey-Leigh worked at the Legal Resources Centre, one of South Africa's preeminent legal rights organizations, on a case that SWEAT filed in the Western Cape High Court against eight police stations, the Metro Police, and the Minister of Safety and Security, requesting a court order preventing the police from arresting sex workers and harassing them with ulterior motives (by, for instance, collecting unjust fines and demanding bribes). Stacey-Leigh helped SWEAT achieve a favorable judgment in that case, although the police continue to flout the court order routinely. In light of this, when Stacey-Leigh joined WLC she began to lodge damages claims in court against the Minister of Police for the continued unlawful arrest and wrongful detention of sex workers. WLC has also submitted formal complaints regarding violation of the court order directly to involved police stations, and the offices of the Deputy Minister of Police, the Mayor of Cape Town, and the Provincial Police Commissioner.

On top of this, WLC and SWEAT spearheaded the case *Kylie v Commission for Conciliation Mediation Arbitration and Others*, an important South African labor case and an example of activists' successfully achieving recognition of sex workers' labor rights even under criminalization.[2] The case resulted in a decision from the Labour Appeal Court which reaffirmed that the South African constitutional right to fair labor practices extends to sex workers for purposes of the Labour Relations Act.[3] Aside from litigation, WLC has engaged in additional legal advocacy that has included submissions to the South African Law Reform Commission arguing for the decriminalization of adult sex work, submissions to the South African Parliament characterizing some conditions of sex worker detention as rising to the level of torture, and the 2012 release of a research report on police abuse against sex workers in South Africa.

In addition to providing health and legal assistance, African sex workers' rights organizations are committed to helping their members conduct their work in as professional a manner as possible, including increasing their financial literacy. A part of Crested Crane Lighters' financial empowerment program in Uganda includes teaching their members how to set and negotiate standard prices for their sexual services. Many of their members had not raised their prices in years, even though the prices of other services and commodities in Uganda have continued to increase. Some sex worker groups, like those affiliated with WONETHA and based in Mijera, Uganda, encourage groups of sex workers working in the same area to standardize their rates and raise prices as a group in order to cut down on the fierce competition and resentment that can develop when certain sex workers keep their prices artificially low. Many sex worker groups also encourage their members to increase their financial strength by opening bank accounts to safeguard their savings; participating in sex worker–led money-lending groups; investing in inexpensive, nice attire to enhance their physical presentation and therefore increase what they can charge for their services; and engaging in other income-generating activities to help supplement their sex work.

Sex workers' rights organizations also urge their members to maintain a professional attitude toward their work and respect for the communities they're working in by, for instance, not using vulgar language around children in the community or leaving used condoms and other trash in the residential neighborhoods where they work, activities that can be a source of tension between sex workers and their neighbors in certain African communities. By engaging in these professionalism services, sex workers' rights organizations have shown that they understand that rights and responsibilities go hand-in-hand.

Ensuring Diversity of Outreach

In providing direct services, African sex workers' rights groups are keenly aware of the need to ensure that they reach a wide swath of diverse sex workers and don't focus solely on archetypal sex workers—cisgender female sex workers who are street-based or brothel-based. The internal diversity of the African movement, which is a hallmark of sex worker movements throughout the world, is deeply impressive, but the cultivation of diversity isn't without its obstacles. As discussed in chapter 3, for instance, the African sex work movement must do more to reach out to queer women, trans men, and gender nonconforming people. In addition, the movement is trying to strengthen its outreach to other populations, including non–queer-identified male sex workers, online sex workers, and people engaged in certain forms of transactional sexual relationships.

There are men in Africa, particularly those who are not queer-identified, who engage in the exchange of sex for cash or other reward but don't conceptualize their activities as sex work. One of the challenges of organizing these men is that although male sex workers have diverse sexual orientations, they are often all perceived as gay, and thus stigma concerning homosexuality leads some men involved in the sex industry to reject the sex work label. It is also difficult for some men to identify as sex workers because they view it as a gendered identity and fear being tarnished with the feminized shame and stigma attached to sex work. Furthermore, they are sometimes hesitant to talk about the abuses they face in the industry, particularly those of a sexual nature like client rape, which they perceive as attacks on their masculinity.

To meet some of these challenges, African sex workers' rights organizations have ensured that male sex workers have separate spaces to come together, air their grievances, and share the pain caused by the abuses they face. HOYMAS in Kenya leads multiple monthly small group discussions involving male sex workers, known as ETL or "Education Through Listening." In each session, they gather no more than fifteen male sex workers in order to keep the meetings intimate and discuss topics the group chooses. SWEAT and Sisonke have also long organized support groups targeting male sex workers. Within these safe spaces, they have focused on cultivating the de-stigmatizing understanding of sex work as work, without demanding that all of those engaged in the industry regard themselves as sex workers. This ensures that people who have a difficult time openly identifying as sex workers but who are engaged in the sex trade nonetheless still feel accepted within the movement. It is an enlightened, big-tent understanding of movement building that does not demand sex worker identity-forming for everyone involved in the movement.

Organizing the small but growing number of middle-class sex workers in Africa who are engaging in sex work online is another challenge.

According to Kenyan sexual rights activist Denis, an online sex worker himself, Kenya has seen a rise in online sex work because Kenyans are becoming more sexually liberated (a local nascent but growing pornography industry is one indication of this) and experiencing increased independent access to free online spaces, including websites, blogs, Facebook, Twitter, and apps like Grindr and WhatsApp. He also points to other factors that facilitate online sex work in Kenya:

> There are real advantages to online sex work as opposed to street work. . . . Standing on the streets is more risky than typing on your laptop in your own home or in your office . . . and it actually allows you to get a larger audience. You can market yourself. You can get a lot of people, as opposed to just standing on the street waiting for whoever comes. . . . It also allows you to screen clients. . . . When you are online there is a certain level of anonymity. So you don't have to be afraid of being outed or getting your name in front of any papers or tabloids.

Online sex work is a more likely option for middle-class Kenyan sex workers because they have easier access to the smartphones, laptops, and tablets that make online sex work possible. Sex workers for whom these tools of online engagement are economically out of reach are less likely to operate online. Although the majority of African sex workers are either street- or venue-based, online sex workers could help bring new perspectives and voices to the movement. One of the obstacles to higher visibility of these online sex workers may be class tension and bias. Middle-class, highly educated online sex workers might not want to be associated with street-based sex workers, while street-based sex workers might see themselves as the authentic representatives of African sex work. In addition to class bias, the invisibility of online sex workers also makes them more difficult to organize. Although some organizations like SWEAT have begun online outreach, African sex worker organizations could do more to brainstorm ways to develop movement participation from those engaging in sex work online. "I think the movement should actually be reaching out to them where they are," suggests Denis. "If the movement can craft online programs, or online education infomercials or health services where you can access them online . . . it would be much easier [to reach and organize online sex workers]."

Another neglected group in African sex work activism consists of people involved in transactional sexual relationships that one could appropriately characterize as sex work. One such example is the phenomenon known as "aristocratic" transactional relationships in Nigerian universities. Some female Nigerian undergraduates, known as "runs girls," engage in these transactional sexual relations with older, well-to-do graduate students, wealthy businessmen, politicians, and military men in exchange for cash (often to save money for their university school fees) or expensive consumer goods.[4] Runs girls largely reject the prostitution label, despite the fact that their transactional sexual relations are generally short-term (taking place in hotels and private residences), economic in nature, and arranged discreetly through campus contacts. This rejection is because runs girls often view sex work as a deviant and stigmatized marker and associate prostitution with the brothel- and street-based work of the lower classes.

Although runs girls generally refuse to see themselves as sex workers because of a fear of stigma and class bias, they experience some of the vulnerabilities sex workers in the industry face, including client abuse and susceptibility to HIV because of lack of access to safe-sex information and supplies. Despite runs girls' contested status, sex worker activists I interviewed in Nigeria rightly view them as engaging in sex work: "Once you get paid for rendering those services, it is sex work. What they do out there in the hotel is what we do at the brothel," said Adaora, a brothel-based sex worker and advocate. Nigerian sex worker activists have begun to brainstorm potential outreach programs targeting runs girls, including campus outreach, social media outreach, and the development of runs girls–specific Creative Space workshops, in order to address their particular vulnerabilities and strengthen the movement through the participation of these highly educated people engaged in sex work.

Public Sensitization: Protests, Community Outreach, Sex Work Public Theater, and Media Advocacy

African sex worker activists place serious priority on engaging in public sensitization aimed at influencing societal attitudes about sex work through activities such as public protests; community outreach, including the use of sex worker–led public dramas; and media advocacy.

Protest marches, for instance, because of their very public embrace of sex workers' rights, are deeply powerful and visible actions that directly challenge stigma and shame concerning sex work. But because of their high visibility, protests aren't always a viable strategy for every political environment, particularly in more repressive countries. Daisy Nakato of WONETHA notes that in Uganda, public protests for either sex workers' rights or LGBT rights put involved activists at a serious security risk. So WONETHA has had to improvise in order to develop public activities that are more politically feasible in Uganda. For example, in honor of the International Day to End Violence against Sex Workers the heads of ASWA called on all member groups in different African capitals to lead public protests. Because this was not possible in Uganda, WONETHA members instead went to an orphanage in Kampala to present gifts to children and invited the media to cover the event in order to emphasize publicly that sex workers are valuable members of the community.

There are many ways to cultivate public visibility to dispel shame and stigma concerning sex work. In Kenya, on World AIDS Day 2012, sex worker activists from HOYMAS engaged in community sensitization through the simple but powerful symbolism of a sex worker–led hospital cleanup. Sex workers wanted to sensitize health care providers and the larger community about sex workers' need to gain access to de-stigmatized health care services, so more than 300 sex worker activists, outfitted with brooms and mops, descended on a famous government-run hospital to wash it clean: "We wanted to sensitize the community and the health workers who often stigmatize us; we wanted to show them we need them, but they need us as well," noted John Mathenge.

This sort of positive community messaging is also explored through sex worker–led public dramas. Umzekelo, the SWEAT and Sisonke drama program that uses performances by sex workers to challenge whorephobia, has presented public dramas in many venues, including in drug rehabilitation centers to highlight how substance abuse is something that sex workers, as well as society at large, can struggle with; in hospitals to explore the damaging effects of discrimination from health workers on sex workers' lives; and in front of more than 200 community members in Johannesburg for World AIDS Day to send the message that safe-sex practices are the responsibility of the entire community and not just those of sex workers alone. Umzekelo has not only advanced pro–sex worker rights messaging, but the practice of engaging in public theater has given sex worker participants more confidence to speak and advocate on behalf of their rights.

Media advocacy also plays a fundamental role in challenging sex work myths. African sex workers' rights activists use radio, television, newspapers, and social media in order to challenge the notion of "perfect victimhood" in the eyes of the public. When many people think of typical victims of human rights abuse, they often conjure up stereotypical images of passive and powerless people. They are seen as incapable of self-expression and spotless in terms of their moral posture—supremely innocent, utterly degraded, waiting to be saved. The biases underlying these notions can lead some to favor "perfect victims" and to disregard injustices faced by other marginalized people like sex workers who may inspire more ambivalent and complicated responses from the public. Sex workers' rights activists show how the privileging of perfect victimhood is misguided because all people have human rights regardless of subjective determinations of worthiness.

Radio is a particularly powerful media tool for sex worker activists in Africa because of its wide reach across economic lines. In reflecting on the power of African radio, Tosh Legoreng, a sex workers' rights activist who has appeared on Botswana radio stations, notes that "people tending to the cattle" as well as "people in office buildings" all have easy access to radio, unlike readers of Botswana newspapers, for instance, which are often written entirely in English and therefore inaccessible to many. SWEAT's media team has found that Facebook is good for engaging with other sex work activists, while Twitter has proved a constructive way of developing relationships with journalists whom the team can cultivate as allies. SWEAT's media team has developed a nice interplay between different media by using Facebook and Twitter to draw listeners and viewers to their appearances on traditional media like television and radio and then use social media to continue the conversation started on the traditional media spaces.

Kenyan activists have perfected the use of traditional media venues like television. In 2012, members of the Kenyan movement shocked the nation by participating in a national television documentary series that explored the lives of male sex workers.[5] The series starred

John Mathenge, who has become a charismatic voice for the rights of male sex workers in Kenya as leader of HOYMAS. In the series, John came out as gay, a male sex worker, and HIV-positive. He spoke boldly and intimately about the urgent need to acknowledge lives lived on the margins and to address the intersections of health, sexuality, sex work, the law, and human rights. He highlighted health care and police discrimination against sex workers as well as the fact that many sex workers, like John, are economic breadwinners for their families. It was the first time anything like it had been aired on national television in Kenya.

The series initially sparked uproar, and John received threats of violence on social media. But, as the shock began to wither, as people began to reflect on John's deep reservoirs of courage in sharing his story, some viewed the series through new, enlightened eyes. The Kenya Ministry of Health, for instance, now uses the series for its community sensitization campaigns on health and human rights, also screening it for police and magistrates. When I asked John why he chose to participate in the television documentary, he said that it was a matter of life and death: "Male sex workers were dying in silence, as if we were nothing. We were burying people every month. In one week we buried four male sex workers. We buried some people younger than me, in their late teens and early twenties, and I started to wonder, will I die, too? Silence was killing us. So, I decided we had to come out of the shadows. We had to go to the media. I was not afraid—this is my life. I said, let the community see the male sex workers. No more silence."

No matter what medium they utilize, sex worker activists are sensitive to the ethics of media advocacy involving a group that has been so marginalized. In order to protect sex worker activists, SWEAT's media team screens journalists, reviews potential questions with sex workers before interviews to ensure they are comfortable with the line of questioning, and confirms that sex workers who require anonymity will have their identities protected. In South Africa, sex worker activists have noticed a shift in media representation of sex work as more South African journalists use the term *sex work* in their reporting rather than *prostitution*, slowly moving their understanding of the industry away from vice and sin to labor and human rights, no doubt an example of the effect of sex workers' media advocacy.

John Mathenge. Nairobi, Kenya. Photograph by author.

Reforming the Legal Landscape

African sex worker activists, echoing what is a firm consensus of the global sex workers' rights movement, advocate for the decriminalization of sex work, including both the selling and purchasing of sexual services. This reform of the legal landscape is one of the key goals of the sex worker movement in Africa and would necessitate the removal of sex work–related criminal laws and the nondiscriminatory application of existing and new labor protections to the sex industry. These new protections should be no more cumbersome than regulations applied to other businesses and should be directly aimed at protecting and realizing sex workers' economic rights, health, and safety.

Since 2011, SWEAT and Sisonke have launched a sophisticated campaign to decriminalize sex work in South Africa through legislative repeal of anti-prostitution laws. Theirs is one of the most ambitious sex worker–led law reform campaigns in the world. In their advocacy, SWEAT and Sisonke have rejected two other potential models for sex work law reform: partial criminalization and legalization. Partial criminalization, also known as the "Swedish model," or the "Nordic model,"[6] decriminalizes the selling of sex but makes illegal the purchasing of sex, therefore criminalizing sex workers' clients (as well as all other third parties involved in the sex industry, including brothel managers). Legalization, as practiced by countries like the Netherlands and Senegal, is not driven by the primary goal of protecting sex workers' rights. Instead, legalization has often resulted in stringent regulation of the sex industry that creates a large underground class of sex workers who don't abide by these stigmatizing hyper-regulations, such as mandatory health checks, and therefore effectively remain criminalized. In 2011, SWEAT invited my graduate research students and me to South Africa to assist its members in drafting legal arguments against partial criminalization and legalization, and in favor of decriminalization within the South African context—arguments I lay out below.

In 1999, Sweden became the first country to introduce the legal system of partial criminalization where the purchasing, but not the provision, of sexual services is illegal. Norway and Iceland have also implemented partial criminalization. At no point in the drafting, passage, or review of the Swedish law did governmental actors consult sex worker communities in Sweden.[7] The Swedish government released a 2010 report that made dubious claims about partial criminalization's success. The report asserts, for instance, the belief that partial criminalization has reduced the incidence of prostitution in Sweden, without providing any evidence to prove this assertion.[8] Research with Swedish sex workers has indicated that an initial reduction in the visibility of street-based prostitution is likely the result of Swedish sex work's having largely moved underground, indoors, and online to less visible spaces.[9] Sweden also suggested that fewer men are purchasing sexual services since the law went into effect. But without reliable data regarding the number of people purchasing sexual services before and after partial criminalization's implementation, it is misleading to imply that the number may have decreased.[10]

Partial criminalization is firmly rooted in stigmatizing anti-prostitution sentiments—in the idea that prostitution is violence against women and that targeting and eliminating the "demand" side of the equation will ultimately abolish prostitution itself. Sex workers under partial criminalization are decriminalized not because the law views them as workers deserving of legal recognition (in fact, although sex workers in Sweden are expected to pay income tax on their sex work earnings, they have no access to protective labor and employment laws)[11] but because under partial criminalization they are regarded as victims of patriarchal violence whose victim status should negate any criminal designation. This narrative, however, does not extend to migrant sex workers: It is illegal for foreign women in Sweden to engage in sex work, and in Norway, foreign sex workers who "fail" document checks during raids are deported.[12] It is unsurprising, then, that targeting demand, especially when this targeting is tied to purported efforts to curb trafficking, is criticized as a method of restricting migration.[13]

Sex workers' rights activists roundly reject partial criminalization for many reasons.[14] Because most sex workers are engaged in the industry for economic reasons, blanket criminalization of their client base is essentially an assault on sex workers' economic interests. The threat of police detection gives them less power over their work and may increase their vulnerability to violence because when their clients are criminalized, sex workers must go into more isolated spaces in order to protect their clients from police detection. In these more hidden spaces, sex workers are more vulnerable to potential abuse. While trying to avoid police detection, sex workers are also forced to negotiate more quickly with clients and therefore may have less time to vet potentially dangerous clients. And even though sex workers under partial criminalization are decriminalized in theory, they still face police harassment. Police in Sweden, for instance, have been reported to subject sex workers to intrusive searches and questioning regarding client activity.[15] So, although the idea of "ending demand" and criminalizing clients is all the rage in anti-prostitution quarters, it is simply, like full criminalization, another way to target prostitution, one that does not address the need to uphold sex workers' rights to pursue their economic interests free of violence and discrimination.

There are two avenues to make sex work legal: legalization, like in countries such as the Netherlands and Senegal, or decriminalization, like in New Zealand. Many sex worker organizations, including in Africa, advocate for decriminalization over legalization. South African advocates have also embraced this framework. Whereas the goal of decriminalization in New Zealand was to remove criminal laws attached to sex work between consenting adults and protect sex workers as a marginalized labor class by bringing them under the aegis of employment labor laws and policies via minimal state regulation, legalization efforts have often resulted in hyper-regulations of the sex industry, like mandatory health testing of sex workers and formal government registration of sex workers that in fact limit sex workers' rights. Sex workers who don't adhere to these hyper-regulations and work outside of the strict legalized framework effectively remain criminalized. This universe of *de facto* illegal sex workers can make up a significant portion, if not the majority, of a sex worker community under legalization.[16] Thus, these legalization schemes have in reality resulted in continued criminalization for many sex workers living under them.

Senegal provides an important illustration of the problems with legalization efforts that don't have sex workers' labor rights as their central motivating force, resulting in strict controls that lead to some types of sex work remaining, in effect, illegal. In 1969, Senegal became the only country in Africa to legalize and regulate prostitution. This law has led to hyper-regulation of the Senegalese sex industry and the creation of a hidden population of Senegalese sex workers illegally working outside the bounds of these restrictive and discriminatory policies. One of the main hyper-regulations is the legal requirement that all female sex workers in Senegal undergo mandatory monthly HIV testing by maintaining a *carnet sanitaire*, a health book "proving" that they are free of STIs.[17] It has long been accepted doctrine within the global health field that mandatory HIV testing perpetuates stigma against targeted populations. It isn't only a violation of a person's right to bodily integrity and privacy, but forced testing also pushes vulnerable, stigmatized groups underground and away from health services. Another hyper-regulation in the Senegalese legalization framework is the stringent requirement that all sex workers formally register with the government through the Bureau of Health and Social Services of the Institute of Social Hygiene.[18] Because of deep-seated stigma against sex workers in Senegalese society, many sex workers don't adhere to the mandatory health checks or formally register with the government and thus operate illegally, constituting a large class of sex workers known as *les clandestines*.[19] As I have argued elsewhere, "A legal scheme that results in a parallel legal universe in which sex workers remain effectively criminalized because they refuse to adhere to misguided state regulations that further their stigmatization is not a framework that supports sex workers' rights."[20]

What is needed is a legal environment in which sex workers aren't subject to unfair and stigmatizing hyper-regulations, where all parties involved in the sex industry—sex workers, clients, and managers alike—are not criminalized and where sex work is subject to government regulations that are designed in consultation with sex workers; advance sex workers' health, safety, and well-being; and are no more restrictive than those governing other businesses. This is why South African sex worker activists have rejected partial criminalization and legalization and embraced decriminalization and the New Zealand model of sex work law reform.

In 2003, New Zealand became the first country to decriminalize sex work, through passage of the New Zealand Prostitution Reform Act (NZPRA). The NZPRA, championed by a coalition of sex workers, women's groups, legal and public health advocates, and members of Parliament, clearly states that it "safeguards the human rights of sex workers and protects them from exploitation" and "promotes the welfare and occupational health and safety of sex workers."[21] In 2008, five years after its passage, the New Zealand Prostitution Law Review Committee, which included sex worker representation, released a report documenting the effects of the new law.[22] In its report, the committee found that decriminalization "[had] had a marked effect in safeguarding the rights of sex workers to refuse particular clients and practices, chiefly by empowering sex workers through removing the illegality of their work."[23] They noted that sex workers reported having higher levels of confidence and well-being, greater ability to negotiate safe-sex practices, and an increased willingness to report abuse to the police.[24] The committee also concluded that there is no evidence to suggest that the numbers of sex workers or youth in the sex trade in New Zealand increased as a result of decriminalization.[25]

By choosing New Zealand's path and rejecting partial criminalization's dangers as well as legalization's hyper-regulations, South African sex worker activists also believe that decriminalization will ensure that the country fulfills its constitutional and international human rights commitments.[26] Indeed, any African country that has ratified international and regional human rights treaties, including the International

Covenant on Civil and Political Rights; the International Covenant on Economic, Social and Cultural Rights; the Convention on the Elimination of All Forms of Discrimination against Women; the African Charter on Human and Peoples' Rights; and the Protocol to the African Charter on Human and Peoples' Rights on the Rights of Women in Africa, is obligated to uphold sex workers' rights to free choice of work, association, the highest-attainable standard of health, security of the person, human dignity, and other rights guaranteed in these instruments.[27]

As noted in this book's Introduction, influential international organizations have called for the decriminalization of adult sex work, including WHO, Human Rights Watch, and the Global Commission on HIV and the Law. Furthermore, UNAIDS, UNDP, and UNFPA have released reports that champion decriminalization as the only rights-based legal approach to sex work law reform. Despite this tidal wave of official support for full decriminalization, anti-prostitution activists have stood their ground and continue to call for partial criminalization. In 2013, Equality Now, an international women's rights organization that is firmly anti-prostitution, created an online letter-writing campaign demanding that UNAIDS reverse its stance advocating the decriminalization of sex work.[28] Equality Now claimed that the UN does not listen to the voices of "survivors" of the sex industry, a perplexing argument considering that the UN and affiliated bodies have in fact exhaustively consulted with sex worker groups throughout the world for reports on the legal status of sex work.[29] In response to Equality Now's petition, SWEAT and Sisonke released a strong statement, endorsed by many of their partners in South Africa, reaffirming their commitment to decriminalization, arguing against the Swedish model and refusing to allow anti-prostitution organizations that seek to speak on their behalf drown out their voices: "When Equality Now suggests 'we listen'—who are they suggesting we listen to?" the statement reads, quoting Kholi Buthelezi, a Sisonke leader. "I would like them to listen to me, and other sex workers who participated in the deliberations of the Commission [on HIV and the Law]. The Swedish model has failed."[30] ASWA also released a statement critical of the Equality Now petition: "[M]any women who would otherwise live in poverty support themselves and their families through sex work: those who seek to further criminalize those women have no suggestions for replacing their income."[31]

* * *

In 2011, I witnessed the birth of SWEAT and Sisonke's decriminalization campaign. Early in the campaign, South African activists worked
under the guidance of and in partnership with Tim Barnett, General
Secretary of the New Zealand Labour Party and a former New Zealand
member of Parliament, who was central to the successful legislative push
to decriminalize sex work in New Zealand. Tim spent months working
as a consultant for SWEAT and Sisonke activists in South Africa, helping them design a decriminalization campaign that would target South
African members of Parliament in order to lay the groundwork for what
in the future may lead to the legislative repeal of the parts of the Sexual
Offenses Act criminalizing prostitution. In November 2011, at one of the
first group meetings in Cape Town to develop a framework for the lobbying campaign, I sat next to a sex worker named Yiva who was cradling
her newborn infant daughter in her arms. Early in the discussion, Yiva
tentatively raised her hand and asked Tim what *lobbying* even meant. I
remember his smile when he defined the term and told her she would
soon be intimately familiar with it because she herself would be involved
in lobbying if she chose.

Several years later, the South African sex worker–led decriminalization lobbying experiment is well underway. South African activists
worked with Tim during his time in South Africa to develop the following plan of action: They created four lobbying teams predominantly
comprising sex worker volunteers and trained them in lobbying tech-
niques and legal arguments on sex work law reform to prepare them to
meet one-on-one with South African members of Parliament to explain
why the current paradigm of criminalization is a violation of sex workers' rights and why decriminalization is the right path for South Africa.
During their meetings with members of Parliament, sex workers on the
lobbying teams also speak about their personal experiences of abuse
linked to criminalization.

They are getting high-profile opportunities to make their case. In
2012, they had large and respectful audiences with both the South African Multi-Party Women's Caucus as well as with the African National
Congress (ANC) Women's League, both of which acknowledged that
criminalization has led to a violation of sex workers' rights, even if they

haven't come to formal conclusions about the best way to remedy the situation. In the same year, Cosatu, the country's politically powerful trade union, formally endorsed decriminalization. In May 2013, the South African Commission for Gender Equality, a quasi-governmental entity, called on the South African Parliament to decriminalize sex work.[32] To expand more on SWEAT and Sisonke's decriminalization campaign, in the first-person narrative that follows Nomad Gallant, a charismatic and expressive South African male sex work activist, speaks of his personal journey to become a member of the lobbying team and his thoughts on the decriminalization campaign's challenges and successes.

Nomad Gallant, 46, Cisgender Male Sex Worker and Activist (Cape Town, South Africa)

"The Passion to Defend What's Right"

Nomad is not my real name. I was given that name because of my restless spirit, because of my heart of adventure and spontaneity. A "nomad" for me is someone who grabs on[to] the wings, branches, and wind of life, whether it blows North, South, East, or West. I grab the branches and see things that I haven't seen, hear things that I haven't heard. I became a sex worker in 2006, when I started to work at a bar in town. It was not my plan to do sex work at the bar, but I found many women asking for my number and wanting to spend time with me. I would spend nights with them, and they would take me shopping or pay me some cash the next day. It took a while for me to realize I was actually engaging in the sex trade. I realized it was a good way to make money, so I continued.

In May 2012, a friend of mine invited me to come visit SWEAT, and when I arrived I was very surprised to see so many male sex workers. I kind of felt funny, but I'm very open to learn[ing], and then I realized that there were quite a few faces that I knew from the bars and taverns, so I settled in quickly. The information at SWEAT was empowerment for me. It was a source of motivation. I found myself coming back week after week, and the enlightenment and learning allowed me to be very active in the group sessions, and then ultimately in the decriminalization lobby team.

I was attracted to join the lobbying team because my life, as I grew up, was about fighting for something, believing in something, wanting something that I felt I was entitled to like everyone else. I've always been kind of an activist. It goes back to the apartheid era when my family was forcibly moved out of District Six.[33] My childhood memory is of my family grabbing our belongings, running, screaming, and then standing outside our house in District Six while these big monsters came in. The government thought that because we refused to sell, they'd just destroy the houses and take the land. So from this bad experience in a very bad time, I've always really felt the need to make my voice heard for what I feel is right. So when I was in high school, I volunteered to be an SRC [Student Representative Committee] leader.[34] I was tired of getting on another bus because certain buses were "whites only." I would get flashbacks of my mom trying to change my diaper at the train station when I was young, but she couldn't because [the restroom] was whites only, so she'd have to walk, her feet almost broken, another hour to get to a Coloured toilet to change me. My cause was clear, and I knew what I was fighting for: It was about not wanting apartheid; it was about wanting to have the same privileges like everyone else. It was just about my human rights. In 1985 there was an ANC boycott, where the ANC laid down demands in terms of wanting our right to vote and having our incarcerated political leaders released. It was then the SRC decided that students were going to put our pens down and join the boycott. We went around to different schools to build a huge march with students. I involved myself politically to the point where I was prepared to give up my education, which I did for that year. So I've always had the passion to defend what's right, to speak out and have my voice be heard, in terms of equality, not just for me, but for everyone.

Watering the Soil

Tim Barnett came from New Zealand to South Africa in 2012 with his knowledge, political senses, and skills. Tim was the perfect guy to set us on a path of how to go about lobbying for decriminalization. He gave us the springboard to get things started and was quite a positive influence. I volunteered to join the lobby[ing] team, and because we were a small group, Tim arranged a basic training session for us. We all went away for a weekend for a workshop, and that's how I got to know how to go about . . . effective lobbying. We did our research about what the Constitution says about our basic economic and fundamental rights, as human beings, as citizens—like the right to dignity, the right to equality, the right to choose [our] own work. We sharpened and refreshed our minds and got our facts together.

When we first started meeting with [members of Parliament] a lot of times they had no idea what the situation is like for sex workers. They didn't know sex workers are abused and raped. We would tell them, "Deputy Minister, let Lucy, who is a sex worker, tell you." And he'd say, "Is she really a sex worker?" And we'd say, "Yes." And then he'd stand back and say, "Okay, Lucy, tell me." And Lucy, in her language, would speak to him. And you'd be amazed because at the end there would be a few deputy ministers who would say, "I'm shocked. I can't believe this is happening. Is this really happening out there?" That's what I loved about Tim's strategy. It was real—it was us standing up for our rights, our voices being heard. Trying to defend what's right, face-to-face, in a decent, civil conversation without any barriers.

In lobbying, I've had different experiences with different members [of Parliament], which has made it very interesting and challenging. Some will tell you that they're not very supportive of women selling sex, maybe because of religion, but they will say it without anger. Whereas we come to other deputy ministers who are afraid of the idea of sex work becoming legal, and they literally challenge every word we say. But we've also found that with a lot of the ministers, we have hit the nail, and they are starting to feel what we are saying. They will say, "I see this whole sex worker thing in a different light because of the way you are painting the picture. I feel that I will support you in your fight for decriminalization. But you must understand I cannot make the first move; I can't make the first step. But if somebody else in Parliament is going to say 'decrim,' then I'm going to go with them." We have made a dent in Parliament because when we first started to come to Parliament, that wasn't the reaction. It was more like, "So what is this sex worker thing about?" But then after a few meetings, there was the response of: "Listen, I'm not in a position to [officially endorse decriminalization now], but I'm fully in support, and what I will do is direct you to this other deputy minister [with whom] I think you'll make a difference."

Do I think we're close to achieving decrim? That's the golden question. I would evaluate it this way: If I put anything in the soil, I'd be a fool to just wait for it to arrive. But if I'm digging and toiling and watering, then whatever I've put in, I'm going to get out. I think we've started very well with decrim: It was just a lot of brave hearts that went out there and said what they wanted to say. If I look back at the response from the beginning, and then the response now, I would say that although I don't really know what the chances are, or when, or if, decrim will take place, I do know that there has been movement. I will say that things are happening within Parliament that have never happened before since we've arrived as the SWEAT lobby team. I will say that a lot of [Parliament] members' preconceived ideas and misconceptions have been shaken, even changed. I will say there's definitely movement.

Decriminalization: A First Step, Not a Final One

Activists like Nomad are indeed bravely waging a just campaign for the decriminalization of adult sex work in South Africa, but although the repeal of criminal laws attached to sex work is a necessary and foundational first step, it is not enough on its own to guarantee sex workers' human rights. Just because sex work ceases being criminal does not mean, for instance, that police harboring deep-seated prejudice against sex workers will stop unjustly using other weapons like municipal by-laws regulating public life to harass and abuse sex workers, much in the way they do now, or that sex workers will automatically accrue workers' benefits. What is needed in addition to the repeal of criminal penalties attached to the sex industry is the application and, in some cases, the creation of positive, progressive laws and policies that bring sex workers within the universe of workers' rights.

Some sex worker activists in Africa disagree with this and argue instead for the removal of all criminal penalties attached to sex work matched with a hands-off approach from the government. During Nomad's interview, for instance, he was clear that he wanted the government to have no role in regulating sex work, only in removing criminal penalties. Those who argue for a *laissez-faire* approach often root their analysis in sexual privacy arguments, contending that sex work is indeed work while simultaneously arguing that it is private sexual behavior between consenting adults and therefore the government should have no say regarding the transactions. But as one delves further into viewing sex work through a labor rights framework, it is harder to give primacy to these privacy arguments, because if sex work is labor, this means it is not simply a matter of private sexual behavior.[35]

The stronger argument for sex workers' rights activists' waging decriminalization campaigns is one that demands not only the repeal of criminal laws but also the application of a legal and policy framework firmly centered on the promotion of sex workers' human rights. This can and must be distinguishable from the hyper-regulations we've seen in countries embracing legalization, like Senegal, because in those cases, the motivating factor for law reform is not concern for how sex workers can have more power over their labor, resulting in regulations of the sex industry that are significantly more cumbersome than ones applied to other businesses.

Thinking through what a post-decriminalization framework would look like involves complicated questions of how such things as municipal law, employment law, occupational health and safety standards, tax law and policy, and immigration law would apply to a diverse, decriminalized sex industry. There can't be a "one size fits all" approach in terms of what post-decriminalization sex work industries should look like because laws and policies vary from country to country, as do sex industries themselves. This diversity will necessitate different iterations of decriminalized environments that positively embrace the realization of sex workers' human rights. What should be universal, however, is that sex workers from diverse parts of the sex trade, who are after all the primary experts on the sex industry, must be central to any effort to decide how current laws and new policies should apply to the sex industry.

If sex work is decriminalized in South Africa, and elsewhere in Africa, and a new legal and policy universe governing sex work prevails, many questions will need to be addressed, and sex workers must be at the center of the debates. In its immensely important publication *Beyond Decriminalization: Sex Work, Human Rights, and a New Framework for Law Reform*, Pivot, a Canadian legal and human rights organization with deep experience focusing on sex work law reform, presents an invaluable post-decriminalization guide useful to all sex worker movements engaging in or thinking of beginning serious legal reform advocacy.[36] In the paragraphs that follow, I have posed many of the guiding questions regarding municipal law, employment law, income tax law, criminal law, and immigration law highlighted in the report, while largely refraining from answering them because it is for sex workers in Africa and other parts of the world to decide what would work best within their own legal and political environments.

Regarding municipal law, should businesses employing more than one sex worker participate in any sort of licensing system, and, if so, how many sex workers would a business have to employ in order to trigger such a licensing scheme? Should all street-level sex workers be exempt from potential licensing schemes that are likely impractical because of the ephemeral nature of street-based work, the financial burdens of obtaining licenses on an already impoverished community, and what would certainly be the propensity of police to severely harass street-level sex workers who aren't licensed? In New Zealand, for instance, sex worker–owned businesses employing no more than four sex workers and street-level sex workers don't require licenses.[37]

Should sex work be zoned for particular designated areas or would such segregation add to stigma and inevitably result in the relegation of sex work to isolated areas where sex workers would be more vulnerable to abuse and harm? Should sex work instead be incorporated into already existing zones for commercial businesses, like strip clubs, nightclubs, and bars? How will policymakers ensure that any zoning regulations put in place take into account sex workers' safety, privacy, and autonomy?

Regarding employment law, how will employment contracts between sex workers and their employers lay out sex workers' rights and responsibilities as employees while ensuring that they can't be compelled to engage in any sexual activity without their full consent? The NZPRA addresses this by guaranteeing that "no contract for the provision of . . . commercial sexual services is illegal or void on public policy or other similar grounds" while ensuring that even sex workers under contract can refuse to consent to a specific sexual activity because compelling a sex worker to consent would amount to sexual assault.[38] How will policymakers ensure that sex workers who are legally viewed as employees have the rights to essential employee benefits like overtime pay? How can sex workers become part of workers' compensation schemes so that they can recover lost wages and health care coverage for work-related injuries? How can occupational health and safety standards be applied to sex work? Can occupational health and safety standards be developed in such a way that mitigates drug- and alcohol-related harms within the sex industry? How will lawmakers ensure that sex workers have access to complaint and grievances procedures that other employees enjoy? Sex workers in New Zealand have access to tribunals focused on resolving workplace disputes.[39] Will sex workers who should enjoy the right to

unionize under decriminalization form their own unions or join existing unions?

Because decriminalization would bring sex workers under the aegis
of income tax law, what measures could be implemented to ensure that
sex workers would be exempt from any attempts to retroactively collect
taxes from the time before sex work was decriminalized? How will policymakers ensure that youths in the sex trade will not face criminalization and that sex workers will not face difficulties because of criminal
records related to prostitution? In New Zealand, although a minimum
age for participation in sex work is rightly and clearly delineated in
the NZPRA, it is also stated that youths involved in the sex trade can't
face criminal prosecution for doing so.[40] In addition, the New Zealand
Criminal Records (Clean Slate) Act of 2004 ensures that sex workers can
apply to have former prostitution convictions wiped from their criminal
records.[41] One area where New Zealand has not been progressive regarding the process of decriminalization is that of immigration law—the
country does not grant visas to foreign people who are immigrating to
the country for the purpose of working in the sex industry.[42] How can
immigration law be fashioned in such a way that migrant sex workers
will not face criminalization?

These are only some of the many, varied, and complex questions regarding law and policy that sex worker activists fighting for decriminalization in Africa and beyond must grapple with. If decriminalization
becomes a reality in South Africa, for instance, and new legal and policy
frameworks are debated, the safeguarding of sex workers' human rights
must be at the center of all debates, as must sex workers themselves, who
should be leaders and participants in task forces committed to grappling
with these questions and finding the answers.

7

"Hearts Strong Like Storms"

Confronting Anti-Prostitution Activists, Religious Opposition, and Political Whorephobia

They kept on saying we are not here. But of late, we are here.
—David Kato

I'm marching through the streets of Cape Town as part of a joint protest led by sex workers and tuberculosis activists, and as we near the South African Parliament building I can see a large white makeshift sign with black lettering hanging loosely on the Parliament gates. As we get closer, I can finally make out what the sign says: "The Sex Trade Fuels Trafficking" it reads, in crooked, bold capital letters, obviously written in a furious hand. There are no counter-protesters at the march, but someone was clearly sending us a message in anticipation of our arrival at what's normally the end point of all state-permitted protest routes in the city. The argument that the sex industry is the main driver of trafficking is a rallying cry for anti-prostitution activists. Not all the activists at the march notice the anti–sex work sign, but its significance isn't lost on me. It is a reminder that although African sex worker activists are raising their voices through street protests, community mobilization, the savvy use of media, and law reform campaigns, they are not embarking on this advocacy in an environment free of determined opposition.

This chapter explores how African sex workers' rights activists are confronting political opponents who try to silence them. It highlights the nature, tactics, and resulting harms of anti-prostitution advocacy in Africa, including rehabilitation programs that seek to "save" sex workers but only perpetuate shame and stigma concerning sex work and divert resources from empowerment programs that could actually address the abuses sex workers face; fundamentalist religious leaders who target sex work as a threat to the moral fabric of African societies; and African government officials who wield what I term "political whorephobia," a strategy that seeks to publicly shame sex workers, denounce sex work advocacy, and crack down on what's perceived as sexual and gender nonconformity. This chapter also showcases, particularly through a case study of a high-profile political attack against sex worker activists in northern Uganda's Gulu district, how advocates bravely confront this opposition and hold firm to just assertions that sex workers' rights are, indeed, human rights.

Anti-Prostitution Activists and the Myth of "Rehabilitation"

Anti-prostitution activists have a particularly powerful presence in Europe, where they've tried, in some cases successfully, to advance anti-prostitution legal reform aimed at partial criminalization, which sex workers roundly oppose,[1] and in the United States, where anti-prostitution reformers in bed with right-wing politicians and evangelical Christian activists have successfully made sex work synonymous with trafficking and embrace what sociologist Elizabeth Bernstein refers to as "carceral feminism."[2] Anti-prostitution advocacy in Africa certainly exists, but it's not yet as determined or influential as in Europe and the United States. The American feminist sex wars were never fully replicated in Africa, and this fact could potentially provide African sex workers' rights advocates with an important window of opportunity to dominate the sex work debate on the continent. But this may well become more challenging as anti-prostitution organizations in Africa begin to lay down their roots.

One example of an emerging anti-prostitution organization in Africa, perhaps a harbinger of a larger collectivized African anti-prostitution push that's yet to come, is the South African group Embrace Dignity. The group views sex work as violence against women, cites the often-discredited research of U.S. anti-prostitution activist Melissa Farley as motivation for their advocacy,[3] champions partial criminalization as a legal pathway to ending prostitution, and seeks to help women exit the sex industry. In reference to sex workers in South Africa, Embrace Dignity claims that prostitution "renders them voiceless,"[4] a curious assertion in a country with one of the most vocal, visible, and vibrant sex worker–led movements on the continent.

One of the potential harms of an organization like Embrace Dignity is that its determination to speak on behalf of "voiceless" sex workers could marginalize sex workers' input in political debates that directly affect their lives. Embrace Dignity was founded and is directed by South African politician Nozizwe Madlala-Routledge, who gained political credibility when she lost her post as the Deputy Minister of Health in 2007 after publicly criticizing the crippling AIDS denialism of then-President Thabo Mbeki's administration.[5] Her enduring political clout has meant that as she transitions into anti-prostitution activism, she has the power to usurp spaces wherein sex workers themselves should be the primary expert voices. For instance, in terms of important high-level discussions about HIV prevention in sex worker communities, Embrace Dignity's minority voice could dominate a political space that should be the domain of sex worker activists.

Embrace Dignity is affiliated with the international organization Coalition Against Trafficking in Women (CATW), probably the world's most well-known and influential anti-prostitution organization. Working in partnership, they have stated their goal as using Embrace Dignity's presence in South Africa as a launching pad for the creation of an African-wide anti-prostitution coalition.[6] So as the African sex workers' rights movement grows, the stage is also being set for a nascent anti-prostitution movement.

An anti-prostitution movement would easily find fertile ground in Africa, particularly because anti-prostitution programs that seek to "rehabilitate" sex workers are common on the continent. Rehabilitation programs, sometimes funded through government gender budgets, seek to "save" sex workers from prostitution by providing them with strategies to exit the industry, oftentimes giving them skills-training classes in activities like sewing, candle making, embroidery, cooking, beadwork, and gardening. These alternative livelihoods often embrace gender stereotypes: There's the incorrect assumption that because the majority of sex workers are women, if given the opportunity they would automatically prefer what some view as proper "women's work"—sewing clothes, gardening tomatoes, or making beaded jewelry to sell in the markets—over sex work.

The ultimate goal of rehabilitation programs is to find alternative means of income for sex workers so that they will exit the industry. And in some cases, these programs implement alternative livelihoods as an HIV prevention strategy in sex worker communities. But no reliable evidence suggests that rehabilitation programs in Africa, or elsewhere, succeed on either of these counts or adequately address violations of sex workers' rights. Instead, this savior mentality perpetuates the notion of shame and stigma concerning sex work. It also diverts funding from interventions that could actually address the abuses sex workers face. "We are wasting resources, which we could use for other, better things," argues Grace Kamau, a Kenyan sex worker activist and master's candidate in gender studies at the University of Nairobi. "It's better to empower a sex worker rather than just [tell] her she should go and sell clothes."

In order to be eligible for a rehabilitation program's skills-training courses, participating sex workers often must agree to stop engaging in sex work. But there's long been a running joke among sex workers that participants in these programs do so during the day only to surreptitiously return to the streets at night where they continue to earn more money through sex work. The reason many sex workers in rehabilitation programs revert to sex work is that the income from these programs' alternative livelihoods simply can't match the money sex workers make. As I've noted in earlier chapters, African sex workers who enter the industry are in many cases choosing sex work over other forms of low-wage work because sex work pays more. They are making economic decisions that are utterly rational in light of the financial pressures they face.

This same economic rationale applies to the rehabilitation context. A sex worker with financial responsibilities will likely not permanently leave the industry if the beadwork or candle-making skills she's acquired through a rehabilitation program don't generate the type of income she enjoys as a sex worker. Grace, who also works as a sex work outreach worker with BHESP in Kenya, echoes this sentiment based on her conversations with sex workers who quickly returned to sex work when their forays into alternative livelihoods resulted in financial distress:

> The rehabilitation programs I know take sex workers from the street and take them to the farm where they're taught how to do farming, and at the end of the day they're given the money for whatever food they farmed and exported. But most of the sex workers in these programs would tell

Grace Kamau. Nairobi, Kenya. Photograph by author.

me, "During the day I go to the farm, but this money at the end of the day gives me 500 shillings [$6 USD]. Five hundred shillings is not enough for my use. I need 2,000 [$24 USD]." So at the end of the day, [the sex worker] will go back to the city and do sex work where she will make maybe four times [what she made farming].

If these alternative livelihoods aren't providing superior economic compensation, then rehabilitation programs are simply ensuring that sex workers who join their programs and exit the sex industry are more financially vulnerable than they were before.

Rehabilitation programs are harmful in other ways as well. Some have led to physical abuse of sex workers and shocking breaches of confidentiality. In Nigeria, for instance, raids in areas of the capital city of Abuja have resulted in the arrest, beating, and forced detention of sex workers in skills-acquisition rehabilitation centers.[7] In Kenya, organizations in Mombasa have used hidden cameras in clubs to secretly record sex workers, called in the police to arrest them, invited the media to cover these arrests, given these same women jobs in hair salons in order to "rehabilitate" them, and touted these intrusive "interventions" on Kenyan television programs as actions that save women from prostitution.

"Rehab is violence," asserts Kenyan sex worker activist John Mathenge, who has led campaigns to demand that Kenyan television stations stop broadcasting and championing these actions that often publicly reveal sex workers' identities without concern for their safety.[8] Peninah Mwangi, another Kenyan sex worker activist who has also coordinated these campaigns against irresponsible media that defend rehabilitation, said, "They can't just show us in the public and say, 'Oh, we've done a splendid job! We got the nine strippers you saw last week—oh, and now they're good girls and they've been reformed.'"

During my fieldwork, I often heard similarly disparaging comments from sex workers about the futility of rehabilitation programs. There is no prevailing evidence in the research literature about rehabilitation programs' success in achieving their stated goals of reducing the number of people in the sex industry and providing them with viable economic options. But I wanted to visit one of these programs myself to gain a better understanding of their motivations. While I was doing fieldwork in Gaborone, Botswana, I asked sex worker activist Tosh Legoreng to set up a meeting for me with the oldest rehabilitation group in the country, the Nkalikela Youth Organization. "Oh, the ones who want to put padlocks on our vaginas?" Tosh responded with a playful chuckle.

Tosh eventually organized a meeting with an Nkalikela representative, who graciously agreed to an interview with me even though she knew I was writing a book firmly steeped in the sex workers' rights tradition. She was effervescent, blunt, and convinced of the righteousness of Nkalikela's rehabilitation mission. Some of Nkalikela's work is certainly laudatory: The organization distributes condoms to sex workers, conducts outreach to health workers to try to reduce stigma toward sex workers, and works with police to encourage them to stop the extortion and illegal arrests of sex workers. But Nkalikela's motivating vision and central work is unabashedly prohibitionist. It utilizes a group work model in which it tries to build participating sex workers' "self-efficacy" until the women realize they want to exit the industry so they can "be like other women."

Despite her obviously good intentions, the Nkalikela representative harbored views that only perpetuate stigma. "There's the issue of mental health because of the burdens of having so many sexual partners. Sex work makes you insane," she said matter-of-factly, exhibiting the anti-prostitution preoccupation with the idea that every woman who has numerous sexual partners in exchange for money is in some way psychically destroyed by that experience. I found her emphasis on the number of sexual partners sex workers have disturbing—her supreme anger was not reserved for the police abuse and social stigma that, to Nkalikela's credit, it does address to some extent, but centered on the fact that sex workers have sex with numerous people. The implicit, stigmatizing message is that the biggest degradation one can experience in the sex work context is to be the whore, and that female sexual activity is somehow irrevocably tied to a woman's essence and identity.

From 2004 to 2008, Nkalikela operated an alternative livelihoods project, which focused on teaching sex workers candle-making skills so they could exit the sex industry. The program's failure is an example of many rehabilitation programs' lack of effectiveness. The Nkalikela representative opened the office closet door to reveal a storage space packed to the brim with candles that were made by sex workers but never sold. She acknowledged that most of the sex workers who had been involved in the candle-making initiative never left sex work. She attributed that in part to sex workers' "not knowing how to save money," which was puzzling in light of the obvious fact that the candle-making enterprise was an unworkable economic scheme.

"The sex workers were saying, 'What do I do with candles! I don't know anything about marketing, it's totally useless to me,'" noted a Botswanan AIDS activist who has worked extensively with sex workers and is very familiar with Nkalikela's work. In many ways these types of alternative livelihood programs are often "predestined to fail," as was found in a research study by the Open Society Foundations that looked in part at rehabilitation programs' effectiveness in Botswana, Namibia, and South Africa: "The programs do not match individual skill bases with training and often fail to read the economic and employment market. The programs do not provide follow-up support and many do not provide seed funding or financial assistance to start small businesses. Discrimination from potential employers and the community against current or former sex workers also limits the possibility of program success."[9]

Some sex workers told me that the brand of alternative livelihood programs discussed here are appropriate only for older, retiring sex workers who because of their advanced age could financially survive making less money than during their sex work heyday. But these rehabilitation programs mostly target younger women who are at the peak of their wage-earning potential as sex workers.

Without question, there are certainly sex workers who want economically viable pathways to leave the industry. But participation in alternative livelihood programs should never be dependent on the stigmatizing requirement that sex workers must first exit the industry. To be clear, sex workers' rights groups do not argue against increased economic opportunities for sex workers. On the contrary, many operate economic empowerment programs within their own organizations. For example, SWEAT in South Africa provides its members with computer skills courses and driving lessons. WONETHA in Uganda offers its members bi-weekly literacy and English-language lessons. These efforts are meant to give sex workers tools with which to strengthen and expand their wage-earning capacity—the focus is on increasing economic opportunities, not on shaming sex workers for the decisions they have made. Whether the sex workers in these projects choose to use these newly acquired skills to find opportunities outside the sex industry or strengthen their economic hand while remaining in it is left completely up to them.

What everyone I interviewed spoke about—whether they wanted to leave the sex industry or stay—was that as long as they remain, they want to receive services that would help increase their power over their labor, like legal assistance to confront abuse from managers, clients, and the police; de-stigmatized health care; lessons in management, setting prices for services, and negotiation skills; and help setting up bank accounts. As long as sex work is presently the best financial option for them, they want all of the necessary tools with which to do the work as safely as possible.

Religious Opposition

Another voice of opposition against sex worker activism in Africa comes from religious leaders who fashion sex work as anathema to African culture and an attack on religious mores. At funerals, weddings, and church

Julie Katongole. Kampala, Uganda. Photograph by author.

services, religious leaders in Uganda have condemned sex work and homosexuality as morally corrosive practices. Julie Katongole, a Ugandan sex worker activist who identifies as bisexual, stopped attending the Universal Church of Christ's Kingdom in Kampala after she grew weary of pastors' using Sunday church services as a platform to denigrate the LGBT community and people who have multiple sexual partners like sex workers. "They were referring to . . . how we are receiving bad days from God," Julie recalls. "They were saying, 'The world is changing! People are doing sins. . . . Women are being attracted to women, men are being attracted to men. . . . People selling [their] bodies. People are liking people of the same sex.' So [they are saying] these are just sins that are coming from us, and then God decides to punish us severely."

Muslim leaders in Mombasa, Kenya, have vocally opposed sex worker activism. "I'll see religious leaders in Mombasa, when sex workers are arrested and as activists we go there and start saying we need our sex workers to be free. . . . They [religious leaders] will come and say, 'No, we are Muslims, we are going to ban these activists,'" says Grace regard-

ing the virtual roadblocks Kenyan sex worker activists have faced from
the religious sector. "They will come and say, 'Why are you bailing out
sex workers? These ones are evil. They are unwanted in our society.'"
In northern Nigeria, under Sharia law, Islamic police have arrested and
publicly condemned scores of women accused of prostitution.[10]

Religious organizations also align with anti-prostitution groups to
conflate sex work with trafficking and fund rehabilitation programs
targeting sex workers that sometimes include Christian doctrine training in their programming, stressing the belief that sex work is not only
harmful but also morally repugnant. This focus on sex work's supposed
immorality also serves as an obstacle to progressive AIDS activism
which seeks to ensure that marginalized and stigmatized groups like sex
workers are included in HIV prevention and treatment programs.

Religious leaders' vocal opposition to sex work reinforces stigma and
strengthens the notion that sex workers are sinful people who are outside of God's favor. African societies are generally highly religious, and
thus this moral condemnation of sex work serves as a powerful indictment. Many African sex workers are themselves religious, and in some
cases, their churches have ostracized them when their work has been revealed. This religious judgment and exclusion can cause sex workers internal turmoil. They may struggle to align their faith with the work that
financially supports their families, in the face of attacks from religious
leaders who insist that sex work disqualifies them from membership in
the faith community. When Lina's fellow congregants at her church in
Lagos, Nigeria, discovered she worked in a brothel, they immediately
ostracized her, demanding that she leave the congregation because she
lacked "righteousness." She felt so ashamed after being outed that she left
the church and joined a new congregation, where she has continued to
successfully hide her work. "I believe I'm a sinner," Lina says, "but I will
not just condemn myself. I am helping myself and my family by providing for my two sons' schooling and feeding as a single parent." Other sex
workers also echoed this sentiment—on the one hand, internalizing and
espousing some of the religious moralization concerning sex work yet
still maintaining their right to do their work free of discrimination and
abuse. "I believe that it [sex work] is sinful because the Bible tells me that
my body is the temple of the Holy Spirit," says Pamela, also a Nigerian
sex worker and a practicing Christian. "But at the same time, I need

freedom. My heart is boiling, and I need to speak out about the abuses we face as sex workers." Still others wholly reject the internalization of religious stigma directed at sex work: "There is no righteous man on earth—we are all sinners," proclaimed Pat Abraham, a leading Nigerian sex worker activist. "No one has a right to judge me or condemn me. We are fighting for the rights of human beings."

Sex worker activists in South Africa clearly see how religion and moral conservatism are used to justify whorephobia. "People often have strong reactions against sex workers, and we are just trying to understand the justification for that. And quite often [these reactions come] from what they perceive as the moral high ground," reflects a SWEAT human rights advocate. "You might have a religious belief about someone, and you judge them to be bad and 'other' and that often dictates your behavior towards them. So it justifies the discrimination, justifies your hatred."

SWEAT and Sisonke activists in South Africa have responded to religious opposition by holding public fora to which they've invited progressive religious scholars to argue against stigma toward sex workers. In December 2012, Sisonke and SWEAT organized and hosted a public "open university" seminar entitled "In Bed with Religion: reconciling sex work and faith." The panel of discussants included Dr. John Blevins, a researcher in the Interfaith Health Program at Emory University in the United States; Islamic scholar and celebrated anti-apartheid activist Professor Farid Esack from the University of Johannesburg; and Ivan Lloyd, the National Coordinator of INERELA+, a network of religious and lay leaders who have been infected with or affected by HIV.

In this unique public forum, the panelists stressed the deeply personal nature of religion and criticized religious leaders' top-down engagement with sex workers, instead encouraging a bottom-up approach in which religious leaders would be open to learning about the role spirituality plays in many African sex workers' lives. They also explored de-stigmatized views of sex work based on liberal readings of religious texts. For instance, Professor Esack spoke about the Muslim practice of *nikah mut'ah* or "temporary marriage" in Shia Islam, which can facilitate prostitution, in which parties can contract to be married for as little as a few hours. Historically, neither these transactions nor the women involved in them were stigmatized.[11]

The public seminar also included testimonials from sex workers who proudly spoke of how they reconciled their faith with their work. SWEAT and Sisonke received positive public feedback for this innovative way of addressing religious opposition to sex work, and I'm still moved by the "sex worker prayer" they included in their advertisements for the event. The prayer, written by Reverend Lorrain Tulleken of INERELA+, an organization which understands that religious leaders can play an influential role in encouraging the notion of nonjudgmental inclusivity, reads: "You know me Lord when I am in dark and dangerous situations, when I am unprotected by the laws of the country. I am your creation but I need help to remember that you alone are my judge. It is to you I answer."

Political Whorephobia

Just as some African religious leaders have taken to their pulpits to attack sex workers, so too have certain African political leaders. African government officials' public condemnation of sex workers and sex work activism is a gendered political strategy I label "political whorephobia." The term is inspired by and derived from the concept of "political homophobia" in sexuality studies. Sociologist Ashley Currier, who has published extensive research on LGBT rights activism in Namibia and South Africa, defines political homophobia as the "public denigration of same-sex sexualities, LGBT activism, nonheterosexual persons, and gender and sexual variance" and "a deliberate strategy some leaders use to silence political opponents, to defend cultural sovereignty, and to deflect public attention away from internal conflicts."[12] Some African leaders have indeed used public attacks on LGBT people as a political tool to shore up their nationalist bona fides while diverting the focus from their own political failings. "They want to use LGBT people as scapegoats for all their failures," a Nigerian LGBT rights activist told me regarding political homophobia in Nigeria, where a 2014 law criminalized LGBT rights activism. "Is it the job of LGBT people to create jobs? To provide lights? No, it's the government's job, and they are failing at that. By passing the law, they were playing on people's fantasy, on the idea that our cultural credibility is being threatened. They are chasing shadows."

The ideas underlying the concept of political homophobia are equally applicable to the sex work context. There are many examples of African political leaders on the local, state, and national level who wield political whorephobia by publicly maligning sex workers as gender and sexual nonconformists who are "un-African" and an affront to national authenticity. These attacks also serve as attempts to silence sex workers' rights activism, which, by its very nature, is a form of political resistance.

African politicians who employ political whorephobia, many of whom have checkered backgrounds, often do so in purported defense of cultural sovereignty. In 2000, then–Nigerian governor of Edo State Lucky Igbinedion, who would later be charged with 142 counts of corruption by the Nigerian Economic and Financial Crimes Commission,[13] stated during the ceremonial signing of a draconian anti-prostitution law: "Prostitution is not part of our culture. . . . It is one of the things that came with civilization."[14] In March 2007, in honor of International Women's Day, President Paul Kagame of Rwanda, whose country has been accused of committing crimes against humanity in the conflict in the Democratic Republic of Congo,[15] delivered an anti-prostitution speech in which he characterized sex work as an affront to Rwandan culture and publicly called on sex workers to leave the country: "I have recently been informed that some women and girls are advocating for prostitution to be considered as any other profession in Rwanda. That's an abomination that may contribute to the deterioration of values of the Rwandan culture. If there are people who can't respect their integrity on the ground that prostitution is part of modernisation, they can go and do this trade elsewhere outside Rwanda."[16]

The idea that sex work is "un-African" does not stand up to the historical record. For instance, there is evidence of prostitution in pre-colonial Akan societies in the Gold and Ivory coasts of Africa. European observers documented their presence and mentioned that there were "Elmina, Fetu, Asebu and Fantyn women who dispensed sexual favours for a negotiated price" who were distinguishable because of their "fine appearance and their clothing."[17] One account of early-nineteenth-century Asante practices stated, "Prostitutes are numerous and countenanced."[18] Prostitution also existed during the pre-colonial period in Nigeria and was mostly rural in nature with prostitutes primarily working independently out of their homes.[19] The social view of prostitutes varied from one region to another. For example, in the southern region of Nsukka, communities viewed prostitutes as independent and daring and thus regarded them with a certain amount of deference and admiration.[20] Whereas, in Igalaland, where cultural norms dictated that a woman closely guard her sexuality, the relationship between Igala citizens and prostitutes was strained.[21] There is also ample evidence to suggest that the famous Ahebi Ugbabe, who became the female king of Enugu-Ezike, an Igbo community, was a prostitute in her younger years. She ran away from home as a teenager and is believed to have engaged in prostitution in order to survive financially.[22]

Unsurprisingly, African politicians who embrace political whore-phobia and the "sex work is un-African" meme are also often acolytes of political homophobia, proving that both strategies are deliberate attempts to police communities characterized as gender and sexual dissidents. Gambian President Yahya Jammeh, who has publicly referred to gay people as "vermin" and "malaria-causing mosquitoes,"[23] in 2002 declared an "uncompromising war on prostitution," a pronouncement that triggered police raids and arrests in brothels and bars in the capital city of Banjul.[24] Uganda State Minister of Ethics and Integrity Simon Lokodo, who has publicly stated that child rape is preferable to homosexuality and personally raided LGBT rights workshops in Uganda,[25] in 2012 set his sights on sex worker activism, stating, "Legalizing prostitution is a sign of moral decadence. . . . The choice of a person to sell their bodies for money cannot be considered a human right but a crime, punishable by law."[26] Former and founding president of Namibia Sam Nujoma, whose well-known political homophobia is credited with igniting the LGBT rights movement in Namibia,[27] has publicly endorsed the idea that sex work is an attack on African culture: "Prostitution has never been part of the culture of our people," he argued in public statements made in 2010. "We have destroyed colonialism, why should we maintain it [prostitution]. . . . [Those advocating the legalization of prostitution] better pack up and go with colonialism."[28]

Politicians have also used political whorephobia as a way to scapegoat sex workers for HIV, shifting emphasis from their own governmental shortcomings in HIV prevention and treatment efforts. In Zambia, waves of severe state repression in the late 1990s and between 2004 and 2008 had the effect of literally driving sex workers out of the country and were coupled with politicians' vitriolic public statements blaming sex workers for the spread of HIV.[29] According to a transcript from a

2007 session of Parliament, Zambian politician Chishima Kabwili is on record as stating: "On HIV/AIDS, Mr. Speaker, I have said before that we need to enact laws that will prevent HIV/AIDS. We need to come up with a law that criminalises prostitution. Unless we arrest all the prostitutes on the streets, AIDS in Zambia will never cease. . . . We have to be extremely serious on this issue. Unless prostitutes are done away with, then we shall not fight HIV/AIDS."[30]

In November 2013, public officials in Botswana launched a public whorephobic campaign to scapegoat sex workers for HIV based on recommendations from the Botswanan government's "Draft Strategies to Address Key Populations." The government campaign against sex work includes arrests, detention, and deportation of sex workers as an HIV prevention strategy, and the Health Ministry will place state-sanctioned anti–sex work messages on billboards, branded vehicles, radio and TV, and in newspapers.[31] The campaign was immediately denounced by human rights organizations including ARASA, the Canadian HIV/AIDS Legal Network, and BONELA.[32] The Botswana government had duped BONELA into conducting surveys with sex workers based on the false assurance that the government would use the information to develop inclusive HIV prevention and treatment strategies. Instead, the government surreptitiously used the gathered information to begin a public war against sex workers in Botswana.[33]

Tosh Legoreng, who has publicly spoken out against the recent crackdowns, has personally felt the harsh hand of political whorephobia in her own life. In May 2013, while she was doing peer education outreach to sex workers outside a local nightclub in Gaborone, two undercover members of the Department of Intelligent Services, a special Botswanan police force, attacked, beat, and detained Tosh. They informed her that they had targeted her because she's a well-known activist who appears regularly on Botswana radio and in newspapers advocating for sex workers' rights. In reflecting on the personal costs of political whorephobia, Tosh stoically told me, "I'm prepared for anything."

Confronting Political Whorephobia in Gulu

How are sex worker activists confronting political whorephobia? The story of the human rights defenders of Uganda's leading sex workers' rights group, WONETHA, who experienced and fought against a severe government crackdown that threatened to derail their efforts to organize sex workers in Gulu in northern Uganda, an area recovering from a twenty-year civil war, provides a powerful example of sex worker resistance to political whorephobia.

In May 2012, local government officials, accompanied by the police, unexpectedly raided WONETHA's sex worker drop-in center in Gulu without search or arrest warrants. As the officers falsely accused the center's coordinators of running a brothel and recruiting people into prostitution, smashed their computers, and confiscated their files, the sex worker activists desperately tried to explain that they were running a drop-in center so sex workers could attend monthly meetings about their health and rights, have free access to condoms, and receive voluntary HIV counseling and testing. For an hour and a half, the officials ransacked the office and confiscated computers, flash drives, reams of paper, research reports, and outreach brochures.

"They arrested and detained the staff, including me," says Amira, a soft-spoken, ebony-skinned young woman originally from Gulu who worked as one of two sex worker coordinators at the drop-in center. "When we arrived at the Central police station they called journalists and community members 'to come and see what prostitutes look like.'" Journalists took photos of the arrested activists that they subsequently splashed all over the front pages of local newspapers. A large crowd gathered outside the police station furiously yelling things like, "I wish Idi Amin [the former Ugandan dictator] was still here to issue a firing squad!" "Give them seven years in jail!" "No, give them life imprisonment!"

The state attorney's office, pressured by local government leaders, filed criminal cases against Amira and eventually four other sex worker activists in Gulu affiliated with WONETHA on charges of "living off the earnings of prostitution." "The whole town was on fire," remembers a legal officer with HRAPF, which provided the accused WONETHA activists with legal representation. "They were saying that prostitution is an abomination of Acholi culture.[34] And because of the intense community reaction the Chief Magistrate said this was a case in the 'public interest' and must be held in open court."

The fierce WONETHA activists could recall a time when the idea of a drop-in center's providing a safe space for sex workers was merely a dream. But their efforts over the years had made it a lived reality. Would they be crushed under the weight of a government crackdown intended to send them back to the barrenness of a past devoid of their organizing efforts? WONETHA knew that if it did not confront these political attacks head-on it would be open season on its advocacy efforts throughout the country.

WONETHA shrewdly assembled a devoted team of Ugandan human rights lawyers, academics, and advocates to help strategize how to secure the drop-in center's future and fight the criminal charges. Essential to WONETHA's efforts was its relationship with HRAPF lawyers who convinced them to plead not guilty to the charges, arguing that the prosecution would be unable, as in most prostitution cases, to present evidence or witnesses to prove that the activists were guilty of the charge of living off the earnings of prostitution. WONETHA also deftly organized a media blitz that brought regional and international attention to the crackdown,[35] and it placed ads in national Ugandan newspapers condemning the raid and arrests and defending itself.

In the first-person narrative that follows, WONETHA leader Daisy Nakato describes in her own words how sex worker activists fought back against political whorephobia in Gulu.

Daisy Nakato, 31, Cisgender Female Sex Worker and Activist (Kampala, Uganda)

"Even If It's One Room"

Gulu is in the northern part of the country, far from the city, and had been in a war for twenty-plus years. But Gulu now is almost a new city—there are a lot of organizations, a lot of business[es], a lot of foreigners. The city's booming even more than here in Kampala, so there's a lot of sex work there. WONETHA is based in Kampala, and we started going to Gulu because we wanted to make sure that we also work with sex workers there. We thought, "If we're getting free condoms in Kampala, let other sisters also have free condoms." But Gulu has very conservative religious and cultural leaders who don't want to hear about anything to do with sex work, condoms, nothing.

Starting the group in Gulu was not easy because we did not have a contact person there. I just went to Gulu myself, stayed in a lodge, and started
moving around and saying to *boda-boda* [motorcycle taxi] guys who are all
over, "Oh, I'm looking for people who identify as sex workers around here.
I need to talk to them." These guys were so open and they took me to the
places where sex workers are, and then once I got there those sex workers
led me to other sex workers. We wanted to link them to referral hospitals
in Gulu for free HIV testing and available ARVs. I remember I had some flyers about HIV, about how you should know your status, and if you want to
have an HIV test call this number, which fell into the hands of the wrong
person. I remember a man I didn't know calling me at the number he found
on the flyer and telling me, "I've seen you! You're promoting prostitution in
Gulu. I'm going to arrest you. You should stop recruiting our women. What
you're doing is not right. Go and promote it somewhere else. Don't bring
prostitution in[to] our area."

At that time the only organization working with sex workers in Gulu
ran a rehabilitation program for sex workers, so they had sewing machines,
they had a hair salon. Because they were into rehabilitation and we are
into the human rights approach, we couldn't work directly with them, but
we met sex workers through them and we saw that there was a need for
a drop-in center for sex workers to at least have, even if it's just one room,
somewhere they can come, sit, share ideas, get information on HIV and free
condoms. So we got financial support to rent a room, and we hired two sex
workers named Amira and Patty and gave them stipends to coordinate the
program and to do outreach to inform sex workers about the new available
services.

We trained the coordinators in human rights so they were taking that
message to sex workers. We also trained them in how to run an office and
how to document sex work stories and violations. There was a small membership fee of something like 5,000 Uganda shillings [$1.99 USD] so that sex
worker members would feel like if they contributed this small amount they
owned the office, that it was their own group. In the drop-in center were
flyers with information on how sex workers could protect themselves from
the police, how to protect themselves from rape, how to protect themselves from bad clients and nonpaying clients, how to protect themselves
from HIV. They had all that information.

"You Are Here to Spoil Our Community"

The local government leaders went to the police and said come and help us arrest these people. When they raided the office in 2012, they got the membership list, which listed the names, phone numbers, and 5,000-shilling membership fees of sex worker members. They said that the 5,000 shilling was to recruit people into sex work, and the phone numbers were so sex workers could be called when clients [arrived] because the center was a brothel. They said the condoms were promoting prostitution. They said the information on how to keep safe was promoting prostitution. The local leaders were saying that we put pornographic images on the drop-in center computers, showing people how to enjoy sex. They confiscated everything, including the computers and all the documents, and then they arrested Amira and Patty.

We were not there when they were arrested. We came from Kampala and all had to travel to Gulu where we found them in the police cell. By then they had also arrested three more of our sex worker activists after they had gone to visit Amira and Patty in the cells. We told the officer-in-charge at the police station, "The drop-in center is here to promote health. Those condoms are for health. Open our computers, read our documents, read our flyers. None of them tells people to join sex work. They're all on promoting health and safety." Outside the police station, it seemed like the whole village was there to testify to how these girls have support from Kampala to promote prostitution.

And every [newspaper] within Gulu was there to take photos. So I really felt bad, because Amira's and Patty's and the other activists' pictures were in the paper, and these are young women who are struggling. The journalists would bring them out and take photos of them, and each media house had [its] own headline in the local newspapers, in the local languages, which was very bad. Because of stigma, most sex workers in Uganda don't want people to know they do sex work. Even their close friends might not know; it's something where it takes time for them to open up. So it was not for the media to expose them. They have kids. They have their siblings. And now they were in prison and their life was coming to an end. Who was going to take care of their families? Gulu is not a big town—it's a small town where everyone knows everyone. So I really felt bad, I wanted to take them out from this place. I know they were leaders and those are things you have to expect once you start activism. But it was hard to look into their eyes and tell them, "Everything will be okay; be strong," even though I could not fully promise or grant them that because I was not sure what was going to happen, especially after knowing that their file was taken to the state attorney and there would be a trial.

We managed to get them bail pending the trial, and we rented them a temporary safe house where they started staying. We were afraid for their safety because after they had appeared in all the newspapers we didn't know what was going to happen. And seeing how unhappy the community was with them, I think they would have killed them—that's the feeling we had. It was the influence of the local government leaders on the population because it was the local leaders who gave out the wrong information that the goal of the drop-in center was to promote prostitution. So the local people took that false information and feared that we were trying to recruit all their kids into sex work. The local leaders were getting this information out to people through the media, especially the radio. I even remember the first time when I went to Gulu to hand out the health flyers to sex workers that it was all over the news that some people were here to "promote prostitution." Local leaders were calling in to radio stations, and they were telling everyone to be careful, to be aware, that we have bad people in the community right now.

We were advised by the officer-in-charge at the police station to go and meet with the deputy resident district commissioner, kind of the deputy mayor. He told us she is a very tough lady, and she had been misinformed about our work and she was one of the people pushing all of this. He told us if we could convince her of the true purpose of the drop-in center, maybe she could help change the minds of the other local leaders. Because what we wanted was our drop-in center to reopen and resume work but with their approval. But when we went to see her, she did not listen to us. She said, "Look at yourselves, you are here to spoil our community, to spoil our girls. You are here getting money from donors to come and spoil our community. The only good thing I can do for my community, and for you, is to arrest you. And your people will never see you." I remember I started shaking because then I could see all of these police officers outside the office with guns. She was threatening us. We finally left that day without being arrested. But the case was not yet closed, and we still had to go to court. We decided that we would not stop our advocacy. We said to each other, "We will not stop. Let this old woman arrest us if she wants."

"Hearts Are So Strong, Like a Storm"

Every single month, we went from Kampala to Gulu for the court cases, and eventually we won the criminal cases. At first many people and the local leaders were going to the court cases, but we also kept on going to the court to defend our friends and soon the community and the local leaders lost interest so they stopped coming. I think maybe they stopped coming because we kept on fighting, we wouldn't give up, and we really tried to talk to these people so they would know who a sex worker really is, and I think some of them started understanding.

We went and talked to the local council leaders one by one trying to explain our position to them. We would go to each of their offices in suits without an appointment, and we would just stand at the entrance until they invited us in. We would tell the local leaders, "You need to join forces with us, and if we're talking about HIV, let's work together. There's no way you can fight HIV without involving us sex workers. You are building your community back after the war. You want to refill your community after all of the deaths. If a program comes trying to support the community [to] not get HIV, why would you stop that program?" And they were willing to listen. After talking to them they realized they needed condoms even for themselves.

We fought and we were able to keep the drop-in center open. It's now registered as the Women Support Initiative Gulu. Sex workers can still drop in whenever they want. [It focuses] on economic empowerment and [has] monthly meetings and outreaches. It's all coming from [the drop-in center]. In activism work, you really have to fight. If you fear, if you're not strong in activism, you can't manage. You don't give up. You just have to be ready, and once you're starting this work it has to be at the back of your mind that all these things could happen. Because if you say we are starting a movement, we really want to see sex workers achieving this and that, and then someone threatens you, arrests you, and you just give up? Then you're not an activist. I've seen activists humiliated and stripped naked, and the following day, they're back on the media still fighting. Especially if people have belief in you, if they have trust in you, if they're like, "Please do it on our behalf, we can't do it."

We feel like we can take on anything. And also knowing that what you're fighting for, you haven't achieved it yet. So when the Gulu raid happened, we were like, no, if I stop here, that means I'm a coward. That means I was not serious about what I did. So that's the power that drives us. Sometimes we feel our hearts are so strong, like a storm.

Epilogue

Africa and the Global Sex Workers' Rights Movement

All we can do is go around telling the truth.
—Carson McCullers, *The Heart Is a Lonely Hunter*

The African sex workers' rights movement does not exist in a vacuum. It is the newest manifestation of what has been a decades-long global struggle for sex workers' rights. The international sex workers' rights movement emerged in the 1970s in the United States and western Europe, and in the early years of its growth, sex worker activists from the Global North dominated the movement. But as sex worker organizing has spread to every corner of the world, including Africa, the international movement has become strikingly globalized, and sex workers' rights activists from the Global South have become visible and prominent champions of the struggle. The movement's sheer geographic diversity is breathtaking: Activists have raised red umbrellas in countries as varied as Brazil, Burma, Cameroon, Canada, China, France, India, Kyrgyzstan, Macedonia, Mali, Mexico, New Zealand, Peru, Thailand, Turkey, the United Kingdom, Zimbabwe, and beyond.[1] The fate of the global movement is a key factor in the health and growth of the sex workers' rights movement in Africa.

Anti-prostitution activists have argued that only "nonrepresentative" and economically privileged sex workers champion the idea of sex workers' rights.[2] But this is an untenable and perplexing argument in the face of flourishing formal movements for sex workers' rights in Africa, Asia, the Caribbean, and Latin America that illuminate the global movement's startling national, racial, ethnic, class, sexual orientation, and gender diversity. The participation and leadership of Global South activists in the international movement challenge anti-prostitution activists' one-dimensional depictions of "degraded Third World prostitutes" incapable of exhibiting agency. In fact, it is now sex worker activists from the Global South who are at the vanguard of the international movement, a compelling counter-narrative to anti-prostitution activists' disempowering claims. For example, the success of the 2012 Sex Worker Freedom Festival in Kolkata, India—the largest and most important global gathering of sex workers' rights activists in the history of the international movement—is a potent symbol of the leading role that Global South sex workers now play in defining the international sex workers' rights agenda.

It is impossible to reflect fully on the growth of the young African movement without acknowledging the role the international sex workers' rights movement is playing in its development. This Epilogue briefly traces the global struggle's transformation into the diverse movement it is today and explores how African advocates are learning from and contributing to the international movement while cultivating important and inspiring South–South partnerships with sex worker activists from India. It ends with a concluding meditation on how, as African activists develop these essential global linkages, the heart of their work remains rooted in African sex workers' daily struggles for rights and justice.

The Globalized Movement

The global sex workers' rights movement has morphed from a fledging movement once briefly dominated by sex workers from the Global North into a vibrant, diverse, and inclusive movement with worldwide representation. As the movement gains momentum, the principle of solidarity across the socially constructed lines of race, gender, culture, and nation increasingly guides its growth. The international movement's early history, however, was not always marked by strong representation of Global South sex worker activists. Despite these initial challenges, there has been a steady march toward inclusion, aided in part by (1) donor funding that has enabled sex workers from the Global South to participate in international fora; (2) the rise of celebrated and influential formal sex workers' rights organizations in the Global South in countries like India, South Africa, and Thailand that have elevated the voices of southern sex workers on the global stage; and (3) a cultivated dedication to the principles of inclusivity and intersectionality that have become trademarks of global sex worker activism.

By nurturing a big-tent form of movement building that welcomes sex workers of diverse genders, sexual orientations, nationalities, races, and immigration and HIV statuses, from both the North and South, the international sex workers' rights movement is, in essence, requiring of itself what it demands of governments and societies at large regarding the need to reject the politics of othering.

Some of the earliest global examples of formalized sex workers' rights activism took place in the United States and western Europe in the 1970s. In May 1973, Margo St. James founded Call Off Your Old Tired Ethics (COYOTE), a San Francisco–based prostitutes' rights organization and the first of its kind in the United States.[3] COYOTE provided direct services to sex workers, campaigned for the decriminalization of prostitution, and spurred prostitutes' rights organizing across the United States.[4] In June 1975, a hundred French prostitutes occupied Saint-Nizier church in Lyon, demanding the lifting of prison sentences for solicitation and an end to police abuse and harassment.[5] Their strike quickly spread to Paris and Marseille and led to the creation of the French Collective of Prostitutes.[6] This uprising, which garnered significant media attention, marked the beginning of formal sex worker organizing in Europe.[7]

In the years following the formation of COYOTE in the United States and the French Collective of Prostitutes in Europe, activists formed sex workers' rights organizations throughout the Global North, including the English Collective of Prostitutes (1975), Prostitutes of New York (PONY) (1976), the German Association of Female and Male Prostitutes (HYDRA) (1980), the Italian Committee for the Civil Rights of Prostitutes (1982), and Red Thread in the Netherlands (1984).[8] These organizations and many more staged protests; waged media campaigns; provided legal, health, and social support services to sex workers; and formed relationships and meaningful networks with one another.

In the 1980s, formal sex workers' rights organizations also slowly emerged in the Global South, including the Ecuadorian Association of Autonomous Women (1982), the Uruguayan Association of Public Prostitutes (AMEPU) (1985), and EMPOWER in Thailand (1985).[9] These early examples of formal sex worker organizing in the Global South prove that political struggle and solidarity among sex workers cannot be dismissed as a Western by-product.

However, as Kamala Kempadoo and Jo Doezema argued in their 1998 book *Global Sex Workers: Rights, Resistance, and Redefinition*, sex workers from the Global North did initially dominate international activism in the early years of the global sex workers' rights movement. In some of the first examples of international activism concerning sex workers' rights, the International Committee for Prostitutes' Rights (ICPR) sponsored two World Whores Congresses held in Amsterdam in 1985 and Brussels in 1986, which culminated in the drafting and passage of the World Charter for Prostitutes' Rights. The Congresses, however, did not involve formal participation from sex workers in the Global South, and consequently the Charter mostly reflected the concerns of Western sex workers and their advocates.[10]

Despite these early challenges, in the 1990s the relationship between the North and South in international sex workers' rights organizing underwent a welcome shift from exclusion to inclusion when sex worker activists in the South gained more opportunities to engage in international activism with the convening of the International AIDS Conferences. AIDS activism created an avenue for southern sex workers to build global alliances and acquire the necessary donor funding to participate in international arenas.[11]

The 1990s also welcomed the creation of what would become highly influential formal sex workers' rights organizations in the Global South, including Davida in Brazil (1992), SWEAT in South Africa (1994), and DMSC (1995) and VAMP (1997) in India.[12] The power of these celebrated and innovative organizations has strengthened and amplified the voices of sex worker activists from the Global South on the international stage.

The 1990 formation of the Global Network of Sex Work Projects (NSWP) also marked a turning point in the global movement.[13] NSWP is an international umbrella membership organization for sex workers' rights groups. NSWP has strengthened the global movement's dedication to inclusivity and commitment to strong leadership roles for southern sex worker activists. It has grown into a truly international network with more than 150 member organizations in 60 countries in Africa, Asia and the Pacific, Europe, Latin America, North America, and the Caribbean. NSWP has represented the concerns of its diverse members in their dealings with influential actors on the world stage, including at the 1995 Fourth World Conference on Women in Beijing and in activism within UN bodies.[14]

Part of the reason the global sex workers' rights movement has tried to correct the exclusionary tendencies of its past is that sex workers themselves have been so marginalized by their governments, society, and anti-prostitution segments of the feminist movement. This experience of marginalization has led the maturing global movement for sex workers' rights to develop a hyper-inclusivity and a fierce dedication to intersectionality. African sex worker activists I interviewed about the state of the global movement spoke only of feeling a deep and hard-won global solidarity among sex worker activists.

Over the past four decades of global sex workers' rights organizing, the shift to an ethos of inclusion and the increasing focus on sex worker activists' voices from the Global South culminated in the 2012 Sex Worker Freedom Festival in Kolkata, India, which stands as a major moment in the history of the international sex workers' rights movement. When U.S. travel restrictions barred sex workers from attending the 2012 International AIDS Conference (IAC 2012) in Washington, D.C., outraged sex workers and their allies organized the festival as an alternative conference that ran parallel to the IAC.[15] The Sex Worker Freedom Festival was thus both a protest against sex workers' exclusion and a demand for respect of their human rights.[16] Co-hosted and organized by DMSC, NSWP, and the All India Network of Sex Workers (AINSW), the festival ran from July 21 to 26, 2012, and welcomed more than 667 sex worker activists from 43 countries, the majority of them from the Global South.[17] It was the largest gathering of advocates in the history of the global sex workers' rights struggle.

The Sex Worker Freedom Festival's location in the Global South was an inspiring example of how the international sex workers' rights movement has embraced the leadership of southern sex workers. The festival also exhibited a commitment to inclusion in its programming: Male and transgender female sex workers hosted panels where they discussed how they often feel marginalized in dialogues about sex work, and sessions for HIV-positive sex workers led to the creation of NSWP+ and the Asia Pacific Network of Positive Sex Workers (APNSW+), two new platforms mobilizing sex workers and their advocates concerning HIV/AIDS, sex work, and the right to health. Sex workers also produced a cross-cultural showcase that featured an array of diverse and interdisciplinary performances on the international aspects of sex work, including the freedom to move and migrate.[18]

Global African Sex Workers and South–South Collaboration

The Sex Worker Freedom Festival was also the first time there was significant representation of African sex workers at a global sex workers' rights gathering of this scale. Many of the African activists featured in this book—Tosh Legoreng of Botswana, Phelister Abdalla and John Mathenge of Kenya, Mama Africa of Namibia, Daisy Nakato and Beyonce Karungi of Uganda—attended the festival. They proudly represented the emerging African sex workers' rights movement and marched through the streets of Kolkata and the famous Sonagachi red-light district with hundreds of sex workers from around the world. Funding still has the effect of making these international spaces accessible for southern activists: Just as AIDS activism and its accompanying donor funding helped sex workers from the Global South begin to take leadership roles in the global movement in the 1990s, African activists who participated in the Sex Worker Freedom Festival were able to attend only because of funding from donors committed to sex worker movement building.[19]

Participation in the festival had a strong effect on African advocates. Being in a space with so many diverse sex workers from around the world—who despite their differences in nationality, ethnicity, class, and gender highlighted similar issues their communities face—was empowering for African activists because it confirmed that sex workers' vulnerability is tied to structural forces in society, including criminalization and whorephobia. "[There were] sex workers from all over the world . . . and then when they shared, it's just like the world goes around—we are all the same," remembers Daisy. "All the challenges in Uganda are the same challenges in the U.S., everywhere, in China, everywhere. We all face the same challenges [because] sex work is criminalized everywhere. . . . If not for the global sex work movement . . . I wouldn't have known that sex workers in other countries also go through the same challenges that we do."

The festival also provided African activists with opportunities to brainstorm ways forward based on the common challenges global sex

Tosh Legoreng. Kasane, Botswana. Photograph by author.

workers face; to hear from fellow activists who are also questioning authority without fear, like Canadian sex workers who were in the process of boldly bringing a successful sex workers' rights case before the Canadian Supreme Court;[20] and to witness the inner workings of celebrated sex workers' rights groups like DMSC in Kolkata whose sex worker–led health outreach program targeting tens of thousands of sex workers in the Sonagachi red-light district has been hailed by global health bodies.[21] Experiencing solidarity across national boundaries increased African sex workers' confidence in their activism. "When I got there I just realized, ah, everybody there was proud of being a sex worker," noted Tosh. "And I just felt if these people are proud of their work, why can't [our sex workers in Botswana] be proud of what we are doing? And that's what I mean when I say this is our time."

As they nurture their connection to the global struggle, African activists are also forming exciting South–South collaborations with Indian sex worker activists. Although I live and work in the United States and my human rights work's primary geographic focus has long been Africa, my first experience observing sex workers' rights activism in action was not in the United States or an African country but in India. In 2008, I traveled to the city of Sangli on the banks of the Krishna River in the state of Maharashtra to work on a project with the famous VAMP sex worker collective. VAMP and its sister organization SANGRAM, led by award-winning activist Meena Seshu, who is one of the great allies of the global sex workers' rights movement, had invited my graduate students and me to Sangli to assist with the research and writing of a policy report. Inspired by VAMP's experience running an HIV program in Sangli's red-light district, the report ultimately created guidelines for rights-based and justice-based HIV interventions targeting sex workers.

I was floored by the collective resilience I witnessed among VAMP sex worker activists. They were a group of fiercely empowered sex workers who regarded their *dhanda*—their work—with pride and who rejected the stigma and violence they experienced from their communities. Comprising thousands of sex workers, VAMP long ago determined that the language of rights alone could not deliver justice; only the establishment of a collective model of sex workers working together to demand that rights become a lived reality would prove fruitful. They operate an HIV prevention program targeting not only sex workers in the collective but also their clients, lovers, and people who secretly engage in sex work, including housewives who engage in clandestine sex work. They run an after-school program for their children, showcase a traveling theater program that addresses whorephobia, and routinely conduct outreach to police and health workers to reduce discrimination against sex workers. If a sex worker is unjustly arrested, they arrive en masse to the police station to demand her release. They host weekly meetings for male and female sex workers, cisgender and transgender, as well as sex workers' children, and discuss the unique issues of concern to these communities.

After I returned from my fieldwork in India in 2008, inspired by the collective activism I witnessed in Sangli, I began to focus the majority of my human rights research and activism on sex workers' rights. So I was not surprised to learn that in 2012, sex workers' rights activists from Botswana, Kenya, Uganda, and Zimbabwe chose to engage in exchange visits with activists from VAMP and other Indian sex worker collectives like the organization Ashodaya Samithi, which works with thousands of sex workers in six districts in the Indian state of Karnataka. African activists traveled to Sangli and Karnataka from the Sex Worker Freedom Festival and studied how Indian activists have been organizing since the 1990s. Many of these African activists had benefited greatly from the Africa exchanges I've described in previous chapters, including groundbreaking workshops for African sex worker activists organized by SWEAT, the African Sex Workers Alliance, and Akina Mama wa Afrika, but this was one of the first times they engaged in intense exchanges with sex workers outside the continent.

African activists highlighted many benefits of South–South collaborations with Indian sex workers. For example, they were struck by the prominent role that transgender sex workers play in Indian sex worker organizing. Several African activists cited this as one of the reasons they've attempted to strengthen the presence of African transgender sex workers within their own organizations. Beyonce Karungi, founder and director of Transgender Equality Uganda, stated how witnessing the visibility and prominence of transgender sex worker activists in India strengthened her resolve to fight for the rights of Ugandan transgender sex workers: "I felt so inspired, like I am not alone in the whole world," remembers Beyonce. "There are many people who are like me, so it kept giving me courage and power and bravery to keep doing my activist work."

African activists also spoke admiringly of VAMP's development of after-school programs for sex workers' children designed to address the stigma the children experience because their parents' work is considered shameful by society. The adult children of VAMP sex workers volunteer at the organization and proudly speak of the mothers who worked hard to provide them with an education. African activists were particularly moved by this focus on sex workers' children because in many of my interviews they characterized the economic catalysts that led them to sex work as strongly tied to their parental obligations to provide for their children. These collaborations, however, have not been one-sided. For instance, during a "community-to-community capacity-building" session between Kenyan, Zimbabwean, and Indian sex workers at the Ashodaya Academy in India, African activists shared advocacy experiences against police abuse, condom shortages, and community stigma with their Indian colleagues.[22]

These South–South collaborations have been formalized with the 2014 establishment of the Sex Worker Academy for Africa (SWAA) based in Nairobi, a joint initiative of KESWA, ASWA, VAMP, Ashodaya, and NSWP aimed at strengthening the sex worker movement in Africa. In the first round of SWAA workshops, Kenyan and Indian activists (known as "faculties") worked together to develop a training curriculum on grassroots activism and country-specific legal and policy advocacy strategies aimed at the decriminalization of sex work. The Kenyan faculty members in turn trained other African activists from throughout the continent. SWAA promises to be a laboratory of ideas for global sex worker activism. And by solidifying innovative South–South collaborations, SWAA provides a powerful counterpoint to anti-prostitution characterizations of sex work activism as foreign to the Global South. Anti-prostitution activists' paradigmatic sex worker advocate is white, privileged, Western, and "nonrepresentative." But these creative South–South collaborations between Indian and African sex worker activists, in which U.S. and European sex workers do not play a central role, are further evidence of the truly global nature of the international sex worker movement and the collective self-reliance of southern sex workers.

* * *

During some of the final days of the Sex Worker Freedom Festival, hundreds of participants took to the streets for sex workers' rights marches. African sex workers played a leading role in these marches, singing sex workers' rights songs they had learned in South Africa. They sang one particularly popular song about a garden boy and a kitchen girl who produce a baby, who as an adult chooses not to work in the kitchen like her mother or in the garden like her father but to become a sex worker. "I'm a sex worker! I'm an activist! I'm a feminist!" the song ends. As they marched through the streets under a sea of red umbrellas, participating sex workers repeatedly asked the African contingent to lead them in singing the song. Global sex workers strongly connected to the lyrics because the song underscores and celebrates the concept of sex workers' agency, the idea that sex workers are people who, despite limiting circumstances, are still enormously capable of moving their lives forward, fighting for their rights as workers, and demanding justice.

African activists have been inspired by their participation in international movement building, including South–South collaborations, and through these exercises in solidarity they have become even more confident in the lessons the African movement has to offer the global struggle for sex workers' rights. In general, rates of poverty are higher and education standards lower in Africa compared with those of other regions where sex workers' rights activism has taken root, and therefore this creates bigger hurdles to activism for African sex workers. And yet despite this, African sex workers embrace activism, exhibiting an intense passion and dedication to the sex workers' rights struggle. In highlighting and reflecting on African sex worker activists' resiliency and determination, notwithstanding the inherent challenges to their activism, Daisy remarked, "Someone will be arrested today, stays in a police cell for a week, but the day they come out, before they even get home, they're talking [on behalf of sex workers' rights]. . . . I think that's something to be proud of."

Concluding Meditation: Flowers for Peninah

The sex workers' rights movement in Africa is taking its rightful place in the global struggle and developing fruitful South–South partnerships. But its enduring success will ultimately be determined by its indigenous strivings—by what it accomplishes on the ground in defense of sex workers' rights in African cities, towns, and rural areas, in places like Thika in Kenya where this book began with the murder of a sex worker named Peninah Nyambura, whose killing sparked sex worker-led protests throughout Thika. I chose to open the book with her murder because as feminist debates continue and as harmful laws and policies criminalizing and stigmatizing sex workers remain, we must not forget that sex workers continue to be thrown in jail, that the number of murdered sex workers continues to rise, that this is an issue of life and death for sex workers in Africa and beyond.

I first heard the story of Peninah's murder from sex worker activists in Nairobi. There had already been a number of sex worker killings in Thika at the time of her death in 2012, and there were several more after—sex workers' bodies discovered in drainage ditches, in hotel rooms, thrown out of cars on the side of the road. The body of one woman dressed in a pink shirt and black stockings, wearing gold earrings and a bracelet on her right wrist, was so badly mutilated that the fifty sex workers who came to view the body could not identify her. This still-unnamed sex worker was found under a bridge on the Thika highway, wire wrapped around her neck, her face destroyed.

In the years I spent researching this book, Peninah's death and the serial killing of sex workers in Thika became one of the many stories that I could not shake, so in July 2013 I decided to travel to Thika, a small, dusty town, bustling with muted energy, to learn more about the murders and the sex work community's response. When I arrived there, I met Aisha, Jina, and Njeri, Thika-based sex workers who had known Peninah well. They told me that Peninah's sex-working name was "Ann" and that many sex workers called her "Mama Ann" because she had become a maternal figure to sex workers in Thika. She was the breadwinner for her entire family and an activist who "joined hands with other sex workers," helping them set up "merry-go-round" money-lending groups, whereby they would pool some of their cash together on a weekly basis to lend to whichever sex worker in the group was most in need that week. Mama Ann also encouraged her fellow sex workers to use condoms, save money, go back to school part-time, and supplement their sex work income with other moneymaking endeavors. She was deeply loved and respected within the Thika sex work community for her efforts.

In investigating her life and death, Aisha, Jina, Njeri, and I, along with two of my graduate students, walked through Thika, visiting sex work venues Peninah had frequented. In one dimly lit bar, men sat solo at low wooden tables, meat cooking on skewers, football blaring on the overhead television set. Women stood in small groups, and occasionally a potential client would pass and touch one of them on the hand to make his interest known. A man briefly tapped one of my graduate students on the hand, mistaking her for a sex worker, a fact that was not an affront to her but simply a reasonable misunderstanding. Her reaction (or nonreaction, as it were) was a subtle but powerful statement that being mistaken for a sex worker should not register as scandalous. The societal belief that the worst thing a woman can be, or be mistaken for, is a "whore" is part of the underlying stigma toward sex workers that nullifies their lives and deaths.

At another venue, a large, brightly lit hotel where condom dispensers lined the walls, I was told that the body of one of Thika's murdered sex workers had been found in one of the hotel rooms in 2010. Her murderer was a serial killer named Philip Onyancha, who also confessed to having killed another sex worker in Thika. But Peninah's murderer, who attacked her after Onyancha's arrest and may also be responsible for some of the murders that took place before and since her killing, has not been found.

After leaving the hotel, we walked to the area where Peninah used to work near the Coca-Cola roundabout in the center of town. The day she was killed, she was last seen beyond the roundabout walking down a back-street of stores with a client. Her body was found squeezed into a drainage ditch at the end of the alley. Although there were night watchmen along the alley who must have seen the man who had accompanied Peninah, none of them would describe what he looked like when questioned. Her killer has not been caught, and the Thika police have not taken Peninah's murder or the killing of other Thika sex workers seriously.

After Peninah's murder, sex workers in Thika and beyond pooled their money to pay for her autopsy and burial, buy her new clothes ("A sex worker can't be buried in a funeral dress!" they told me), and donate money to her surviving family members. Hundreds of sex workers came from all over Kenya to Thika to protest Peninah's murder, the other unsolved murders of Thika sex workers, and police inaction on the killings. They faced police beatings and harassment during the protest, but they were not deterred. The protest was the first time women in the Thika sex industry publicly referred to themselves as sex workers. "We wanted people to know that we call ourselves sex workers because it is the wheat our families depend on," said Aisha. "The community should know that we exist. And there's no going back." The bravery of activists like Peninah, Aisha, Jina, and Njeri, and that of the many sex workers profiled in this book, who fight for their right to dignity, to health, to work, to reject violence and discrimination—to live freely—will remain the heart of the sex workers' rights movement in Africa.

On that July afternoon in Thika, in the fading sunlight, Aisha, Jina, Njeri, and I walked down the alleyway where Peninah last walked and stood over the ditch at the end of the alley where her body had been discovered. "The day of the protest march, we moved all through Thika holding flowers," they told me, solemnly, hopefully, defiantly. "We brought the flowers to this ditch where she was found and threw them in."

NOTES

INTRODUCTION

1 Cisgender is generally defined as a gender identity that aligns with social expectations of assigned sex at birth.

2 Anna-Louise Crago and Jayne Arnott, *Rights Not Rescue: A Report on Female, Trans, and Male Sex Workers' Human Rights in Botswana, Namibia, and South Africa* (New York: Open Society Institute, 2009), http://www.opensocietyfoundations.org/sites/default/files/rightsnotrescue_20090706.pdf, accessed April 10, 2014; *Documenting Human Rights Violations of Sex Workers in Kenya: A Study Conducted in Nairobi, Kisumu, Busia, Nanyuki, Mombasa and Malindi* (Kenya: Federation of Women Lawyers in Kenya, 2008), 16–19, http://www.opensocietyfoundations.org/sites/default/files/fida_20081201.pdf, accessed April 10, 2014; Fiona Scorgie et al., "Human rights abuses and collective resilience among sex workers in four African countries: a qualitative study," *Globalization and Health* 9, no. 33 (2013), doi:10.1186/1744–8603-9–33; Kathambi Kinoti, "Sex Work in Southern Africa: Criminalization Provides Screen for Other Rights Violations," *Association for Women's Rights in Development*, February 20, 2009, http://awid.org/eng/Library/Review-of-Rights-not-Rescue, accessed April 10, 2014; *"Treat Us Like Human Beings": Discrimination against Sex Workers, Sexual and Gender Minorities, and People Who Use Drugs in Tanzania* (New York: Human Rights Watch, 2013), http://www.hrw.org/sites/default/files/reports/tanzania0613webwcover_0_0.pdf, accessed April 10, 2014; Vivienne Lalu, "Considering decriminalization of sex work as a health issue in South Africa: The experience of SWEAT," *Exchange on HIV/AIDS, Sexuality and Gender* (Cape Town, South Africa: Oxfam, 2007), 11–13, http://www.kit.nl/net/KIT_Publicaties_output/ShowFile2.aspx?e=1280, accessed April 10, 2014.

3 Kathleen Barry, "Female Sexual Slavery: Understanding the International Dimensions of Women's Oppression," *Human Rights Quarterly* 3, no. 2 (May 1981), doi:10.2307/761856; Kathleen L. Barry, *The Prostitution of Sexuality* (New York and London: New York University Press, 1996); Andrea Dworkin, "Prostitution and Male Supremacy," *Michigan Journal of Gender & Law* 1 (1993): 1–12; Melissa Farley, "Prostitution, Trafficking, and Cultural Amnesia: What We Must Not Know in Order to Keep the Business of Sexual Exploitation Running Smoothly," *Yale Journal of Law & Feminism* 18 (2006): 102–36; Melissa Farley, "Prostitution and the Invisibility of Harm," *Women & Therapy* 26 (2003): 247–80, doi:10.1300/J015v26n03_06; Catharine MacKinnon, "Prostitution and Civil Rights," *Michigan Journal of Gender*

& *Law* 1 (1993): 13–31; Catharine A. MacKinnon, "Trafficking, Prostitution, and Inequality," *Harvard Civil Rights–Civil Liberties Law Review* 46 (2011): 271–309.

4 Aziza Ahmed and Meena Seshu, "'We Have the Right Not to Be Rescued': When Anti-Trafficking Programmes Undermine the Health and Well-Being of Sex Workers," *Anti-Trafficking Review*, no. 1 (2012): 149–65; Melissa Ditmore, "Trafficking and Sex Work: A Problematic Conflation" (PhD dissertation, City University of New York, 2002), Proquest Central (Document Number: 276259451); Melissa Ditmore, "Sex Work, Trafficking: Understanding the Difference," *RH Reality Check*, May 6, 2008, http://rhrealitycheck.org/article/2008/05/06/sex-work-trafficking-understanding-difference/, accessed April 10, 2014; Ann Jordan, "Human Rights or Wrongs? The Struggle for a Rights-Based Response to Trafficking in Human Beings," *Gender and Development* 10, no. 1 (2002): 28–37, doi:10.1080/13552070215891; Juhu Thukral, "To Address Human Trafficking, the United States Must Take a New Approach," *RH Reality Check*, October 2, 2012, http://rhrealitycheck.org/article/2012/10/02/in-handling-sex-trafficking-crisis-president-obama-may-not-be-getting-it-right/, accessed April 10, 2014; Juhu Thukral, "Human Rights and Trafficking," *Sh'ma: A Journal of Jewish Ideas* 39, no. 653 (2008): 6–7; Aziza Ahmed, "Think Again: Prostitution: Why Zero Tolerance Makes for Bad Policy on World's Oldest Profession," *Foreign Policy*, January 19, 2014, http://www.foreignpolicy.com/articles/2014/01/19/think_again_prostitution, accessed April 10, 2014.

5 "Laws and Policies Affecting Sex Work: A Reference Brief" (Open Society Foundations, New York, 2012), http://www.opensocietyfoundations.org/sites/default/files/sex-work-laws-policies-20120713.pdf, accessed April 10, 2014; *HIV and the Law: Risks, Rights and Health* (New York: Global Commission on HIV and the Law, July 2012), 36–38, http://www.hivlawcommission.org/resources/report/FinalReport-Risks,Rights&Health-EN.pdf, accessed April 10, 2014. According to the Global Commission on HIV and the Law, of the 196 countries and territories in the world, 116 of them criminalize sex work. Only 80 countries and territories provide some form of legal protection for sex work, while 13 countries have no information available. Ibid.

6 Kamala Kempadoo and Jo Doezema, eds., *Global Sex Workers: Rights, Resistance, and Redefinition* (New York: Routledge, 1998). The history of the global sex workers' rights movement will be covered in more detail in the Epilogue. The growing international sex workers' rights movement can be seen in the members of the Global Network of Sex Work Projects, which hosts more than 150 organizations from Africa, Asia and the Pacific, Europe, Latin America and the Caribbean, and North America. Specifically, members hail from Antigua and Barbuda, Australia, Austria, Bangladesh, Bosnia and Herzegovina, Botswana, Brazil, Cambodia, Cameroon, Canada, China, Côte d'Ivoire, the Democratic Republic of the Congo, East Timor, Ecuador, Ethiopia, Fiji, France, Georgia, Germany, Guyana, Hong Kong, Hungary, India, Indonesia, Jamaica, Japan, Kazakhstan, Kenya, Kyrgyzstan, Lithuania, Macedonia, Mexico, Montenegro, Myanmar, the Netherlands, Netherlands Antilles, Nigeria, Norway, Pakistan, Papua New Guinea, Peru, Portugal, Russia, Saint Lucia,

Serbia, South Africa, Spain, Sweden, Switzerland, Tajikistan, Tanzania, Thailand, Trinidad and Tobago, Turkey, Uganda, Ukraine, the United Kingdom, the United States, and Zimbabwe. "Where Our Members Work," *NSWP: Global Network of Sex Work Projects*, n.d., http://www.nswp.org/members, accessed April 10, 2014.

7 During a trip to Poipet, a small town in northwestern Cambodia, Nicholas Kristof met two female teenagers—Srey Neth and Srey Mom. Kristof characterized them as indebted to their brothel owners and forced to work as prostitutes. Kristof writes that he bought both Srey Neth and Srey Mom for $150 USD and $203 USD, respectively. He then drove them back to their home villages, where they were reunited with their families and given $100 USD each to start small businesses. In "Loss of Innocence," Kristof reveals that, after a fight with her mother, Srey Mom returned to work at her old brothel. Nicholas Kristof, "Girls for Sale," *New York Times*, January 17, 2004, http://www.nytimes.com/2004/01/17/opinion/girls-for-sale.html, accessed April 10, 2014; Nicholas Kristof, "Bargaining for Freedom," *New York Times*, January 21, 2004, http://www.nytimes.com/2004/01/21/opinion/bargaining-for-freedom.html, accessed April 10, 2014; Nicholas Kristof, "Going Home, with Hope," *New York Times*, January 24, 2004, http://www.nytimes.com/2004/01/24/opinion/going-home-with-hope.html, accessed April 10, 2014; Nicholas Kristof, "Loss of Innocence," *New York Times*, January 28, 2004, http://www.nytimes.com/2004/01/28/opinion/loss-of-innocence.html, accessed April 10, 2014. Critics of Kristof argued that his actions and writings regarding Srey Neth and Srey Mom oversimplified the socioeconomic factors surrounding the sex industry in an attempt to justify his neocolonial intervention in these young women's lives. Katha Pollitt, "Kristof to the Rescue?," *The Nation*, February 12, 2004, http://www.thenation.com/article/kristof-rescue#, accessed April 10, 2014; Larissa Sandy, "Just Choices: Representations of Choice and Coercion in Sex Work in Cambodia," *The Australian Journal of Anthropology* 18, no. 2 (2007): 194–206, doi:10.1111/j.1835–9310.2007.tb00088.x.

8 Kathleen Barry has called sex workers' rights activists the "pro-prostitution lobby" and argues that such activists perpetuate the continued control of sex workers by "pimps." Kathleen Barry, "Pimping: The World's Oldest Profession," *On the Issues Magazine*, Summer 1995, http://www.ontheissuesmagazine.com/1995summer/pimping.php, accessed April 10, 2014. Gloria Steinem called sex worker activist groups and the foundations that support them in India the "trafficking lobby." "'This Trip Was Life-Changing,'" *The Telegraph*, April 22, 2012, http://www.telegraphindia.com/1120422/jsp/calcutta/story_15393912.jsp#.Uz3HJ1cVBz, accessed April 10, 2014.

9 The Global Coalition on Women and AIDS, "Violence against Women and HIV/AIDS: Critical Intersections: Violence against Sex Workers and HIV Prevention," Information Bulletin Series (citing the WHO HIV/AIDS Sex Work Toolkit) (World Health Organization, 2005), no. 3, http://www.who.int/gender/documents/sex-workers.pdf, accessed April 10, 2014; WHO Department of HIV/AIDS, *Prevention and Treatment of HIV and Other Sexually Transmitted Infections for Sex Workers in Low- and Middle-Income Countries* (World Health Organization, 2012) 8, 17, http://www.who.int/hiv/pub/guidelines/sex_worker/en/, accessed April 10, 2014;

Consolidated Guidelines on HIV Prevention, Diagnosis, Treatment and Care for Key Populations (World Health Organization, 2014) 91, http://apps.who.int/iris/bitstr eam/10665/128048/1/9789241507431_eng.pdf?ua=1&ua=1, accessed April 10, 2014.

10 *Sex Work and the Law in Asia and the Pacific: Laws, HIV and Human Rights in the Context of Sex Work* (United Nations Development Programme, 2012), http://www.snap-undp.org/elibrary/Publications/HIV-2012-SexWorkAndLaw.pdf, accessed April 10, 2014.

11 UN Women, "Note on Sex Work, Sexual Exploitation and Trafficking" (United Nations Entity for Gender Equality and the Empowerment of Women, 2014), http://www.nswp.org/sites/nswp.org/files/UN%20Women's%20note%20on%20sex%20 work%20sexual%20exploitation%20and%20trafficking.pdf, accessed April 10, 2014.

12 UNAIDS, "UNAIDS Guidance Note on HIV and Sex Work" (Joint United Nations Programme on HIV/AIDS, 2009), 16–17, http://www.unaids.org/en/media/unaids/contentassets/documents/unaidspublication/2009/JC2306_UNAIDS-guidance-note-HIV-sex-work_en.pdf, accessed April 10, 2014; "UNAIDS Briefing Note: The Legal Status of Sex Work: Key Human Rights and Public Health Considerations" (UNAIDS, February 2014) 2, http://www.nswp.org/sites/nswp.org/files/sexwork_brief-21feb2014.pdf, accessed April 10, 2014.

13 ILO, "Leaving No One Behind: Reaching Key Populations through Workplace Action on HIV and AIDS" (International Labour Organization, 2014) 34–36, http://www.ilo.org/wcmsp5/groups/public/—-ed_protect/—-protrav/—-ilo_aids/documents/publication/wcms_249782.pdf, accessed April 10, 2014.

14 United Nations Human Rights Council (HRC), Session 23/36, "Report of the Special Rapporteur on Extreme Poverty and Human Rights, Ms. Magdalena Sepúlveda Carmona," 12, May 17, 2013, http://www.ohchr.org/Documents/HRBodies/HRCouncil/RegularSession/Session23/A-HRC-23-36-Add1_en.pdf, accessed April 10, 2014; United Nations Human Rights Council (HRC), Session 14/20, "Report of the Special Rapporteur on the right of everyone to the enjoyment of the highest attainable standard of physical and mental health, Anand Grover," April 27, 2010, http://www2.ohchr.org/english/bodies/hrcouncil/docs/14session/A.HRC.14.20.pdf, accessed April 10, 2014; United Nations Human Rights Council (HRC), Session 22/53, "Report of the Special Rapporteur on torture and other cruel, inhuman or degrading treatment or punishment, Juan E. Méndez," 18, February 1, 2013, http://www.ohchr.org/Documents/HRBodies/HRCouncil/RegularSession/Session22/A.HRC.22.53_English.pdf, accessed April 10, 2014.

15 The Lancet Editorial Board, "Sex Workers and HIV—Forgotten and Ostracised," *The Lancet* 380, no. 9838 (July 21, 2012): 188, doi:10.1016/S0140-6736(12)61197-0.

16 "HIV and Sex Workers," *The Lancet* (July 22, 2014), http://www.thelancet.com/series/HIV-and-sex-workers, accessed April 10, 2014; Kate Shannon et al., "Global epidemiology of HIV among female sex workers: influence of structural determinants," *The Lancet*, Early Online Publication (July 22, 2014), doi:10.1016/S0140-6736(14)60931-4.

17 *HIV and the Law: Risks, Rights and Health*, 38.

18 Ibid., 39.

19 Ibid., 10.

20 Margaret H. Wurth et al., "Condoms as Evidence of Prostitution in the United States and the Criminalization of Sex Work," *Journal of the International AIDS Society* 16 (1), 2 (May 24, 2013), doi:10.7448/IAS.16.1.18626; *World Report 2014* 47 (Human Rights Watch, 2014), http://www.hrw.org/sites/default/files/reports/wr2014_web_0.pdf, accessed April 10, 2014.

21 "East African Sex Workers Share Their Stories in a New Publication," *Open Society Foundations*, July 6, 2010, http://www.opensocietyfoundations.org/press-releases/east-african-sex-workers-share-their-stories-new-publication, accessed April 10, 2014; "Fighting Violence against Sex Workers in Central and Eastern Europe and Central Asia," *Open Society Foundations*, December 17, 2008, http://www.opensocietyfoundations.org/press-releases/fighting-violence-against-sex-workers-central-and-eastern-europe-and-central-asia, accessed April 10, 2014; "Fostering Enabling Legal and Policy Environments for Sex Workers' Health and Human Rights," *Open Society Foundations*, June 22, 2006, http://www.opensocietyfounda-tions.org/events/fostering-enabling-legal-and-policy-environments-sex-workers-health-and-human-rights, accessed April 10, 2014; "Legal Empowerment Program Increases Access to Justice for Sex Workers in South Africa," *Open Society Founda-tions*, September 5, 2011, http://www.opensocietyfoundations.org/press-releases/legal-empowerment-program-increases-access-justice-sex-workers-south-africa, accessed April 10, 2014.

22 Chi Mgbako, "Why the Women's Rights Movement Must Listen to Sex Workers," *RH Reality Check*, May 22, 2012, http://rhrealitycheck.org/article/2012/05/22/why-women%E2%80%99s-rights-movement-must-listen-to-sex-workers/, accessed April 10, 2014.

23 Kay Thi Win, "Chairperson of APNSW Address at AWID Forum" (Istanbul, Turkey, April 21, 2012), http://apnsw.wordpress.com/2012/04/21/plenary-speech-by-kaythi-win-chairperson-of-apnsw-at-awid-forum-in-istanbul-21-april-2012/, accessed April 10, 2014; Mgbako, "Why the Women's Rights Movement Must Listen to Sex Workers."

24 "GCWA: Statement of support on the International Day for Sex Workers: June 2, 2014," *Global Coalition on Women and AIDS*, June 2, 2014, http://gcwa.unaids.org/news/gcwa-statement-support-international-day-sex-workers-june-2–2014, ac-cessed April 10, 2014.

25 A precursor to this study is the book *Global Sex Workers: Rights, Resistance, and Redefinition*, edited by Kamala Kempadoo and Jo Doezema, which focuses on sex work in Côte d'Ivoire, Ghana, Senegal, and South Africa, among many oth-ers countries in the Global South. It was the first book that explored sex worker organizing in the Global South. Another precursor is a booklet entitled *When I Dare to Be Powerful: On the Road to a Sexual Rights Movement in East Africa*, by Zawadi Nyong'o and published by Akina Mama wa Afrika, an East African women's rights NGO. The booklet sought to dispel the many stereotypes and misconceptions about sex workers in Africa by presenting alternative narratives from sex workers themselves. *When I Dare to Be Powerful: On the Road to a Sexual Rights Movement in East Africa* (Nairobi, Kenya: Akina Mama wa Afrika, 2010), http://www.oozebap.org/dones/biblio/Sex_Worker.pdf, accessed April 10, 2014.

26 Because sex workers are a criminalized population, it is difficult to assess accurately the number of people working in the sex industries in all of the countries in this study. Sex workers in Kenya are thought to number roughly 200,000, while sex workers in South Africa number more than 182,000. "Good Practice in Sex Worker–Led HIV Programming" (Global Network of Sex Work Projects, Edinburgh, Scotland, UK, 2014), 10, 16, http://www.nswp.org/sites/nswp.org/files/Global%20Report%20English.pdf, accessed April 10, 2014. There is very little evidence on the number of sex workers in Botswana, Mauritius, Namibia, Nigeria, and Uganda.

27 Sylvia Tamale, "Paradoxes of Sex Work and Sexuality in Modern-Day Uganda," *East African Journal of Peace and Human Rights* 15, no. 1 (2009): 69–109. Tamale notes that the literature on feminist engagement with sex work in Uganda specifically and Africa generally is very slim. Ibid., 10, 12.

28 Sociologist Carol Queen has argued that "sex-positive" feminism does not "denigrate, medicalize, or demonize any form of sexual expression except that which is not consensual." Carol Queen, "Sex Radical Politics, Sex-Positive Feminist Thought, and Whore Stigma," in *Identity Politics in the Women's Movement*, ed. Barbara Ryan (New York and London: New York University Press, 2001), 94. In general, though, my interviewees did not predominantly appeal to a sex-positive or sexual liberation framework when crafting sex workers' rights arguments within the African context. They overwhelmingly placed more emphasis on a labor rights appeal and their right to work safely.

29 Marlise Richter, "Sex Work as a Test Case for African Feminism," *BUWA! A Journal on African Women's Experiences*, 2012, 66 (internal citations omitted), http://www.osisa.org/sites/default/files/sex_work_as_a_test_case_for_african_feminism62–69.pdf, accessed April 10, 2014.

30 I explore the early history of feminist solidarity with sex worker movement building in Uganda in chapter 5.

31 *Revolving Door: An Analysis of Street-Based Prostitution in New York City* (Urban Justice Center's Sex Workers Project, 2003), 44, 47, http://sexworkersproject.org/publications/reports/revolving-door/, accessed April 10, 2014.

32 *Sex Workers at Risk: Condoms as Evidence of Prostitution in Four US Cities* (New York: Human Rights Watch, 2012), http://www.hrw.org/sites/default/files/reports/us0712ForUpload_1.pdf, accessed April 10, 2014; Acacia Shields, *Criminalizing Condoms: How Policing Practices Put Sex Workers and HIV Services at Risk in Kenya, Namibia, Russia, South Africa, the United States, and Zimbabwe* (Open Society Foundations, July 2012), http://www.opensocietyfoundations.org/sites/default/files/criminalizing-condoms-20120717.pdf, accessed April 10, 2014.

33 "About December 17," *December 17: International Day to End Violence against Sex Workers*, 2014, http://www.december17.org/about/, accessed April 10, 2014. Gary

Ridgway murdered forty-eight young women over the course of sixteen years during the 1980s and 1990s. Many of the women, some as young as sixteen, were sex workers or youth involved in the sex industry whom Ridgway strangled. He then disposed of their bodies in wooded areas around Kings County, Washington. It took two decades for the police to solve these murders and bring Ridgway to justice. Matthew Preusch, "Families Speak as Green River Killer Gets 48 Life Terms," *New York Times*, December 19, 2003, http://www.nytimes.com/2003/12/19/us/families-speak-as-green-river-killer-gets-48-life-terms.html?ref=garyleonridgway, accessed April 10, 2014.

34 Kathleen N. Deering et al., "A Systematic Review of the Correlates of Violence against Sex Workers," *American Journal of Public Health* E-View ahead of Print (2014), doi:10.2105/AJPH.2014.301909; Michael D.E. Goodyear and Linda Cusick, "Protection of Sex Workers: Decriminalisation Could Restore Public Health Priorities and Human Rights," *BMJ* 334 (2007): 52–53, doi:10.1136/bmj.39063.645532.BE; *Westminster Sex Worker Task Group: Violence Faced by Sex Workers in Westminster: Recommendations Report* (Westminster Sex Worker Task Group, 2012), https://www.westminster.gov.uk/sites/default/files/uploads/workspace/assets/publications/FINAL-Westminster-Sex-Workers-Rep-1365592773.pdf, accessed April 10, 2014; Kate Shannon et al., "Prevalence and Structural Correlates of Gender Based Violence Among a Prospective Cohort of Female Sex Workers," *BMJ* 339, no. 442–49 (2009), doi:10.1136/bmj.b2939; *VIH et commerce du sexe. Garantir l'accès universel à la prévention et aux soins* (France: Conseil national du sida, Septembre 2010), 14–20, http://www.cns.sante.fr/IMG/pdf/2010–09–16_avi_fr_prevention-2.pdf, accessed April 10, 2014.

35 *Arrest the Violence: Human Rights Abuses against Sex Workers in Central and Eastern Europe and Central Asia* (Sex Workers' Rights Advocacy Network in Central and Eastern Europe and Central Asia, November 2009), 20, http://www.opensocietyfoundations.org/sites/default/files/arrest-violence-20091217.pdf, accessed April 10, 2014.

36 Carol Jenkins, *Violence and Exposure to HIV Among Sex Workers in Phnom Penh, Cambodia* (USAID, March 2006), 26, tbl. 11, http://www.hivpolicy.org/Library/HPP001702.pdf, accessed April 10, 2014.

37 *"Swept Away": Abuses against Sex Workers in China* (Human Rights Watch, 2013), http://www.hrw.org/sites/default/files/reports/china0513_ForUpload_0.pdf, accessed April 10, 2014. The international media extensively covered this report. See, for example, Tania Branigan, "China's Anti-Prostitution Policies 'Lead to Increase in Abuse of Sex Workers,'" *The Guardian*, May 13, 2013, http://www.theguardian.com/world/2013/may/14/china-prostitution-increase-abuse-workers, accessed April 10, 2014; Deborah Kan, "Report Says China Police Abuse Sex Workers," Interview (*Wall Street Journal*, n.d.), http://live.wsj.com/video/report-says-china-police-abuse-sex-workers/E4AB79AD-C0BB-44EF-8F2A-61B633A5C6DE.html#!E4AB79AD-C0BB-44EF-8F2A-61B633A5C6DE, accessed April 10, 2014; Grace Li, "Rights Group Urges China to Repeal Penalties against Sex Workers," *Reuters*, May 14, 2013, http://www.reuters.com/article/2013/05/14/china-sexworker-

idUSL3N0DV04V20130514, accessed April 10, 2014; Louise Watt, "Sex Workers in China Subject to Police Abuse, Human Rights Watch Says," *Huffington Post*, May 13, 2013, http://www.huffingtonpost.com/2013/05/15/sex-workers-in-china-subj_n_3278228.html, accessed April 10, 2014.

38 Jo Doezema argues that anti-trafficking activists and scholars who view and portray sex workers as disempowered victims perpetuate a single-story narrative that is not only exclusionary in nature but also imperialist. Jo Doezema, "Ouch! Western Feminists' 'Wounded Attachment' to the 'Third World Prostitute,'" *Feminist Review* 67 (2001): 16–38. Doezema argues that the identity of "third world prostitutes" is orientalist and imperialist, using Liddle and Rai's definition that orientalist power is exercised discursively when the author (1) "denies the subject the opportunity for self representation" and (2) Western civilization is portrayed as "more advanced." Ibid., 28 (quoting Joanna Liddle and Shirin Rai, "Feminism, Imperialism and Orientalism: The Challenge of the 'Indian Woman,'" *Women's History Review*, December 2006, 512). Abolitionist scholars often portray sex workers as victims of their "backward" cultures, which drive women into sex work by devaluing their humanity. See, for example, Barry, *The Prostitution of Sexuality*, 49–52 (trafficking of women "prevails especially in pre-industrial feudal societies . . . where women are excluded from the public sphere. Women's reduction to sex is a fact of their status as the property of their husbands"). Doezema and others argue that, viewed through this lens of analysis, Western abolitionists can be seen as neo-imperialists seeking to "rescue" the "degraded third-world prostitute." Doezema, "Ouch! Western Feminists' 'Wounded Attachment' to the 'Third World Prostitute,'" 16–32; Svati P. Shah, "Prostitution, Sex Work and Violence: Discursive and Political Contexts for Five Texts on Paid Sex, 1987–2001," *Gender & History* 16, no. 3 (November 2004): 794–812; Prabha Kotiswaran, *Dangerous Sex, Invisible Labor: Sex Work and the Law in India* (Princeton and London: Princeton University Press, 2011).

39 I edited the six first-person narratives included in this study for length, clarity, and narrative flow, ensuring that these edits did not change the meaning or intention of the interviewees' words.

40 I did not include representation from North Africa in this study because of a lack of visible formal sex worker–led organizing in the countries in that region.

41 I use the term *prostitute* in this study only in the historical sense, because *sex worker* was not a term used during pre-colonial or colonial times. The Mau Mau uprising against the British colonial state took place between 1952 and 1960. According to historian Luise White, in the early 1950s around 400 prostitutes took oaths of loyalty to the Mau Mau, agreeing to collect information for or contribute money to the Mau Mau revolt. Prostitutes' activism during the colonial era, White argues, was part of a significant and larger history of women's political activism. Luise White, *The Comforts of Home: Prostitution in Colonial Nairobi* (Chicago and London: University of Chicago Press, 1990), 204–7.

42 I asked the interviewees questions on a wide range of topics, including entry into sex work, attitudes regarding traditional feminist debates over prostitution, hu-

man rights abuses experienced by sex workers, history of formal and informal sex worker organizing, movement strategies, diversity within the movement, and the global sex workers' rights movement.

CHAPTER 1. "OUR HOUSE'S FOUNDATION"

1 I explore the relationship between SWEAT and Sisonke in detail in chapter 4.

2 World Health Organization, "Category 3: Implementation: Implementation Basics," *HIV/AIDS Sex Work Toolkit*, http://www.who.int/hiv/topics/vct/sw_toolkit/implementation/en/, accessed April 10, 2014; UNAIDS, "UNAIDS Guidance Note on HIV and Sex Work."

3 DMSC runs a variety of outreach programs focused on sex workers and their families. These programs include combating the HIV/AIDS epidemic through medical intervention, community building, and social services; running education programs for sex workers' children; organizing and putting on cultural performances; running a vocational training program; and providing micro-credit loans to sex workers. "Activities," *Durbar Mahila Samanwaya Committee*, n.d., http://durbar.org, accessed April 10, 2014.

4 MacKinnon argues that the noun *prostitute* is misleading in that it doesn't sufficiently express all the social forces that act on women involved in prostitution. She claims that *prostituted* is more accurate because these women are prostitutes only because of "choices precluded, options restricted, possibilities denied." MacKinnon, "Trafficking, Prostitution, and Inequality," 273–74; in a talk at Carleton College, Norma Ramos, the executive director of the anti-prostitution organization Coalition against Trafficking in Women (CATW), noted that she used the term *prostituted women* to demonstrate how women cannot choose to enter prostitution but rather are forced into it. Beth Budnick, "Convo Speaker Deals with 'the World's Oldest Oppression,'" *The Carletonian*, April 6, 2010, http://apps.carleton.edu/carletonian/?story_id=624530&issue_id=624502, accessed April 10, 2014.

5 Rachira Gupta, the founder and president of Apne Aap, an anti-prostitution organization in India, denounced DMSC's work, saying that the Sonagachi model "actually disempowers girls and protects the sex industry, which is not helping the girls." Mohua Das, "Workshop Focus on Sex Trafficking," *Calcutta Telegraph*, December 15, 2012, http://www.telegraphindia.com/1121215/jsp/calcutta/story_16312582.jsp#.U3KTIygVBzs, accessed April 10, 2014. Gupta argues that organizations seeking to provide condoms to sex workers for HIV/AIDS prevention help to legitimize the prostitution industry, which she sees as inextricably tied to sex trafficking. Richard Wolf, "Fights against AIDS, Sex Traffic Collide at High Court," *USA Today*, April 21, 2013, http://www.usatoday.com/story/news/politics/2013/04/21/supreme-court-prostitution-sex-trafficking-hiv-aids/2097619/, accessed April 10, 2014. Norma Ramos of CATW argues that "HIV policy is designed to protect men from disease rather than women from violence" and advocates against U.S. funding for human rights and health organizations that provide essential lifesaving services to sex workers. Ibid.

6 Fatoumata Sire Diakite, "Prostitution in Mali" (February 1999), http://www.uri.edu/artsci/wms/hughes/mhvmali.htm, accessed April 10, 2014.

7 Chimamanda Ngozi Adichie, *The Danger of a Single Story*, Ted Talk Global, 2009, http://www.ted.com/talks/chimamanda_adichie_the_danger_of_a_single_story, accessed April 10, 2014.

8 Ibid., 5:00.

9 Ibid., 6:27.

10 Ibid., 13:27.

11 There are disputed definitions of what constitutes trafficking. The United Nations Protocol to Prevent, Suppress and Punish Trafficking in Persons, Especially Women and Children (Palermo Protocol) defines trafficking as:

> [T]he recruitment, transportation, transfer, harbouring or receipt of persons, by means of the threat or use of force or other forms of coercion, of abduction, of fraud, of deception, of the abuse of power or of a position of vulnerability or of the giving or receiving of payments or benefits to achieve the consent of a person having control over another person, for the purpose of exploitation. Exploitation shall include, at a minimum, the exploitation of the prostitution of others or other forms of sexual exploitation, forced labour or services, slavery or practices similar to slavery, servitude or the removal of organs.

12 Agustín, *Sex at the Margins*, 36–41; Aziza Ahmed, "'We Have the Right Not to Be Rescued'"; Janie A. Chuang, "Rescuing Trafficking from Ideological Capture: Prostitution Reform and Anti-Trafficking Law and Policy," *University of Pennsylvania Law Review* 158 (2010): 1655–728; Ditmore, "Sex Work, Trafficking"; Ditmore, "Trafficking and Sex Work"; Melissa Gira Grant, "The War on Sex Workers," *Reason* 44, no. 9 (February 2013): 31–36; Melissa Gira Grant, "The Truth about Trafficking: It's Not Just about Sexual Exploitation," *The Guardian*, October 24, 2012, http://www.theguardian.com/commentisfree/2012/oct/24/truth-about-trafficking-sexual-exploitation, accessed April 10, 2014; Ann Jordan, "Human Rights or Wrongs?"; Ann Jordan, "Sex Trafficking: The Abolitionist Fallacy," *Foreign Policy in Focus*, March 18, 2009, http://fpif.org/sex_trafficking_the_abolitionist_fallacy/, accessed April 10, 2014; Prabha Kotiswaran, "Vulnerability in Domestic Discourses on Trafficking: Lessons from the Indian Experience," *Feminist Legal Studies* 20 (2012): 245–62, doi:10.1007/s10691-012-9211-z; Svati P. Shah, "Prostitution, Sex Work and Violence"; Svati P. Shah, "Sex Work in the Global Economy," *New Labor Forum* 12, no. 1 (Spring 2003): 78–81; Ronald Weitzer, "The Mythology of Prostitution: Advocacy Research and Public Policy," *Sexuality Research & Social Policy* 7, no. 1 (15–29); Ronald Weitzer, "Sex Trafficking and the Sex Industry: The Need for Evidence-Based Theory and Legislation," *The Journal of Criminal Law and Criminology* 101, no. 4 (2012): 1337–69.

13 For a recent and interesting exploration of trafficking into forced labor, see Denise Brennan, *Life Interrupted: Trafficking into Forced Labor in the United States* (Durham and London: Duke University Press, 2014).

14 CD4 is a type of white blood cell count that is an important indicator of the immune system's strength.

15 Barry, *The Prostitution of Sexuality*, 23; Farley, "Prostitution and the Invisibility of Harm," 249; MacKinnon, "Trafficking, Prostitution, and Inequality," 281.

16 Laura Agustín, "Naked Musings on Borders, Illegality and Personal Identity," *The Naked Anthropologist*, May 12, 2013, http://www.lauraagustin.com/naked-musings-on-borders-illegality-and-personal-identity, accessed April 10, 2014.

17 White, *The Comforts of Home*, 2.

18 Ibid., 2, 29–50, 119–24.

19 Melinda Chateauvert, *Sex Workers Unite: A History of the Movement from Stonewall to SlutWalk* (New York: Beacon Press, 2014), 2.

20 Joseph E. Davis, *Stories of Change: Narrative and Social Movements* (Albany: State University of New York Press, 2002), 4; Sidney Tarrow, *The Language of Contention: Revolutions in Words, 1688–2012* (Cambridge: Cambridge University Press, 2013).

21 "*Amandla!*" is a Xhosa and Zulu word meaning "power." "Amandla!" was the rallying cry of the anti-apartheid movement led by the African National Congress (ANC) in South Africa.

22 Umkhonto we Sizwe, which means "spear of the nation," was the armed wing of the ANC. It was co-founded by Nelson Mandela and carried out guerrilla attacks against government installations beginning in December 1961.

23 The Commission on the Status of Women is a functional commission of the United Nations Economic and Social Council. It is the main international policymaking organization that is dedicated to gender equality and the advancement of women. "Overview," *Commission on the Status of Women*, n.d., http://www.un.org/womenwatch/daw/csw/index.html, accessed April 10, 2014.

24 South Africa Const. Ch. 2, § 22.

CHAPTER 2. "IN A DARK PLACE THERE'S NO LIGHT"

1 "Ten Reasons to Decriminalize Sex Work," *Open Society Foundations*, accessed March 19, 2014, http://www.opensocietyfoundations.org/sites/default/files/decriminalize-sex-work-20120713.pdf, accessed March 24, 2014; *Arrest the Violence*; Acacia Shields, *Criminalizing Condoms*; Crago and Arnott, *Rights Not Rescue*; UNAIDS, "UNAIDS Guidance Note on HIV and Sex Work," 5; Kate Shannon and Joanne Ceste, "Condom Negotiation and HIV/STI Risk Among Sex Workers," *The Journal of the American Medical Association* 304 (August 2010): 573–74, doi:10.1001/jama.2010.1090; UNAIDS Advisory Group on HIV and Sex Work, "Report of the UNAIDS Advisory Group on HIV and Sex Work, Geneva, 2011" Health Systems Trust, http://www.hst.org.za/sites/default/files/20111215_Report-UNAIDS-Advisory-group-HIV-Sex-Work_en.pdf, accessed March 24, 2014.

2 Mauritius, *Criminal Code (Cap 195), 253*, 1838; South Africa, *Sexual Offences Act (Act No. 23)*, 2, 9, 12A, 15, 19, 20, 1957 (amended 1988); Uganda, *Penal Code Act of 1950*, 131, 132, 136–39, 1950.

3 Richter, "Sex Work as a Test Case for African Feminism."

4 Sylvia Tamale, "Paradoxes of Sex Work and Sexuality in Modern-Day Uganda," in *African Sexualities: A Reader*, ed. Sylvia Tamale, 154 (Cape Town: Pambazuka Press, 2011).

5 Botswana, *Offences against Morality*, http://www.wipo.int/wipolex/en/text.jsp?file_id=238601, accessed March 24, 2014; Namibia, *Combating Immoral Practices Act (Act 21 of 1980)*, 2, 5, 10, 1980; Nigeria, *Offences against Morality*. Chapter 21, http://www.nigeria-law.org/Criminal%20Code%20Act-PartIII-IV.htm#Chapter%20 21, accessed March 24, 2014; Kenya, *Woman Living on Earnings of Prostitution or Aiding, Etc., Prostitution*, Chapter XV, http://www.kenyalaw.org/Downloads/Grey-Book/8.%20The%20Penal%20Code.pdf, accessed March 24, 2014.

6 Prostitution is legalized in Senegal, but it is not decriminalized. Chapter 6 explores the difference between legalization and decriminalization in detail.

7 Angelique Arde, "It's the Oldest Form of Oppression," Coalition Against Trafficking in Women, August 22, 2011, http://www.catwinternational.org/Home/Article/214-its-the-oldest-form-of-oppression, accessed March 24, 2014.

8 Martha C. Nussbaum, "Whether from Reason or Prejudice: Taking Money for Bodily Services," *The Journal of Legal Studies* 27 (1998): 707.

9 Gail Pheterson, *The Prostitution Prism* (Amsterdam: Amsterdam University Press, 1996).

10 In fact, anti-prostitution reformers seem to believe that more police presence in sex workers' lives is the answer. Anti-prostitution activists along with Christian evangelicals and conservative policymakers have made the sex industry a prime target of their anti-trafficking initiatives, both in the United States and abroad. Sociologist Elizabeth Bernstein has termed this form of activism focusing primarily on penal solutions "carceral feminism." Bernstein argues that one of the consequences of carceral feminism has been an "unprecedented police crackdown on people of color who are involved in the street-based sexual economy—including pimps, clients and sex workers alike." Elizabeth Bernstein, "Militarized Humanitarianism Meets Carceral Feminism: The Politics of Sex, Rights, and Freedom in Contemporary Antitrafficking Campaigns," *Signs: Journal of Women in Culture and Society* 36:1 (2010): 57.

11 *"Welcome to Hell Fire": Torture and Other Ill-Treatment in Nigeria* (London: Amnesty International, 2014), 32–34.

12 South Africa, *Criminal Procedure Act of 1977*, 252A, 1977.

13 "Whore stigma" in particular extends to all women who are perceived to go against "compulsory virtue." Melissa Gira Grant, *Playing the Whore: The Work of Sex Work* (New York and London: Verso, 2014), 75–77; Pheterson, *The Prostitution Prism*; Jill Nagle, ed., *Whores and Other Feminists* (New York: Routledge, 1997). I use the term *whorephobia* specifically to describe the phenomenon of the social fear and hatred of sex workers.

14 Emmanuel Akyeampong, "Sexuality and Prostitution among the Akan of the Gold Coast c. 1650–1950," *Past and Present* 156 (1997): 156; Nwando Achebe, *The Female King of Colonial Nigeria: Ahebi Ugbabe* (Bloomington: Indiana University Press,

2011), 77–86. Chapter 7 includes a more in-depth exploration of pre-colonial prostitution in Africa.

15 Makalo, "Gambia: Prostitutes Heighten Danger of HIV/Aids," February 14, 2003, http://allafrica.com/stories/200302140179.html, accessed March 24, 2014; Elizabeth Adinoyi, "Nigeria: Eradicating Prostitution in Our Societies," *Daily Trust (Abuja)*, October 17, 2002, http://allafrica.com/stories/200210170187.html, accessed March 24, 2014; Barolong Seboni, "Botswana: Male Prostitution," *Mmegi/The Reporter (Gaborone)*, December 2, 2006, http://allafrica.com/stories/200612040259.html, accessed March 24, 2014; Martha Eshun-Oppong, "Ghana: Women Say No to Legalisation of Prostitution," *Accra Mail (Accra)*, April 22, 2005, http://allafrica.com/stories/200504220611.html, accessed March 24, 2014; Grace Mutandwa, "Zimbabwe: Child Prostitutes—A Reflection of Bad Parenting," *Zimbabwe Standard (Harare)*, September 18, 2011, http://allafrica.com/stories/201109190322.html, accessed March 24, 2014; Alfred Byenkya, "Uganda: Avoid the Temptation to Legalise Prostitution," *New Vision (Kampala)*, September 24, 2006, http://allafrica.com/stories/200609250343.html, accessed March 24, 2014.

16 The medical faculties of the University of Manitoba and the University of Nairobi launched research and treatment clinics known as the Sex Worker Outreach Program (SWOP). SWOP clinics provide public health services such as HIV and STI treatment and prevention services. "Kenya AIDS Control Project," http://unitid.uonbi.ac.ke/sites/default/files/chs/unitid/unitid/KACP%20informant_2.pdf, accessed March 24, 2014; Wits Reproductive Health and HIV Institute (WHRI) is an institute of the Faculty of Health and Sciences of the University of Witwatersrand. WHRI works extensively in the southern African region in collaboration with WHO and UNAIDS, providing services and outreach to male and female sex workers. "WHRI," Wits Reproductive Health and HIV Institutes, http://www.wrhi.ac.za/Pages/default.aspx, accessed March 24, 2014.

17 "Preventing HIV among Sex Workers in Sub-Saharan Africa: A Literature Review," *WHO*, http://www.who.int/hiv/pub/sti/sex_workers_afro/en/, accessed March 27, 2014; "Prevention and Treatment of HIV and Other Sexual Transmitted Infections for Sex Workers in Low and Middle Income Countries," *UNAIDS*, December 2012, http://apps.who.int/iris/bitstream/10665/77745/1/9789241504744_eng.pdf, accessed March 24, 2014; *HIV and the Law: Risks, Rights and Health*.

18 John Agaba, "Activists Oppose Mandatory HIV Testing Plan," *New Vision*, September 12, 2013, http://www.newvision.co.ug/news/647162-activists-oppose-mandatory-hiv-testing-plan.html, accessed March 24, 2014; "Uganda: Bill Threatens Progress on HIV/AIDS," *Human Rights Watch*, November 6, 2009, http://www.hrw.org/news/2009/11/06/uganda-bill-threatens-progress-hivaids, accessed March 24, 2014; "Uganda: Bill Criminalizing HIV/AIDS Transmission Advances in Parliament," *Library of Congress*, July 20, 2011, http://www.loc.gov/lawweb/servlet/lloc_news?disp3_l205402749_text, accessed March 24, 2014.

19 "UNAIDS/WHO Policy Statement on HIV Testing," *UNAIDS*, June 2004, http://data.unaids.org/una-docs/hivtestingpolicy_en.pdf, accessed March 24, 2014.

CHAPTER 3. OUT OF THE SHADOWS

1 Homosexuality is illegal in the following African countries: Algeria, Angola, Benin, Botswana, Burundi, Cameroon, Comoros, Egypt, Eritrea, Ethiopia, Gambia, Ghana, Guinea, Kenya, Lesotho, Liberia, Libya, Malawi, Mauritania, Mauritius, Morocco, Mozambique, Namibia, Nigeria, Sao Tome and Principe, Senegal, Seychelles, Sierra Leone, Somalia, South Sudan, Sudan, Swaziland, Tanzania, Togo, Tunisia, Uganda, Zambia, Zimbabwe. "Amnesty International Facts and Figures," *Amnesty International*, http://www.amnestyusa.org/sites/default/files/making_love_a_crime_-_facts__figures.pdf, accessed March 18, 2014.

2 "Homosexuality is against African norms and traditions, even in religion it is considered a great sin," former Kenyan President Daniel Arap Moi once said. "Being Gay in Kenya," news24 Archives, February 22, 2006, http://www.news24.com/Africa/Features/Being-gay-in-Kenya-20060222, accessed March 18, 2014; Robert Mugabe has called homosexuality "un-African" and a "white disease." Bernardine Evaristo, "The Idea That African Homosexuality Was a Colonial Import Is a Myth," *The Guardian*, March 8, 2014, http://www.theguardian.com/commentisfree/2014/mar/08/african-homosexuality-colonial-import-myth, accessed March 18, 2014; former Nigerian President Olusegun Obasanjo called "homosexual practice and same-sex marriages . . . clearly un-Biblical, unnatural and definitely un-African." "Obasanjo Backs Bishops over Gays," *BBC News*, October 27, 2004, http://news.bbc.co.uk/2/hi/africa/3955145.stm, accessed March 18, 2014; Ugandan MP David Bahati, who was the sponsor of Uganda's anti-homosexuality bill, has said that homosexuality is "un-African because it is inconsistent with African values, of procreation and of the belief in the continuity of family and clan." Aarti Divani, "Is Homosexuality 'un-African'?" *Think Africa Press*, October 12, 2011, http://thinkafricapress.com/gender/homosexuality-un-african-colonialism, accessed March 18, 2014; Sam Nujoma, former president of Namibia, claimed that lesbians and gay men were unpatriotic and thus unworthy of citizenship rights, stating "where were they [LGBT people] when we sacrificed our lives during the bitter liberation struggle?" Ashley Currier, *Out in Africa: LGBT Organizing in Namibia and South Africa* (Minneapolis and London: University of Minnesota Press, 2012), 47, 49, 131.

3 Despite an international outcry and opposition from rights groups, Uganda passed the Anti-Homosexuality Act in February 2014. The law imposed severe penalties for gay people, such as life imprisonment for engaging in gay sex, life imprisonment for living in a same-sex marriage, and up to seven years' imprisonment for "attempting to commit homosexuality." "Museveni Signs Uganda Anti-Gay Bill," *BBC News*, February 24, 2014, http://www.bbc.com/news/world-africa-26320102, accessed March 18, 2014. In August 2014, Uganda's Constitutional Court overturned the act on procedural grounds. "Uganda court annuls anti-homosexuality law," *BBC News*, August 1, 2014, http://www.bbc.com/news/world-africa-28605400, accessed March 18, 2014.

4 A gender nonconforming person is an individual who does not conform to stereotypical notions of male or female gender expression, especially regarding the sex the individual was assigned at birth.

5 The law officially bans same-sex marriage and calls for up to ten years' imprisonment for membership in LGBT organizations. Owen Bowcott, "Nigeria Arrests Dozens as Anti-Gay Law Comes into Force," *The Guardian*, January 14, 2014, http://www.theguardian.com/world/2014/jan/14/nigeria-arrests-dozens-anti-gay-law, accessed March 18, 2014.

6 Chuang, "Rescuing Trafficking from Ideological Capture"; Aziza Ahmed, "The Unintended Consequences of Nick Kristof's Anti-Sex Trafficking Crusade," *The Guardian*, March 26, 2012, http://www.theguardian.com/commentisfree/cifamerica/2012/mar/26/nick-kristof-anti-sex-trafficking-crusade, accessed March 18, 2014; Jordan, "Sex Trafficking"; Julie Hamm, *Moving Beyond "Supply and Demand" Catchphrases*, GAATW, 2011, http://www.gaatw.org/publications/MovingBeyond_SupplyandDemand_GAATW2011.pdf, accessed March 18, 2014; Ditmore, "Sex Work, Trafficking."

7 Ditmore, "Sex Work, Trafficking"; Melissa Gira Grant, "U.S. Policy and the Unjust Approach to Human Trafficking of the International Justice Mission," *RH Reality Check*, October 2, 2012, http://rhrealitycheck.org/article/2012/10/02/unjust-approach-international-justice-mission/, accessed March 18, 2014; Melissa Ditmore and Juhu Thukral, "To Address Human Trafficking, the United States Must Take a New Approach," *RH Reality Check*, October 2, 2012, http://rhrealitycheck.org/article/2012/10/02/in-handling-sex-trafficking-crisis-president-obama-may-not-be-getting-it-right/, accessed March 18, 2014.

8 *Collateral Damage: The Impact of Anti-Trafficking Measures on Human Rights around the World*, GAATW, 2007, http://www.gaatw.org/Collateral%20Damage_Final/singlefile_CollateralDamagefinal.pdf, accessed March 18, 2014; Melissa Ditmore, *The Use of Raids to Fight Trafficking in Persons*, Sex Workers Project, 2009, http://sexworkersproject.org/downloads/swp-2009-raids-and-trafficking-report.pdf, accessed March 18, 2014.

9 Ronald Weitzer, "The Social Construction of Sex Trafficking: Ideology and Institutionalization of a Moral Crusade," *Politics & Society* 35, no. 3 (September 1, 2007): 456, doi:10.1177/0032329207304319; Jordan, "Sex Trafficking."

10 In Europe, Nigerian economic migrants whom the state characterizes as either victims of human trafficking or undocumented migrants are both subject to state deportation back to Nigeria. Those who receive the trafficking and thus "victim" designation, however, receive a "humanitarian deportation" that includes a resource package, while those who are classified as undocumented migrants or "criminals" do not. Sine Plambech, "Between 'Victims' and 'Criminals': Rescue, Deportation, and Everyday Violence Among Nigerian Migrants," *Soc Pol* 21 (3)(Fall 2014): 382–402, doi:10.1093/sp/jxu021.

11 "WHO | HIV/AIDS." *WHO*. http://www.who.int/gho/hiv/en/, accessed March 31, 2014.

12 Kenya and South Africa: *The Global HIV Epidemic Among Sex Workers*, World Bank, 2013, 92, 16, http://www.worldbank.org/content/dam/Worldbank/document/ GlobalHIVEpidemicsAmongSexWorkers.pdf, accessed March 31, 2014; Nigeria: Erin Papworth et al., "Epidemiology of HIV among Female Sex Workers, Their Clients, Men Who Have Sex with Men and People Who Inject Drugs in West and Central Africa," *Journal of the International AIDS Society* 16, no. 4 Suppl 3 (December 2, 2013), doi:10.7448/IAS.16.4.18751; Uganda: "AIDSInfo- Data." *UNAIDS*, http://www.aidsinfoonline.org/devinfo/libraries/aspx/dataview.aspx, accessed March 31, 2014.

13 Shifa Mwesigye, "Uganda: HIV Bill—Here's What Constitutes a Crime," *AllAfrica. com*, May 12, 2014, http://allafrica.com/stories/201405131206.html, accessed March 31, 2014.

14 UNAIDS, "UNAIDS Guidance Note on HIV and Sex Work."

15 "WHO | HIV/AIDS," *WHO*, http://www.who.int/mediacentre/factsheets/fs360/en/, accessed March 31, 2014.

16 A 2013 study in Zimbabwe assessed factors behind the low usage of HIV prevention and treatment facilities by sex workers. Researchers found that sex workers face barriers such as being demeaned and humiliated by health workers in health care facilities. Sibongile Mtetwa et al., "'You Are Wasting Our Drugs': Health Service Barriers to HIV Treatment for Sex Workers in Zimbabwe," *BMC Public Health* 13, no. 1 (July 31, 2013): 698. doi:10.1186/1471-2458-13-698.

17 In the early 2000s, researchers conducted a study on the HIV epidemic in Ghana, Kenya, Lesotho, Malawi, and Rwanda which revealed that sex workers play a limited role in the transmission of HIV in mature epidemics. Only 1.3 to 9.4 percent of infections in the general population could be attributed to sex workers. Pauline M. Leclerc and Michael Garenne, "Commercial Sex and HIV Transmission in Mature Epidemics: A Study of Five African Countries," *International Journal of STD and AIDS* 19, no. 10 (October 2008): 660–64, doi:10.1258/ijsa.2008.008099.

CHAPTER 4. "EACH OTHER'S KEEPERS"

1 Benin: Association Biowa, "Red Umbrella Fund Grantees," *Mama Cash*, http://www.mamacash.org/what-we-do-2/special-initiatives/red-umbrella-fund/red-umbrella-fund-grantees/, accessed April 11, 2014. Cameroon: Aids Acodev and Nkwen Association of Sex Workers (NASEW). Anne Mireille Nzouankeu, "Male Sex Workers in Cameroon Face Social Stigma and Poor Access to Care," *The Guardian*, December 1, 2011, sec. Global development, http://www.theguardian.com/global-development/2011/dec/01/hiv-aids-cameroon-male-sex-workers, accessed April 11, 2014; Martin Nkematabong, "Cameroon: Sex Workers Strike!" *Cameroon Tribune (Yaoundé)*, November 28, 2007, http://allafrica.com/stories/200711280787.html, accessed April 11, 2014. Côte d'Ivoire: Blety and Alternative Côte d'Ivoire. Nina Benedicte Kouassi, "Cote d'Ivoire: Sex Workers Attacked in Abidjan," *Key Correspondents (Hove)*, March 7, 2014, http://allafrica.com/stories/201403100912.html,

accessed April 11, 2014; "Scourge of Violence against Transgender Sex Workers in Cote d'Ivoire," *The M&G Online*, http://mg.co.za/article/2012–12–10-scourge-of-violence-against-transgender-sex-workers-in-ivory-coast, accessed April 3, 2014. Democratic Republic of Congo: Collective for Integrated Economic, Social and Cultural Development (CODESCI). Stephanie Plasse, "DRC: Prostitutes Claim Their Rights," *Afrik News*, March 4, 2010, http://www.afrik-news.com/article17092. html, accessed April 3, 2014. Ethiopia: Nikat. Meron Tekleberhan, "Organization Founded by Former Ethiopian Sex Workers Receives UNAIDS Award," *Ezega*, May 12, 2011, http://www.ezega.com/news/NewsDetails.aspx?Page=news&NewsID=2891, accessed April 3, 2014. Lesotho: Alliance of Lesotho Sex Workers. "Alliance of Lesotho Sex Workers (ALSW)." *Topix*, http://www.topix.com/forum/world/lesotho/ T59J2LE3HPR53L29P, accessed April 3, 2014. Madagascar: *Integration of HIV and Sexual and Reproductive Health and Rights* (International HIV/AIDS Alliance, n.d.), 34, http://www.aidsalliance.org/assets/000/000/417/507-Good-Practice-Guide-Integration-of-HIV-and-Sexual-and-Reproductive-Health-and-Rights_original. pdf?1405586821, accessed April 3, 2014; "FIMIZORE," *Red Ribbon Award- UNAIDS*, http://redribbonaward.org/index.php?option=com_content&view=article&id=7 4%3Afimizore-fikambanana-miaro-ny-zonny-rehetra-madagascar&catid=36%3A winners&lang=en#.Uz2VRKhdUuc, accessed April 3, 2014. Malawi: National Sex Workers Alliance. "Malawi Sex Workers Alliance Demand Respect, Legalisation of Prostitution," *Malawi Nyasa Times*, http://www.nyasatimes.com/2012/11/10/malawi-sex-workers-alliance-demand-respect-legalisation-of-prostitution, accessed April 3, 2014; "Malawi Sex Workers Unite in Push for Better Health Care," http://www. africareview.com/News/Malawi-sex-workers-unite-in-push-for-better-health-care/-/979180/1616712/-/lbm2f5/-/index.html, accessed April 3, 2014. Mali: Danaya So. Katja Remane, "Preventing Teenage Prostitution in Mali," *Swissinfo.ch*, September 26, 2011, http://www.swissinfo.ch/eng/politics/Preventing_teenage_prostitution_in_ Mali.html?cid=31211214, accessed April 3, 2014. Mozambique: ASWA. "Sex Workers March in Africa," *GlobalPost*, http://www.globalpost.com/dispatches/globalpost-blogs/africa-emerges/sex-workers-rights-day-marked-africa, accessed April 3, 2014. Sierra Leone: Movement of Vulnerability and Empowerment (MVE) and the Foundation for Democratic Initiatives and Development (FDID). Vickie Remoe, "On International Sex Workers Day Sierra Leonean Women in the Trade Want It Legalized," *The Everything Sierra Leone News Blog*, http://www.switsalone.com/19269_ on-international-sex-workers-day-sierra-leonean-women-in-the-trade-want-it-legalized, accessed April 3, 2014; "Sierra Leone News: Commercial Sex Workers Deserve Health Facilities–FDID," Awoko Newspaper, http://awoko.org/2013/09/23/ sierra-leone-news-commercial-sex-workers-deserve-health-facilities-fdid, accessed April 3, 2014. Tanzania: Wake up and Step Forward Coalition. Katy Migiro, "Police Rape Tanzanians Most at Risk of HIV, Health Workers Deny Them Services— HRW," June 18, 2013, http://www.trust.org/item/20130617141942-r5lwo, accessed April 3, 2014; Human Rights Watch, "'Treat Us Like Human Beings.'" Togo: Forum on the Rights of Sex Workers in Togo. "The Rights of Sex Workers in Togo," *NSWP*:

Global Network of Sex Work Projects, February 2, 2012, http://www.nswp.org/news-story/the-rights-sex-workers-togo, accessed April 4, 2014. Zambia: "African Sex Workers to March for Their Day as Zambia Says No Immorality Here," *Zambian Watchdog*, March 12, 2011, http://zwd.cums.in/african-sex-workers-to-march-for-their-day-as-zambia-says-no-immorality-here, accessed April 3, 2014. Zimbabwe: The Centre for Sexual Health, HIV and Aids Research (CeSHHAR). Paidamoyo Chipunza, "Zimbabwe: 12, 383 Sex Workers Register," *AllAfrica*, November 12, 2013, http://allafrica.com/stories/201311121137.html, accessed April 3, 2014.

2 Danaya So in Mali, founded in 1994, is the oldest sex workers' rights organization in West Africa. Katja Remane, "Preventing Teenage Prostitution in Mali," *Swissinfo. ch*, September 26, 2011, http://www.swissinfo.ch/eng/politics/Preventing_teen-age_prostitution_in_Mali.html?cid=31211214, accessed April 3, 2014.

3 Shane Petzer and Gordon Isaacs, "The Development and Implementation of a Sex Worker Advocacy and Intervention Programme in Post-Apartheid South Africa with Special Reference to the Western Cape City of Cape Town," http://www.wal-net.org/csis/groups/sweat/la_abstract.html, last modified April 20, 1998, accessed April 3, 2014.

4 Samantha Majic refers to the ability of sex work activists to maintain a radical posture even when formalized into nonprofits as "resistance maintenance." Samantha Majic, *Sex Work Politics: From Protest to Service Provision* (Philadelphia: University of Pennsylvania Press, 2014).

5 RHRU merged with a unit at the University of Witwatersrand, Enhancing Children's HIV Outcomes (ECHO), to form WRHI in October 2010. "Our History," *Wits Reproductive Health and HIV Unit*, http://www.wrhi.ac.za/Pages/OurHistory. aspx, accessed March 30, 2014.

6 Anne McClintock, "The Scandal of the Whorearchy: Prostitution in Colonial Nairobi," *Transition* No. 52, 1991, 96–97; White, *The Comforts of Home*, 73–78, 119–24.

7 The WHO, the International AIDS Society, Population Council, and the World Bank have all argued that sex worker peer outreach and support is a highly effective tool in HIV prevention and awareness. *Community Empowerment*, WHO, 9, http://www.who.int/hiv/pub/sti/swit_chpt1.pdf, accessed March 30, 2014; Florence Akanle, "Effect of Peer Education as a Key Strategy for Safe Sexual Behavior Among Female Sex Workers: Implication for HIV Prevention in Nigeria," 2010, http://www.iasociety.org/Abstracts/A200735392.aspx, accessed March 30, 2014; *Peer Education and HIV/AIDS: Past Experience, Future Directions*, Population Council, 2000. http://www.popcouncil.org/pdfs/peer_ed.pdf, accessed March 30, 2014; "India: Community Empowerment Key to Turning Tide on HIV," *The World Bank*, November 28, 2011, http://www.worldbank.org/en/news/feature/2012/11/27/india-community-empowerment-key-to-turning-tide-on-hiv, accessed March 30, 2014; *The Global HIV Epidemics Among Sex Workers*.

8 For more detailed information on the Creative Space methodology, see Jo Monson and Morgan Mitchell, *Creative Space Manual* (Cape Town: SWEAT and Red Umbrella Programme, 2014), https://materialsdevelopmentafrica.files.wordpress.

com/2014/06/red-umbrella-creative-space-manual-2014.pdf, accessed March 30, 2014.

9 Chapter 6 spotlights Sisonke and SWEAT's national campaign to decriminalize sex work in South Africa.

10 Gillian Schutte, "Johannesburg's Gay Pride Parade, Not Much to Be Proud Of," *The South African Civil Society Information Service*, October 8, 2012, http://sacsis.org.za/site/article/1450, accessed March 30, 2014.

11 UNAIDS, *Country Report—Kenya*, 2008, 11, http://www.unaids.org/en/dataanalysis/knowyourresponse/countryprogressreports/2008countries/kenya_2008_country_progress_report_en.pdf, accessed March 30, 2014.

12 I explore the workshop organized by Akina Mama wa Afrika in more detail in chapter 5.

13 "Sex Worker Health and Rights: Where Is the Funding?" http://www.opensocietyfoundations.org/publications/sex-worker-health-and-rights-where-funding, accessed April 4, 2014.

14 Melissa Hope Ditmore and Dan Allman, "An analysis of the implementation of PEPFAR's anti-prostitution pledge and its implications for successful HIV prevention among organizations working with sex workers," *Journal of the International AIDS Society* 16 (17354), March 28, 2013, doi:10.7448/IAS.16.1.17354. In 2013, the U.S. Supreme Court held that the application of the anti-prostitution pledge to U.S.-based organizations is a violation of First Amendment rights. *Agency for International Development et al v. Alliance for Open Society International, Inc., et al.*, 133 S. Ct. 2321 (2013).

15 "Funding for sex worker rights," *Mama Cash*, http://www.mamacash.org/what-we-do-2/special-initiatives/red-umbrella-fund/funding-sex-worker-rights/, accessed June 2, 2014.

16 Matthew Greenall et al., *Sex work and HIV—Reality on the ground: Rapid assessments in five towns in Namibia* (Namibia: UNFPA and UNAIDS, 2011), http://africa.unfpa.org/public/pid/10231, accessed April 4, 2014.

17 United Nations HRC, "Report of the Special Rapporteur on Extreme Poverty," 12.

CHAPTER 5. SOLIDARITY IS BEAUTIFUL

1 Gift Phiri, "Zimbabwe cracks down on the oldest profession," *Al Jazeera*, May 20, 2013, http://www.aljazeera.com/indepth/features/2013/05/20135151409826571.html, accessed May 13, 2014.

2 Ibid.; Dan Moshenberg, "The Real Housewives of Harare," *Africa Is a Country*, May 22, 2013, http://africasacountry.com/the-real-housewives-of-harare/, accessed May 13, 2014.

3 Moshenberg, "Real Housewives of Harare."

4 Phiri, "Zimbabwe cracks down."

5 "Zimbabwe: Policing Sex Work—An Appropriate Response?" *Southern African Litigation Centre* and *Sexual Rights Centre*, August 17, 2012, http://www.souther-

nafricalitigationcentre.org/2012/08/17/salc-in-the-news-policing-sex-work-in-zimbabwe-an-appropriate-response/, accessed May 13, 2014.

6 Shields, *Criminalizing Condoms*, 4.

7 Daniel Nemukuyu, "Loitering Laws Challenged," *The Herald*, March 16, 2014, http://www.herald.co.zw/loitering-laws-challenged/, accessed May 13, 2014.

8 Grant, *Playing the Whore*, 127.

9 Nyong'o, *When I Dare to Be Powerful*, vii–viii.

10 Ibid., vii.

11 Zawadi Nyong'o, *Breaking Boundaries: Collective Organising for a Just Society* (Kampala, Uganda: Akina Mama wa Afrika, 2010), 10.

12 Ibid., 15.

13 Ibid., 10.

14 Nyong'o, *When I Dare to Be Powerful*, 118.

15 "Women's movement attempts a rebound," *The Observer*, May 22, 2011, http://www.observer.ug/index.php?option=com_content&view=article&id=13521:womens-movement-attempts-a-rebound, accessed May 13, 2014.

16 "Botswana HIV: Mogae in Call to Legalise Homosexuality," *BBC News*, October 19, 2011, News Africa edition, http://www.bbc.com/news/world-africa-15368752, accessed May 13, 2014.

17 Aziza Ahmed, "'Rugged Vaginas' and 'Vulnerable Rectums': The Sexual Identity, Epidemiology, and Law of the Global HIV Epidemic," *Columbia Journal of Gender and Law* 26, no. 1 (2012): 1–57.

18 Bowcott, "Nigeria Arrests Dozens as Anti-Gay Law Comes into Force"; Alan Cowell, "Uganda's President Signs Antigay Bill," *New York Times*, February 24, 2014, http://www.nytimes.com/2014/02/25/world/africa/ugandan-president-to-sign-antigay-law.html, accessed May 13, 2014; Andy Kopsa, "Abandoned and Imprisoned for Being Gay in Cameroon," *The Nation*, March 4, 2014, http://www.thenation.com/article/178630/abandoned-and-imprisoned-being-gay-cameroon#, accessed May 13, 2014; Drew Hinshaw, "Anti-Gay Violence on the Rise in Senegal, Rights Group Says," *Bloomberg*, November 30, 2010, http://www.bloomberg.com/news/2010–11–30/anti-gay-violence-on-the-rise-in-senegal-rights-group-says.html, accessed May 13, 2014.

19 Chi Mgbako, "Africa's LGBT Rights Movement," *Huffington Post*, May 3, 2011, http://www.huffingtonpost.com/chi-mgbako/africas-lgbt-rights-movement_b_856695.html, accessed May 13, 2014.

20 Solome Nakaweesi and Hope Chigudu, *The LGBTIQ and Sex Worker Movements in East Africa* 1 (BRIDGE, April 2013), http://socialmovements.bridge.ids.ac.uk/sites/socialmovements.bridge.ids.ac.uk/files/case-studies/East%20african%20case%20study%20final.pdf, accessed May 13, 2014.

21 Currier, *Out in Africa*, 46.

22 Ibid., 33–37.

23 "Survival sex" involves individuals' engaging in the exchange of sex for food, housing, and other basic needs as a result of extreme conditions of deprivation.

24 Nakaweesi and Chigudu, *The LGBTIQ and Sex Worker Movements in East Africa*, 2; "Uganda Miniskirt Ban: Police Stop Protest March," *BBC News*, February 26, 2014, News Africa edition, http://www.bbc.com/news/world-africa-26351087, accessed May 13, 2014; Jeffrey Gettleman, "Uganda Anti-Gay Law Struck Down by Court," *New York Times*, August 1, 2014, http://www.nytimes.com/2014/08/02/world/africa/uganda-anti-gay-law-struck-down-by-court.html?hp&action=click&pgtype=Homepage&version=LargeMediaHeadlineSum&module=photo-spot-region&region=photo-spot&WT.nav=photo-spot, accessed May 13, 2014.

25 MSM in South Africa: Kevin Kelly, Nolwazi Mkhwanazi, and Rethabile Mashale, *Synthesis of Research on Prevention of Sexual Transmission of HIV in South Africa* (Centre for AIDS Development, Research and Evaluation, 2012), 28, http://futures-group.com/files/publications/Synthesis_of_Research_on_Prevention_of_Sexual_Transmission_of_HIV_in_SA.pdf, accessed May 13, 2014; MSM in Kenya: *MSM, HIV, and the Road to Universal Access—How Far Have We Come?* (amFAR: The Foundation for AIDS Research, August 2008), http://www.amfar.org/uploaded-Files/In_the_Community/Publications/MSM%20HIV%20and%20the%20Road%20to%20Universal%20Access.pdf, accessed May 13, 2014; Female sex workers in Kenya and South Africa: *The Global HIV Epidemic Among Sex Workers*, 16.

26 Nakaweesi and Chigudu, *The LGBTIQ and Sex Worker Movements in East Africa*, 6.

27 Melissa Hope Ditmore, *When Sex Work and Drug Use Overlap: Considerations for Advocacy and Practice*, 14 (Harm Reduction International, 2013), http://www.ihra.net/files/2014/08/06/Sex_work_report_ƒ4_WEB.pdf, accessed June 2, 2015.

CHAPTER 6. WATERING THE SOIL

1 Zawadi Nyong'o, *A Nascent Movement: Sex Worker Organising in East Africa*, Print, July 5, 2010, http://www.awid.org/eng/News-Analysis/Issues-and-Analysis/A-Nascent-Movement-Sex-Worker-Organising-in-East-Africa, accessed May 13, 2014.

2 *Kylie v Commission for Conciliation Mediation and Arbitration and Others* (Labour Appeal Court of South Africa 2010), http://www.saflii.org/za/cases/ZALAC/2010/8.html, accessed May 13, 2014.

3 Kylie was dismissed from the brothel where she lived and worked for allegations of misconduct. On her behalf, SWEAT and WLC first submitted a formal complaint to the Commission for Conciliation, Mediation and Arbitration, which is the legal body that mediates and arbitrates labor disputes before the South African Labour Court. The Commission refused to order Kylie's reemployment or reinstatement because sex work is illegal in South Africa. SWEAT and WLC appealed the ruling to the Labour Court, which upheld the Commission's ruling. However, upon appeal to the Labour Appeal Court, the Court ruled in Kylie's favor, accepting the argument that Kylie is entitled to fair labor practices under the Labour Relations Act as an informal worker. Kylie and the brothel owner eventually agreed on a settlement.

4 Oludayo Tade and Adeshemwa Jheminat Adekoya, "Transactional sex and the 'aristo' phenomenon in Nigerian Universities," *Human Affairs* 22 (2012): 239–55,

http://link.springer.com/article/10.2478%2Fs13374-012-0020-5, accessed May 13, 2014.

5 Anne Soy-Mwendia, *Muffled Killer, Part 1*, Documentary (KTN, 2012), http://www. youtube.com/watch?v=IDJkd7J3SBU, accessed May 13, 2014; Anne Soy-Mwendia, *Muffled Killer, Parts 2 and 3*, Documentary (KTN, 2012), http://www.youtube.com/watch?v=xra7iQNga90, accessed May 13, 2014.

6 The "Nordic model," which unilaterally criminalizes the purchase of sex, exists in three Nordic countries: Sweden, Norway, and Iceland. May-Len Skilbrei and Charlotta Holmström, "The 'Nordic Model' of Prostitution Law Is a Myth," *The Conversation*, December 16, 2013, http://theconversation.com/the-nordic-model-of-prostitution-law-is-a-myth-21351, accessed May 13, 2014.

7 Ann Jordan, *The Swedish Law to Criminalize Clients: A Failed Experiment in Social Engineering*, Center for Humanitarian Rights and Humanitarian Law, April 2012, 3–4.

8 Ibid., 7.

9 Elizabeth Bernstein, *Temporarily Yours: Intimacy, Authenticity, and the Commerce of Sex* (Chicago and London: University of Chicago Press, 2007), 153.

10 Jordan, *The Swedish Law to Criminalize Clients*, 6.

11 Ibid., 4–5.

12 Skilbrei and Holmström, "The 'Nordic Model' of Prostitution Law Is a Myth."

13 Bernstein, *Temporarily Yours*, 150–51.

14 Chi Mgbako et al., "The Case for the Decriminalization of Sex Work in South Africa," *Georgetown Journal of International Law* 44 (2013): 1433–34, https://www.law.georgetown.edu/academics/law-journals/gjil/recent/upload/zsx00413001423.PDF, accessed May 13, 2014.

15 Jordan, *The Swedish Law to Criminalize Clients*, 12.

16 For example, 90 percent of all sex workers in Queensland, Australia, where sex work is legalized and regulated, work illegally. Chi Mgbako et al., "The Case for the Decriminalization of Sex Work in South Africa," 1434–35.

17 Chi Mgbako and Laura Smith, "Sex Work and Human Rights in Africa," *Fordham International Law Journal* 33 (2010): 1212, http://papers.ssrn.com/sol3/papers.cfm?abstract_id=1710654, accessed May 13, 2014.

18 Oumar Tandia, "Prostitution in Senegal," in *Global Sex Workers*, ed. Kempadoo and Doezema, 242–43.

19 Mgbako and Smith, "Sex Work and Human Rights in Africa," 1213–14.

20 Mgbako et al., "The Case for the Decriminalization of Sex Work in South Africa," 1436.

21 *Prostitution Reform Act 2003. New Zealand*, 2003, http://www.legislation.govt.nz/act/public/2003/0028/latest/whole.html#DLM197821, accessed May 13, 2014.

22 *Report of the Prostitution Law Review Committee on the Operation of the Prostitution Reform Act 2003*, 14 (New Zealand Government, May 2008), http://www.justice.govt.nz/policy/commercial-property-and-regulatory/prostitution/prostitution-law-review-committee/publications/plrc-report/documents/report.pdf, accessed May 13, 2014.

23 Ibid.

24 Ibid., 14, 50.

25 *Report of the Prostitution Law Review Committee*, 40–41, 102.

26 Mgbako et al., "The Case for the Decriminalization of Sex Work in South Africa," 1446–54.

27 *International Covenant on Civil and Political Rights*, arts. 6, 9, 22, 155, Dec.16, 1966, 999 U.N.T.S. 171; *International Covenant on Economic, Social and Cultural Rights*, arts. 6(1), 12, Dec. 16, 1966, 993 U.N.T.S. 9; *Convention on the Elimination of All Forms of Discrimination against Women*, arts. 11(1)(a), 145, Dec. 18, 1979, 1249 U.N.T.S. 13; *African Charter on Human and Peoples' Rights*, arts. 4, 6, 5, 10, 15, 16, June 27, 1981, OAU Doc. CAB/LEG/67/3 rev. 5, 21 I.L.M. 58 (1982); *Protocol to the African Charter on Human and Peoples' Rights on the Rights of Women in Africa*, arts. 3, 4, 14, Sept. 13, 2000, CAB/LEG/66.6.

28 "United Nations: Listen to Survivors—Don't Jeopardize Efforts to Prevent Sex Trafficking," *Equality Now*, September 20, 2013, http://www.equalitynow.org/take_action/sex_trafficking_action511, accessed May 13, 2014.

29 *Sex Work and the Law in Asia and the Pacific*, v (United Nations Development Programme, 2012). In the process of researching and drafting its 2012 watershed report arguing for the decriminalization of sex work, the Global Commission on HIV and the Law, an independent expert body convened by UNDP and UNAIDS, received numerous regional dialogue submissions from sex workers' rights organizations. Following are examples of submissions from Africa: Global Commission on HIV and the Law, Regional Dialogue Submission—Africa, "46. Mozambique: African Alliance of Sex Workers (ASWA), August 3–4, 2011, 79–82, http://www.hivlawcommission.org/index.php/submissions?task=document.viewdoc&id= 82, accessed May 13, 2014; Global Commission on HIV and the Law, "56. Namibia: The Red Umbrella ASWA Namibia,"107–8; Global Commission on HIV and the Law, "57. Nigeria: ASWA Nigeria," 108–14; Global Commission on HIV and the Law, "70. Mauritius: Chrysalide," 140–41; Global Commission on HIV and the Law, "72. Mali: Danaya So," 144–47; Global Commission on HIV and the Law, "84. Kenya: Kenya Sex Workers Alliance (KESWA)," 172–74; Global Commission on HIV and the Law, "128. Zimbabwe: Sex Workers in Zimbabwe," 269–71; Global Commission on HIV and the Law, "129. Zimbabwe: Sexual Rights Centre Zimbabwe," 271–74; Global Commission on HIV and the Law, "130. Botswana: Sisonke Botswana," 274–78; Global Commission on HIV and the Law, "131. South Africa: SISONKE Sex Worker Movement, supported by SWEAT (Sex Worker Education & Advocacy Taskforce)," 278–91; Global Commission on HIV and the Law, "139. South Africa: SWEAT," 305–15; Global Commission on HIV and the Law, "157. Uganda: Women's Organization for Human Rights Advocacy (WONETHA)," 354–57; Global Commission on HIV and the Law, "168. Zimbabwe: Female Sex Workers Network of Zimbabwe (FSWNZ)," 377–78.

30 "Response to the Misguided Petition by Equality Now and Allies Attacking Sex Worker Human Rights and the Decriminalisation of Sex Work," *SWEAT*, October

7, 2013, http://www.sweat.org.za/index.php/item/474-response-to-the-misguided-petition-by-equality-now-and-allies-attacking-sex-worker-human-rights-and-the-decriminalisation-of-sex-work, accessed May 13, 2014.

31 "ASWA statement to the United Nations protest against Decriminalization," *African Sex Workers Alliance*, September 24, 2013, http://www.africansexworkeralliance. org/content/aswa-statement-united-nations-protests-against-decriminalization, accessed May 13, 2014.

32 "South African Commission for Gender Equality Calls for Decriminalisation and Protection of Sex Workers Rights," *Global Commission on HIV and the Law*, May 31, 2013, http://www.hivlawcommission.org/index.php/news/news/185-south-african-commission-for-gender-equality-calls-for-decriminalisation-and-protection-of-sex-workers-rights, accessed May 13, 2014.

33 District Six was a neighborhood in Cape Town, South Africa, that was originally known as a Coloured neighborhood in the early 1900s. In 1966, the apartheid government declared District Six a "whites only" zone under the Great Areas Act. All residents, including Coloured people, Black Africans, Indians, Chinese, and Malays, were forcibly removed from their homes, which were razed, and relocated to the Cape Flats on the outskirts of Cape Town by the apartheid government. Scott C. Johnson, "The Real District 9: Cape Town's District Six," *Newsweek*, August 26, 2009, http://www.newsweek.com/real-district-9-cape-towns-district-six-78939, accessed May 13, 2014.

34 The Soweto Students' Representative Council was an action committee that planned and coordinated protests against the use of Afrikaans in school instruction.

35 Adrienne D. Davis, "Regulating Sex Work: Assimilationism, Erotic Exceptionalism and Beyond," *California Law Review*, March 21, 2014, February 2015, Forthcoming, http://papers.ssrn.com/sol3/papers.cfm?abstract_id=2412713, accessed May 13, 2014.

36 *Beyond Decriminalization: Sex Work, Human Rights and a New Framework for Law Reform* (Pivot Legal Society, June 2006), http://d3n8a8pro7vhmx.cloudfront.net/pivotlegal/legacy_url/275/BeyondDecrimLongReport.pdf?1345765615, accessed May 13, 2014.

37 *Prostitution Reform Act 2003. New Zealand*, s 4, 5, 34, 35. In circumstances in which licensing is deemed appropriate, what sort of privacy protections should be put in place to ensure that sex workers are able to maintain anonymity because of what will surely be continued stigma attached to sex work even after decriminalization? What sort of safeguards should be implemented and what kinds of sensitivity training should licensing bodies receive to ensure that discriminatory attitudes regarding sex work don't influence their decisions? What legal remedies will sex workers have in the face of licensing remedies that are discriminatory toward sex work?

38 *Prostitution Reform Act 2003*, s 7.

39 Ibid., s 7, 10, 16, 17, 18.

40 Ibid., s 23.

41 *Criminal Records (Clean Slate) Act 2004, New Zealand*, s 7, 14.

42 *Prostitution Reform Act 2003. New Zealand*, s 19(1)(a).

CHAPTER 7. "HEARTS STRONG LIKE STORMS"

1 Alexandra Topping, "Tough or Tolerant? Scotland Turns up Heat on Prostitution Debate," *The Guardian*, July 15, 2013, http://www.theguardian.com/society/2013/jul/15/scotland-prostitution-debate-criminalisation-legalisation, accessed May 13, 2014; Laura Lynch, "Prostitution Laws: Europeans Debate Whether Criminalization or Legalization Works Better," *CBS News*, December 19, 2013, http://www.cbc.ca/news/world/prostitution-laws-europeans-debate-whether-criminalization-or-legalization-works-better-1.2470190, accessed May 13, 2014.

2 Janie Chuang, "Rescuing Trafficking from Ideological Capture"; Bernstein, "Militarized Humanitarianism Meets Carceral Feminism," 45–72.

3 Scholars and researchers have often asserted that Melissa Farley's research methodology is problematic in numerous ways. Sociologist Ronald Weitzer has argued that much of Farley's work has methodological flaws, including sampling biases and lack of transparency in her research and ethical methods. For example, he argues that in Farley's "Bad for the Body, Bad for the Heart: Prostitution Harms Women Even if Legalized or Decriminalized," she fails to disclose the demographics of samples, the specific questions asked of respondents, how interview locations are selected, and how interview subjects are approached. "Flawed Theory and Method in Studies of Prostitution," *Violence against Women* 11, no. 7 (July 2005): 934–49, doi:10.1177/1077801205276986.

Wendy Lyons astutely notes that an oft-cited Farley study of sex workers in nine countries which concluded that 89 percent of study participants wanted to leave sex work is tainted by a heavy selection bias in respondents that likely skewed the responses:

It is not clear that *any* of the sex workers interviewed came from the less vulnerable sectors (i.e. independent indoor workers, or brothel workers in countries where they have labour, health and safety rights). The large majority clearly did not. Some of them were selected from agencies that cater to people wishing to leave prostitution, which is a bit like selecting people at a jobs fair to find out if they're looking for work. . . . In short, this study does not tell us how *sex workers* feel about their work. At most, it may tell us how *sex workers in particularly vulnerable sectors* feel about their work. That 89 percent figure simply cannot be generalised to sex workers as a whole.

Wendy Lyons, "What is a 'representative' sex worker?" *Feminist Ire*, November 13, 2011, http://feministire.wordpress.com/2011/11/13/what-is-a-representative-sex-worker/, accessed May 13, 2014.

Dr. Calum Bennachie of the New Zealand Prostitutes' Collective filed a complaint with the American Psychological Association against Farley in 2011. Bennachie asserted that Farley has attempted to mislead people by publishing errors as fact and selectively reporting parts of the Report of the Prostitution Law Review Commission. He argued that despite her use of flawed questionnaires and conducting only cursory interviews, Farley claimed that she could diagnose sex workers with post-traumatic stress disorder. Finally, Bennachie noted that

Canadian courts have deemed Farley an unreliable witness. Calum Bennachie, "Complaint to the APA against Melissa Farley," 2011, http://cybersolidaires.type-pad.com/files/complaint-to-apa-against-mfarley.pdf, accessed May 13, 2014.

4 "Why Embrace Dignity?," *Embrace Dignity*, http://embracedignity.org.za/site/our-vision/, accessed May 13, 2014.

5 Michael Wines, "AIDS Activist Nozizwe Madlala-Routledge Keeps Her Convictions but Loses Her Job," *New York Times*, September 7, 2007, http://www.nytimes.com/2007/09/07/world/africa/07iht-profile.4.7423546.html?pagewanted=all, accessed May 13, 2014.

6 "Why Embrace Dignity?"

7 "NGO, Mbu Clash Over Sex Workers in Abuja," *Business World Intelligence*, April 14, 2014, http://businessworldng.com/new/?p=9363, accessed May 13, 2014.

8 "Kenyan Sex Workers Demand Removal of TV Documentary That Outs Sex Workers and Violates Our Rights!," *Global Network of Sex Work Projects*, July 9, 2013, http://www.nswp.org/news-story/kenyan-sex-workers-demand-removal-tv-documentary-outs-sex-workers-and-violates-our-rights, accessed May 13, 2014.

9 *Rights Not Rescue*, 70–71.

10 "Islamic police arrest 150 in Nigeria accused of indecent dress, prostitution and cross-dressing." *The Telegraph*, October 23, 2013, http://www.telegraph.co.uk/news/worldnews/africaandindianocean/nigeria/10398365/Islamic-police-arrest-150-in-Nigeria-accused-of-indecent-dress-prostitution-and-cross-dressing.html, accessed May 13, 2014.

11 *Nikah mut'ah* refers to the practice of temporary marriage accepted in Shia Islam. A man and woman entering into *nikah mut'ah* must first specify the duration of the marriage and the material compensation that the man will give to the woman. There are no limits on how long a couple can agree to be married under *nikah mut'ah*—it can be for one hour or one century. Originally, the practice was used to accommodate men who traveled far distances and spent long periods of time away from their wives and families while fighting in the army. The marriage contract can specify additional conditions, including the number of acts of sexual intercourse. Neither person can claim inheritance, maintenance, or entitlement rights. Children born from a *mut'ah* marriage are deemed legitimate and have inheritance rights. Dawoud el-Alami, "Marriage," in *Modern Muslim Societies*, Muslim World (Cavendish Square Publishing, 2011), 49–50; Shabnam Mahmood and Catrin Nye, "I Do . . . for Now. UK Muslims Revive Temporary Marriages," *BBC News*, May 13, 2013, http://www.bbc.com/news/uk-22354201, accessed May 13, 2014.

12 Currier, *Out in Africa*, 175–76 (internal citations omitted).

13 "Wanted Nigerian Hands Himself In," *BBC News*, January 21, 2008, sec. Africa, http://news.bbc.co.uk/2/hi/africa/7201026.stm, accessed May 13, 2014.

14 Mgbako and Smith, *Sex Work and Human Rights in Africa*, 1191.

15 "DR Congo: UN Report Exposes Grave Crimes," *Human Rights Watch*, October 1, 2010, http://www.hrw.org/news/2010/10/01/dr-congo-un-report-exposes-grave-crimes, accessed May 13, 2014.

16 "President Kagame Rules out Prostitution in Rwanda," *Panapress*, March 9, 2007, http://www.panapress.com/President-Kagame-rules-out-prostitution-in-Rwanda—13–503340–18-lang2-index.html, accessed May 13, 2014.

17 Akyeampong, "Sexuality and Prostitution among the Akan of the Gold Coast c. 1650–1950," 156.

18 Ibid.

19 Achebe, *The Female King of Colonial Nigeria*, 78.

20 Ibid., 80.

21 Ibid., 81.

22 Ibid., 76–77.

23 "John Kerry Denounces Yahya Jammeh's 'Unacceptable' Anti-LGBT Comments," *Huffington Post*, February 19, 2014, http://www.huffingtonpost.com/2014/02/19/john-kerry-yahya-jammeh_n_4819310.html, accessed May 13, 2014.

24 Mgbako and Smith, *Sex Work and Human Rights in Africa*, 1190.

25 "Ugandan Reverend Simon Lokodo: 'Child Rape Better than Homosexuality' [VIDEO]," *International Business Times*, http://www.ibtimes.co.uk/ugandan-reverend-simon-lokodo-child-rape-better-homosexuality-video-1437976, accessed May 13, 2014.

26 Joyce Nyakato, "37 Percent Sex Workers Are HIV Positive," *New Vision*, March 24, 2012. PDF on file; Elizabeth Acaye, "Ugandan Sex Workers Post Highest HIV Rates, Community Considers Expanding Care," *Global Press Journal*, December 13, 2012, http://www.globalpressjournal.com/africa/uganda/ugandan-sex-workers-post-highest-hiv-rates/page/0/2, accessed May 13, 2014.

27 Currier, *Out in Africa*, 46.

28 Luqman Cloete, "Nujoma Condemns Attempts to Legalise Prostitution," *The Namibian*, October 19, 2010, http://www.namibian.com.na/indexx.php?archive_id=71927&page_type=archive_story_detail&page=2710, accessed May 13, 2014.

29 Anna-Louise Crago, "'Bitches Killing the Nation': The State-Sponsored Scapegoat-ing of Sex Workers for HIV in Zambia 2004–2008." (Library and Archives Canada = Bibliothèque et Archives Canada, 2011), 108–9.

30 Ibid., 110.

31 Mtokozisi Dube, "Botswana Starts Purge against Sex Workers," *Daily Nation*, November 5, 2013, http://mobile.nation.co.ke/News/Botswana-starts-purge-against-sex-workers/-/1950946/2061984/-/format/xhtml/-/13g0x20/-/index.html, accessed May 13, 2014.

32 "Human Rights Organizations Condemn the Campaign of the Botswana Gov-ernment to Crack Down on Sex Workers," *Canadian HIV/AIDS Legal Network*, November 13, 2013, http://www.aidslaw.ca/publications/interfaces/downloadDocu-mentFile.php?ref=1393, accessed May 13, 2014; "Ministry of Health Acts in Bad Faith," *BONELA*, October 28, 2013, http://www.bonela.org/index.php?option=com_k2&view=item&Itemid=223&id=109:28-october-2013, accessed May 13, 2014.

33 "Ministry of Health Acts in Bad Faith," *BONELA*.

34 The Acholi people are the dominant ethnic group in Gulu.

35 "International Coalition Condemns Human Rights Violations against W.O.N.E.T.H.A.," *Women's Global Network for Reproductive Rights*, July 31, 2012, http://wgnrr.org/international-coalition-condemns-human-rights-violations-against-w-o-n-e-t-h-a/, accessed May 13, 2014.

EPILOGUE

1 "Where Our Members Work," *Global Network of Sex Work Projects*, http://www.nswp.org/members, accessed May 22, 2014.

2 MacKinnon, "Trafficking, Prostitution, and Inequality," 272–78; Melissa Farley, "The Real Harms of Prostitution," *MercatorNet*, October 19, 2010, http://www.mercator-net.com/articles/view/the_real_harms_of_prostitution, accessed May 22, 2014.

3 For an in-depth history of COYOTE, see Chateauvert, *Sex Workers Unite*, 47–82.

4 Ibid.; Valerie Jenness, *Making It Work: The Prostitute's Rights Movement in Perspective* (Chicago: Aldine Transaction, 1993), 42–47.

5 Lilian Mathieu, "An Unlikely Mobilization: The Occupation of Saint-Nizier Church by the Prostitutes of Lyon," *Revue Française de Sociologie* 42, no. 1 (2001): 107–31.

6 Ibid., 128; Gregor Gall, *Sex Worker Union Organizing: An International Study* (New York: Palgrave Macmillan, 2006), 53–54.

7 Gall, *Sex Worker Union Organizing*, 53–54.

8 Kempadoo and Doezema, *Global Sex Workers*, 19; Gall, *Sex Worker Union Organizing*, 50, 133–34, 140; "Prostitutes of New York (PONY)," *Global Network of Sex Work Projects*, accessed May 22, 2014, http://www.nswp.org/members/north-america-and-the-caribbean/prostitutes-new-york-pony, accessed May 22, 2014.

9 Kate Sutherland, "Work, Sex, and Sex-Work: Competing Feminist Discourses on the International Sex Trade," *Osgoode Hall Law Journal* 42 (2004): 26; "Portraits of Empowerment Exhibition Targets Stigma of Asian Sex Workers," *Bangkok Post*, April 7, 2013, http://www.bangkokpost.com/print/344318/, accessed May 22, 2014.

10 Kempadoo and Doezema, *Global Sex Workers*, 19–20.

11 Ibid., 21–22.

12 "História," *Davida*, http://www.davida.org.br/, accessed May 22, 2014; for the history of SWEAT, see chapter 4; Teela Sanders, Maggie O'Neill, and Jane Pitcher, *Prostitution: Sex Work, Policy and Politics* (London: SAGE Publications, 2009), 104; "History," *Durbar Mahila Samanwaya Committee*, http://durbar.org/html/history.aspx, accessed May 9, 2014; Andrea Cornwall, "Indian Sex Workers Are a Shining Example of Women's Empowerment," *The Guardian*, July 26, 2012, http://www.theguardian.com/global-development/poverty-matters/2012/jul/26/india-sex-workers-female-empowerment, accessed May 22, 2014.

13 Kempadoo and Doezema, *Global Sex Workers*, 20; "History," *Global Network of Sex Work Projects*, http://www.nswp.org/page/history, accessed May 22, 2014. Kempadoo and Doezema write that the founding of NSWP was in 1991, while NSWP cites 1990 on its website.

14 "History," *Global Network of Sex Work Projects*; "What We Do," *Global Network of Sex Work Projects*, http://www.nswp.org/page/what-we-do, accessed May 22, 2014; "UNAIDS Advisory Group," *Global Network of Sex Work Projects*, http://www.nswp.org/unaids-advisory-group, accessed May 22, 2014.

15 Zoe Scorgings et al., *Solidarity Is Not a Crime: Sex Worker Freedom Festival, Kolkata, India 2012* (Global Network of Sex Work Projects, April 2014), 1, 14, http://www.nswp.org/sites/nswp.org/files/SWFF%20Report_PDF%20version_0. pdf, accessed May 22, 2014; U.S. immigration law prohibits entry of "aliens" who have engaged in sex work in the past ten years. 8 U.S.C. § 1182(a)(2)(D)(i) (Supp. 2013).

16 The Sex Worker Freedom Festival Manifesto calls for seven basic freedoms of sex workers to be respected: the freedom of association and to unionize, the freedom to be protected by the law, freedom from abuse and violence, freedom from stigma and discrimination, freedom to access quality health services, freedom of movement and to migrate, and freedom to work and choose an occupation. Scorgings et al., *Solidarity Is Not a Crime*, 37–47.

17 Scorgings et al., *Solidarity Is Not a Crime*, 2.

18 Mariko Passion, *Kolkata to DC Transmission of StarWhores Go Intergalactic at the International AIDS Conference 2012*, Video, Uploaded October 17, 2013, http://www.youtube.com/watch?v=_1UUOib_fsM, accessed May 22, 2014; Scorgings et al., *Solidarity Is Not a Crime*, 15, 24–25, 29–35.

19 Mama Cash is an example of one of the few international organizations that support sex worker movement building that is not tied solely to HIV/AIDS advocacy. Mama Cash administers the Red Umbrella Fund, which is run by and for sex workers, to support the strengthening of the global sex workers' rights movement. "A New Fund for and By Sex Workers: The Red Umbrella Fund," Mama Cash, http://www.mamacash.org/what-we-do/special-initiatives/red-umbrella-fund/about-the-red-umbrella-fund/, accessed September 11, 2014.

20 *Bedford v. Canada* (Attorney General), 3 S.C.R. 1101 (2012).

21 Claire Provost, "Fight against HIV Empowering Sex Workers in India, Says UN Aids Envoy," *The Guardian*, July 23, 2012, http://www.theguardian.com/global-development/2012/jul/23/hiv-sex-workers-india-aids, accessed September 11, 2014; "Operationalizing an Effective Community Development Intervention for Reducing HIV Vulnerability in Female Sex Work: Lessons Learned from The Sonagachi Project in Kolkata, India.," *WHO*, http://www.who.int/hiv/topics/vct/sw_toolkit/sonagachi_operationalizing_copy_1.pdf, accessed September 11, 2014; Dallas Swendeman et al., "Empowering Sex Workers in India to Reduce Vulnerability to HIV and Sexually Transmitted Diseases," *Social Science & Medicine (1982)* 69, no. 8 (October 2009): 1157–66, doi:10.1016/j.socscimed.2009.07.035.

22 "Sex workers from Africa visit Mysore peers," *The Hindu*, August 4, 2012, http://www.thehindu.com/todays-paper/tp-national/tp-karnataka/sex-workers-from-africa-visit-mysore-peers/article3725747.ece, accessed September 11, 2014.

SELECTED BIBLIOGRAPHY

Achebe, Nwando. *The Female King of Colonial Nigeria: Ahebi Ugbabe*. Bloomington: Indiana University Press, 2011.

Adichie, Chimamanda Ngozi. *The Danger of a Single Story*. Ted Talk Global, 2009. http://www.ted.com/talks/chimamanda_adichie_the_danger_of_a_single_story (accessed April 10, 2014).

Agustín, Laura. "Naked Musings on Borders, Illegality and Personal Identity." *The Naked Anthropologist*, May 12, 2013. http://www.lauraagustin.com/naked-musings-on-borders-illegality-and-personal-identity (accessed April 10, 2014).

Ahmed, Aziza. "'Rugged Vaginas' and 'Vulnerable Rectums': The Sexual Identity, Epidemiology, and Law of the Global HIV Epidemic." *Columbia Journal of Gender and Law* 26 (2012): 1–57.

Ahmed, Aziza, and Meena Seshu. "'We Have the Right Not to Be Rescued': When Anti-Trafficking Programmes Undermine the Health and Well-Being of Sex Workers." *Anti-Trafficking Review*, no. 1 (2012): 149–65.

Akyeampong, Emmanuel. "Sexuality and Prostitution among the Akan of the Gold Coast c. 1650–1950." *Past and Present* 156 (1997): 156.

"ASWA statement to the United Nations protest against Decriminalization," African Sex Workers Alliance, September 24, 2013. http://www.africansexworkeralliance.org/content/aswa-statement-united-nations-protests-against-decriminalization (accessed May 13, 2014).

Bernstein, Elizabeth. "Militarized Humanitarianism Meets Carceral Feminism: The Politics of Sex, Rights, and Freedom in Contemporary Anti-Trafficking Campaigns." *SIGNS* 36, no. 1 (Autumn 2010): 45–72.

———. *Temporarily Yours: Intimacy, Authenticity, and the Commerce of Sex*. Chicago and London: University of Chicago Press, 2007.

Beyond Decriminalization: Sex Work, Human Rights and a New Framework for Law Reform. Pivot Legal Society, June 2006. http://d3n8a8pro7vhmx.cloudfront.net/pivotlegal/legacy_url/275/BeyondDecrimLongReport.pdf?1345765615 (accessed May 13, 2014).

Chateauvert, Melinda. *Sex Workers Unite: A History of the Movement from Stonewall to SlutWalk*. New York: Beacon Press, 2014.

Chuang, Janie A. "Rescuing Trafficking from Ideological Capture: Prostitution Reform and Anti-Trafficking Law and Policy." *University of Pennsylvania Law Review* 158 (2010): 1655–728.

Collateral Damage: The Impact of Anti-Trafficking Measures on Human Rights around the World. GAATW, 2007. http://www.gaatw.org/Collateral%20Damage_Final/singlefile_CollateralDamagefinal.pdf (accessed March 18, 2014).

Crago, Anna-Louise. "'Bitches Killing the Nation': The State-Sponsored Scapegoating of Sex Workers for HIV in Zambia 2004–2008." Library and Archives Canada = Bibliothèque et Archives Canada, 2011.

Crago, Anna-Louise, and Jayne Arnott. *Rights Not Rescue: A Report on Female, Trans, and Male Sex Workers' Human Rights in Botswana, Namibia, and South Africa*. New York: Open Society Institute, 2009. http://www.opensocietyfoundations.org/sites/default/files/rightsnotrescue_20090706.pdf (accessed April 10, 2014).

Currier, Ashley. *Out in Africa: LGBT Organizing in Namibia and South Africa*. Minneapolis and London: University of Minnesota Press, 2012.

Davis, Adrienne D. "Regulating Sex Work: Assimilationism, Erotic Exceptionalism and Beyond." *California Law Review* (2015).

Ditmore, Melissa. "Trafficking and Sex Work: A Problematic Conflation." PhD dissertation, City University of New York, 2002. Proquest Central, Document Number 276259451.

——. *The Use of Raids to Fight Trafficking in Persons*. Sex Workers Project, 2009. http://sexworkersproject.org/downloads/swp-2009-raids-and-trafficking-report.pdf (accessed March 18, 2014).

——. *When Sex Work and Drug Use Overlap: Considerations for Advocacy and Practice*. Harm Reduction International, 2013. http://www.ihra.net/files/2013/11/20/Sex_work_report_ƒ4_WEB.pdf (accessed May 13, 2014).

Documenting Human Rights Violations of Sex Workers in Kenya: A Study Conducted in Nairobi, Kisumu, Busia, Nanyuki, Mombasa and Malindi. Kenya: Federation of Women Lawyers in Kenya, 2008. http://www.opensocietyfoundations.org/sites/default/files/fida_20081201.pdf (accessed April 10, 2014).

Doezema, Jo. "Ouch! Western Feminists' 'Wounded Attachment' to the 'Third World Prostitute.'" *Feminist Review* 67 (2001): 16–38.

Gall, Gregor. *Sex Worker Union Organizing: An International Study*. New York: Palgrave Macmillan, 2006.

"GCWA: Statement of Support on the International Day for Sex Workers: June 2, 2014," *Global Coalition on Women and AIDS*, June 2, 2014. http://gcwa.unaids.org/news/gcwa-statement-support-international-day-sex-workers-june-2-2014 (accessed April 10, 2014).

Goodyear, Michael D.E., and Linda Cusick. "Protection of Sex Workers: Decriminalisation Could Restore Public Health Priorities and Human Rights." *BMJ* 334 (2007): 52–53. doi:10.1136/bmj.39063.645532.BE.

Grant, Melissa Gira. *Playing the Whore: The Work of Sex Work*. New York and London: Verso, 2014.

Greenall, Matthew, et al. *Sex work and HIV—Reality on the ground: Rapid assessments in five towns in Namibia*. Namibia: UNFPA and UNAIDS, 2011. http://africa.unfpa.org/public/pid/10231 (accessed April 4, 2014).

Hamm, Julie. *Moving Beyond "Supply and Demand" Catchphrases.* GAATW, 2011. http://www.gaatw.org/publications/MovingBeyond_SupplyandDemand_ GAATW2011.pdf (accessed March 18, 2014).

HIV and the Law: Risks, Rights and Health. New York: Global Commission on HIV and the Law, July 2012, 36–38. http://www.hivlawcommission.org/resources/report/ FinalReport-Risks,Rights&Health-EN.pdf (accessed April 10, 2014).

"Human Rights Organizations Condemn the Campaign of the Botswana Government to Crack Down on Sex Workers." *Canadian HIV/AIDS Legal Network,* November 13, 2013. http://www.aidslaw.ca/publications/interfaces/downloadDocumentFile. php?ref=1393 (accessed May 13, 2014).

"International Coalition Condemns Human Rights Violations against W.O.N.E.T.H.A." *Women's Global Network for Reproductive Rights,* July 31, 2012. http://www.wgnrr. org/news/international-coalition-condemns-human-rights-violations-against- wonetha (accessed May 13, 2014).

Jenness, Valerie. *Making It Work: The Prostitutes' Rights Movement in Perspective.* Chicago: Aldine Transaction, 1993: 42–47.

Jordan, Ann. "Human Rights or Wrongs? The Struggle for a Rights-Based Response to Trafficking in Human Beings." *Gender and Development* 10, no. 1 (2002): 28–37. doi:10.1080/13552070215891.

———. *The Swedish Law to Criminalize Clients: A Failed Experiment in Social Engineering.* Center for Humanitarian Rights and Humanitarian Law, April 2012.

Kempadoo, Kamala, and Jo Doezema, eds. *Global Sex Workers: Rights, Resistance, and Redefinition.* New York: Routledge, 1998.

"Kenyan Sex Workers Demand Removal of TV Documentary That Outs Sex Workers and Violates Our Rights!" *Global Network of Sex Work Projects,* July 9, 2013. http://www.nswp.org/news-story/kenyan-sex-workers-demand-removal-tv- documentary-outs-sex-workers-and-violates-our-rights (accessed May 13, 2014).

Kotiswaran, Prabha. *Dangerous Sex, Invisible Labor: Sex Work and the Law in India.* Princeton and Oxford: Princeton University Press, 2011.

———. "Vulnerability in Domestic Discourses on Trafficking: Lessons from the Indian Experience." *Feminist Legal Studies* 20 (2012): 245–62. doi:10.1007/ s10691-012-9211-z.

"Leaving No One Behind: Reaching Key Populations through Workplace Action on HIV and AIDS." *International Labour Organization,* 2014. http://www.nswp.org/ sites/nswp.org/files/ILO_Leaving_No_One_Behind.pdf (accessed April 10, 2014).

"Legal Empowerment Program Increases Access to Justice for Sex Workers in South Africa." *Open Society Foundations,* September 5, 2011. http://www.opensocietyfoun- dations.org/press-releases/legal-empowerment-program-increases-access-justice- sex-workers-south-africa (accessed April 10, 2014).

Mathieu, Lilian. "An Unlikely Mobilization: The Occupation of Saint-Nizier Church by the Prostitutes of Lyon." *Revue Française de Sociologie* 42, no. 1 (2001): 107–31.

McClintock, Anne. "The Scandal of the Whorearchy: Prostitution in Colonial Nairobi." *Transition* no. 52 (1991): 96–97.

Mgbako, Chi, et al. "The Case for the Decriminalization of Sex Work in South Africa." *Georgetown Journal of International Law* 44 (2013): 1433–36, 1446–54.

Mgbako, Chi, and Laura Smith. "Sex Work and Human Rights in Africa." *Fordham International Law Journal* 33 (2010): 1190–91, 1212–14.

Monson, Jo, and Morgan Mitchell. *Creative Space Manual.* Cape Town: SWEAT and Red Umbrella Programme, 2014. https://materialsdevelopmentafrica.files.word-press.com/2014/06/red-umbrella-creative-space-manual-2014.pdf (accessed March 30, 2014).

Mtetwa, Sibongile, et al. "'You Are Wasting Our Drugs': Health Service Barriers to HIV Treatment for Sex Workers in Zimbabwe." *BMC Public Health* 13, no. 1 (July 31, 2013). doi:10.1186/1471–2458–13–698.

Nagle, Jill, ed. *Whores and Other Feminists.* New York: Routledge, 1997.

Nakaweesi, Solome, and Hope Chigudu. *The LGBTIQ and Sex Worker Movements in East Africa.* BRIDGE, April 2013. http://socialmovements.bridge.ids.ac.uk/sites/socialmovements.bridge.ids.ac.uk/files/case-studies/East%20african%20case%20study%20final.pdf (accessed May 13, 2014).

"Note on Sex Work, Sexual Exploitation and Trafficking." *United Nations Entity for Gender Equality and the Empowerment of Women,* 2014. http://www.nswp.org/sites/nswp.org/files/UN%20Women's%20note%20on%20sex%20work%20sexual%20ex-ploitation%20and%20trafficking.pdf (accessed April 10, 2014).

Nussbaum, Martha C. "Whether from Reason or Prejudice: Taking Money for Bodily Services." *The Journal of Legal Studies* 27 (1998): 707.

Nyong'o, Zawadi. *Breaking Boundaries: Collective Organising for a Just Society.* Kampala, Uganda: Akina Mama wa Afrika (AMwA), 2010.

———. *When I Dare to Be Powerful: On the Road to a Sexual Rights Movement in East Africa.* Nairobi, Kenya: Akina Mama wa Afrika, 2010. http://www.oozebap.org/dones/biblio/Sex_Worker.pdf (accessed April 10, 2014).

Papworth, Erin, et al. "Epidemiology of HIV among Female Sex Workers, Their Clients, Men Who Have Sex with Men and People Who Inject Drugs in West and Central Africa." *Journal of the International AIDS Society* 16, no. 4 Suppl 3 (December 2, 2013). doi:10.7448/IAS.16.4.18751.

Pheterson, Gail. *The Prostitution Prism.* Amsterdam: Amsterdam University Press, 1996.

Plambech, Sine. "Between 'Victims' and 'Criminals': Rescue, Deportation, and Everyday Violence Among Nigerian Migrants." *Soc Pol* 21 (3)(Fall 2014): 382–402. doi:10.1093/sp/jxu021.

"Prevention and Treatment of HIV and Other Sexually Transmitted Infections for Sex Workers in Low and Middle Income Countries." *UNAIDS,* December 2012. http://apps.who.int/iris/bitstream/10665/77745/1/9789241504744_eng.pdf (accessed April 10, 2014).

Public Health Crisis: The Impact of Using Condoms as Evidence of Prostitution in New York City. New York: Sex Workers Project at the Urban Justice Center, April 2012. http://sexworkersproject.org/downloads/2012/20120417-public-health-crisis.pdf (accessed April 11, 2014).

Queen, Carol. "Sex Radical Politics, Sex-Positive Feminist Thought, and Whore Stigma." In *Identity Politics in the Women's Movement*, ed. Barbara Ryan, 94–99. New York and London: New York University Press, 2001.

Report of the Prostitution Law Review Committee on the Operation of the Prostitution Reform Act 2003. New Zealand Government, May 2008. http://www.justice.govt.nz/ policy/commercial-property-and-regulatory/prostitution/prostitution-law-review-committee/publications/plrc-report/documents/report.pdf (accessed May 13, 2014).

"Response to the Misguided Petition by Equality Now and Allies Attacking Sex Worker Human Rights and the Decriminalisation of Sex Work." *SWEAT*, October 7, 2013. http://www.sweat.org.za/index.php/item/474-response-to-the-misguided-petition-by-equality-now-and-allies-attacking-sex-worker-human-rights-and-the-decriminalisation-of-sex-work (accessed May 13, 2014).

Revolving Door: An Analysis of Street-Based Prostitution in New York City. New York: Sex Workers Project at the Urban Justice Center, 2003, 44. http://sexworkersproject. org/publications/reports/revolving-door/ (accessed April 10, 2014).

Richter, Marlise. "Sex Work as a Test Case for African Feminism." *BUWA! A Journal on African Women's Experiences at the Open Society Initiative for Southern Africa* (2012): 62–69.

Richter, Marlise, and Pamela Chakuvinga. "Being Pimped Out: How South Africa's AIDS Response Fails Sex Workers." *Agenda: Empowering Women for Gender Equity* 26, no. 2 (2012): 65–79.

Scorgie, Fiona, et al. "Human rights abuses and collective resilience among sex workers in four African countries: a qualitative study." *Globalization and Health* 9, no. 33 (2013). doi:10.1186/1744-8603-9-33.

Scorgings, Zoe, et al. *Solidarity Is Not a Crime: Sex Worker Freedom Festival, Kolkata, India 2012*. Global Network of Sex Work Projects, April 2014. http://www.nswp.org/ sites/nswp.org/files/SWFF%20Report_PDF%20version_0.pdf (accessed May 22, 2014).

Sex Work and the Law in Asia and the Pacific: Laws, HIV and Human Rights in the Context of Sex Work. United Nations Development Programme, 2012. http://www. snap-undp.org/elibrary/Publications/HIV-2012-SexWorkAndLaw.pdf (accessed April 10, 2014).

"Sex Worker Health and Rights: Where Is the Funding?" *Open Society Foundations*, June 2006. http://www.opensocietyfoundations.org/publications/sex-worker-health-and-rights-where-funding (accessed April 4, 2014).

Sex Workers at Risk: Condoms as Evidence of Prostitution in Four US Cities. New York: Human Rights Watch, 2012. http://www.hrw.org/sites/default/files/reports/us-0712ForUpload_1.pdf (accessed April 10, 2014).

Shah, Svati P. "Prostitution, Sex Work and Violence: Discursive and Political Contexts for Five Texts on Paid Sex, 1987–2001." *Gender & History* 16, no. 3 (November 2004): 794–812.

———. "Sex Work in the Global Economy." *New Labor Forum* 12, no. 1 (Spring 2003): 78–81.

Shannon, Kate, et al. "Global epidemiology of HIV among female sex workers: influence of structural determinants." *The Lancet*, Early Online Publication (July 22, 2014). doi:10.1016/S0140-6736(14)60931-4.

Shields, Acacia. *Criminalizing Condoms: How Policing Practices Put Sex Workers and HIV Services at Risk in Kenya, Namibia, Russia, South Africa, the United States, and Zimbabwe.* New York: Open Society Foundations, July 2012. http://www.open-societyfoundations.org/sites/default/files/criminalizing-condoms-20120717.pdf (accessed April 10, 2014).

"South African Commission for Gender Equality Calls for Decriminalisation and Protection of Sex Workers Rights." *Global Commission on HIV and the Law,* May 31, 2013. http://www.hivlawcommission.org/index.php/news/news/185-south-african-commission-for-gender-equality-calls-for-decriminalisation-and-protection-of-sex-workers-rights (accessed April 10, 2014).

Sutherland, Kate. "Work, Sex, and Sex-Work: Competing Feminist Discourses on the International Sex Trade." *Osgoode Hall Law Journal* 42 (2004): 139–67.

Tade, Oludayo, and Adeshemwa Jheminat Adekoya. "Transactional sex and the 'aristo' phenomenon in Nigerian Universities." *Human Affairs* 22 (2012): 239–55.

Tamale, Sylvia. "Paradoxes of Sex Work and Sexuality in Modern-Day Uganda." In *African Sexualities: A Reader*, ed. Sylvia Tamale. Cape Town: Pambazuka Press, 2011.

Tandia, Oumar. "Prostitution in Senegal." In *Global Sex Workers: Rights, Resistance, and Redefinition*, ed. Kamala Kempadoo and Jo Doezema, 240–45. New York: Routledge, 1998.

The Lancet Editorial Board. "Sex Workers and HIV—Forgotten and Ostracised." *The Lancet* 380, no. 9838 (July 21, 2012): 188. doi:10.1016/S0140-6736(12)61197-0.

Thukral, Juhu. "Human Rights and Trafficking." *Sh'ma: A Journal of Jewish Ideas* 39, no. 653 (2008): 6–7.

"'Treat Us Like Human Beings': Discrimination against Sex Workers, Sexual and Gender Minorities, and People Who Use Drugs in Tanzania." New York: *Human Rights Watch*, June 18, 2013. http://www.ecoi.net/local_link/250605/361390_en.html (accessed April 10, 2014).

"Uganda: Bill Threatens Progress on HIV/AIDS." *Human Rights Watch*, November 6, 2009. http://www.hrw.org/news/2009/11/06/uganda-bill-threatens-progress-hivaids (accessed March 24, 2014).

"UNAIDS Briefing Note: The Legal Status of Sex Work: Key Human Rights and Public Health Considerations." *UNAIDS*, February 2014. http://www.nswp.org/sites/nswp.org/files/sexwork_brief-21feb2014.pdf (accessed April 10, 2014).

United Nations Human Rights Council (HRC), Session 23/36. "Report of the Special Rapporteur on Extreme Poverty and Human Rights, Ms. Magdalena Sepúlveda Carmona," May 17, 2013. http://www.ohchr.org/Documents/HRBodies/HRCouncil/RegularSession/Session23/A-HRC-23-36-Add1_en.pdf (accessed April 10, 2014).

United Nations Human Rights Council (HRC), Session 22/53, "Report of the Special Rapporteur on torture and other cruel, inhuman or degrading treatment or punishment, Juan E. Méndez," February 1, 2013. http://www.ohchr.org/Documents/HR-

Bodies/HRCouncil/RegularSession/Session22/A.HRC.22.53_English.pdf (accessed April 10, 2014).

Weitzer, Ronald. "Flawed Theory and Method in Studies of Prostitution." *Violence against Women* 11, no. 7 (July 2005): 934–49. doi:10.1177/1077801205276986.

———. "The Social Construction of Sex Trafficking: Ideology and Institutionalization of a Moral Crusade." *Politics & Society* 35, no. 3, September 1, 2007. doi:10.1177/0032329207304319.

White, Luise. *The Comforts of Home: Prostitution in Colonial Nairobi*. Chicago and London: University of Chicago Press, 1990.

"Preventing HIV among Sex Workers in Sub-Saharan Africa: A Literature Review." *World Health Organization*. http://www.who.int/hiv/pub/sti/sex_workers_afro/en/ (accessed March 27, 2014).

"Zimbabwe: Policing Sex Work—An Appropriate Response?" *Southern African Litigation Centre* and *Sexual Rights Centre*, August 17, 2012. http://www.southernafricalitigationcentre.org/2012/08/17/salc-in-the-news-policing-sex-work-in-zimbabwe-an-appropriate-response/ (accessed May 13, 2014).

INDEX

Abdalla, Phelister, 1–3, 97–102, 188

Abortion, 137

Abraham, Pat, 79, 171

Abuja, 165

Access to justice: denial of, 12, 57; fight for increased, 30; lack of, 4, 11, 49, 51–52, 56, 86; police not a source of, 55, 58–59, 82–83, 195

Acholi, 176, 223n34

Activism, 11, 69, 87, 90, 97–98, 102, 108, 110, 119, 121, 136, 180–181, 186–187, 189, 208n10; HIV/AIDS, 84, 128, 170, 188; anti-prostitution, 163; feminist, 124; formal sex work, 16–17; grassroots sex work, 9, 98, 192; informal sex work, 5; intersectional, 115; LGBT, 132; media, 88; of prostitutes in Nairobi during colonial era, 204n41; sex work, 6, 10, 12–14, 16, 73, 94, 118, 123, 133–134, 143, 168–169, 172–174, 184–185, 190, 193. *See also* Movements

Adichie, Chimamanda Ngozi, 1, 23

African Charter on Human and Peoples' Rights, 152

African National Congress (ANC), 41, 155, 207n21; and Umkhonto we Sizwe, 41, 207n22; Women's League, 153

African Sex Worker Alliance (ASWA), 97, 104–105, 144, 152, 191–192

African Women's Leadership Institute (AWLI), 119–122

Agency, 13, 18, 83; African women's, 118; choice and, 35; coercion and, 29; collective, 18; consent and, 24; exhibiting,

184; human, 12, 30, 32; individual, 8; individual and community, 5; lack of, 33; limited economic opportunities not a negation of, 31; notion of, 119; sex workers', 21, 192

AIDS and Rights Alliance of Southern Africa, 104, 106, 175

AIDS Support and Education Trust, 88

Akina Mama wa Afrika, 97, 118–119, 123, 191

Allies, 2–3, 6, 9, 13, 73, 107, 110, 115, 139, 145, 187, 190; as farm workers, 114; in the NGO and intergovernmental field, 105; support and dedication of, 113; as trade unionists, 35

All India Network of Sex Workers, 187

Alternative livelihoods, 163–165, 167. *See also* Rehabilitation programs

Amnesty International, 55

Analysis, 13, 125, 157, 304n38; feminist, 11; of the focus countries' social and political histories, 14; sex workers' rights, 116

ANC. *See* African National Congress

Anti-homosexuality laws, 3, 210n1; in Nigeria, 79, 130; in Uganda, 69, 130, 131

Anti-prostitution activists, 4, 7, 10, 12, 23, 30–31, 53, 63, 152, 161–162, 183–184, 192; and co-option of anti-trafficking language and movements, 24, 80

Anti-prostitution pledge, 104

Anti-retroviral medication (ARVs), 27, 64, 178

ABOUT THE AUTHOR

Chi Adanna Mgbako is Clinical Professor of Law and Director of the Walter Leitner International Human Rights Clinic in the Leitner Center for International Law and Justice at Fordham Law School. She earned her J.D. from Harvard Law School and her B.A. from Columbia University.

CPSIA information can be obtained
at www.ICGtesting.com
Printed in the USA
JSHW011802240720
6888JS00003B/144